Federal Judiciary Appropriations, 1792–2010

compiled by

Daniel S. Holt

Assistant Historian

Federal Judicial Center
Federal Judicial History Office
2012

This Federal Judicial Center publication was undertaken in furtherance of the Center's statutory mission to "conduct, coordinate, and encourage programs relating to the history of the judicial branch of the United States government." While the Center regards the content as responsible and valuable, it does not reflect policy or recommendations of the Board of the Federal Judicial Center.

Contents

iii

Acknowledgments

Bruce Ragsdale oversaw this project from start to finish and worked closely with me to determine the scope and presentation of this wealth of data. Matthew Axtell conducted a substantial amount of the preliminary research for this volume, including collecting the relevant congressional statutes up to 1921 and surveying the archival materials related to the appropriations process in the nineteenth century. Jake Kobrick assisted with proofing the data. Thanks to Geoff Erwin for formatting the tables and closely editing them for greater consistency and clarity of presentation.

Appropriations and Financial Administration in the Courts: An Historical Overview

Throughout its history, the chief source of funding for the federal judiciary of the United States has been money authorized by Congress to be expended out of the general funds of the federal treasury. The federal judiciary has also received support from other sources, such as litigant fees and the fines, forfeitures, and penalties collected by the courts in the course of government litigation. This brief introductory essay surveys the changing procedures for determining the level of congressional appropriations and for disbursing appropriated funds throughout the federal judicial system. The essay also examines the historical relationship between the federal courts, Congress, and the executive agencies charged with supervising judicial expenditures and budgeting.

1789–1870

In each annual appropriations statute, Congress appropriated funds to pay the salaries of federal judges, the Attorney General of the United States, and district attorneys and district marshals. Congress also appropriated money—referred to by lawmakers and Treasury Department officials as the "Judiciary Fund"—to pay for the operating expenses of courts.

The expenses paid for out of the Judiciary Fund included per diem and travel expenses of jurors, witnesses, clerks, district attorneys, commissioners, and district marshals. The Judiciary Fund also covered the expenses and fees charged by the district attorneys and marshals in the prosecution of crimes against the United States and the detention and maintenance of prisoners. In 1830, the statutory language for court expenses was expanded to include those related to "suits in which the United States are concerned." In 1867, the Judiciary Fund was designated also for "legal assistance to the Attorney-General, and other special and extraordinary expenditures, in cases of the Supreme Court of the United States, in which the United States are concerned." The cost of operating the courts, then, also included the expenses of the United States government as a litigant in the courts.

The funds specified in the annual appropriations statutes were only a portion of the total amount of money available to the judiciary at the start of each fiscal year. Congress also appropriated for court expenses the "funds arising from fines, penalties, and forfeitures" that were collected by the courts and turned over to the Treasury, the amount of which varied from year to year. The courts also began each year with unexpended balances of appropriations carried over from previous years. Under an act passed in 1795, unexpended balances could be carried over for two years after the expiration of the fiscal year for which the funds were appropriated, at which point the Treasury was required to transfer the balances to the so-called "surplus fund." Money in the surplus fund was unavailable to the Treasury and had to be reappropriated by Congress.[1]

---

1. *U.S. Statutes at Large* 1 (1795): 437.

The district marshals and the Department of the Treasury worked together to estimate the upcoming financial needs of the courts and to disburse appropriated funds. Marshals were the disbursing agents for the district and circuit courts and were thus responsible for distributing from the Treasury the fees, per diem, and travel allowances of jurors, witnesses, clerks, and attorneys. Marshals paid for all contingent expenses of the courts as well, such as rental of courtrooms, furnishings, and the transport, housing, and subsistence of prisoners.

Marshals were responsible for communicating to the Secretary of the Treasury estimates of expenses for the coming fiscal year. The Treasury Department—after 1818, specifically, the Register's Office—reviewed the estimates submitted by marshals as well as the accounts maintained on each district court by Treasury accounting officers to estimate the needs of the entire judiciary for each coming fiscal year. The Register presented the estimates to the Secretary of the Treasury, who submitted them along with those for the other government agencies to the appropriate committee in Congress: between 1794 and 1865, the Ways and Means Committee of the House of Representatives; after 1865, the House Committee on Appropriations.

Once funds were appropriated, district marshals submitted to the Secretary of the Treasury estimates of upcoming expenses prior to each term of court and requested advances of funds. Each marshal posted a bond and could receive advances only up to that amount. The First Auditor of the Treasury and the Comptroller reviewed the estimates and the Secretary of the Treasury would sign a warrant for a specific amount of money to be remitted to the marshal; that amount was then deposited by the marshal in a national bank or other approved depository. Upon disbursing the funds, the marshal submitted returns to the Treasury, certified by the district judge, accounting for court expenses and the marshal's expenditures. The First Auditor, who maintained accounts for each judicial district, made a preliminary review of the returns to ensure that the funds were properly accounted for. The Comptroller of the Treasury then reviewed and "adjusted" the accounts if he found any expenditures to be inconsistent with the appropriation statutes. If the auditor or the Comptroller found that the fees or expenses claimed by the marshal were not provided for by statute or were charged at a higher rate than that fixed by Congress, he could disapprove the account and not credit the marshal with the money spent. In those cases, the Treasury would inform the marshal that a portion of the funds advanced was owed to the government. The amount would usually be deducted from the advances for the next term of court. In cases where marshals had exhausted their advances, they submitted requisitions to the Treasury to be able to meet outstanding expenses or to be reimbursed for expenses paid for out of pocket. In 1849, Congress created the Department of the Interior, which began supervising judicial accounts. The Comptroller of the Treasury continued to review and "adjust" accounts prior to final settlement.

In the 1840s, Congress placed caps on the amount of fees that court officers could retain as compensation and, in so doing, brought key changes to the supervision of accounts. Prior to 1841, clerks, commissioners, district attorneys, and marshals kept as their compensation the fees collected from private litigants. In the 1841 appropriation statute, Congress set a maximum compensation for marshals, district attorneys, and clerks, and it required court officers to return all fees to the Treasury above that amount, less the expenses of their offices and pay to deputies. A section in the 1842 appropriation act required all court officers to submit accounts twice a year at fixed times and to disclose all fees and emoluments received by themselves, as well as by their deputies. The new limits on compensation meant that the fees collected above the set maximum were considered revenue of the United States government. The Comptroller of the Treasury ruled as well that court officers owed the government not just the actual cash collected above the statutory compensation limit, but all recorded fees above that limit whether they were able to collect them or not.[2]

The changes in compensation and accounting arose from congressional concern, dating back to 1830, that the expenses of the federal courts were growing too quickly and that court officers were earning exorbitant fees. A congressional committee investigated court expenditures and concluded that courts were instituting unnecessary proceedings and requiring excessive forms and procedures as a way to generate more fees. For example, the investigators charged that attorneys prosecuted several suits or indictments where a consolidation into a single case would have been more appropriate, or clerks issued multiple writs where a single one would have been sufficient. The committee recommended a bill that would increase compensation for basic duties and equalize them among the courts so that officers would be paid more for their work and end the temptation to abuse the system with extra forms and proceedings.[3] Congress responded with an 1853 statute that set out a uniform fee schedule for all court officers and placed specific limits on the amount of money that marshals could spend on certain contingent expenses without the prior approval of the Secretary of the Interior.[4]

1871–1939

In 1870, Congress established the Department of Justice and assigned to it the administrative responsibility over the courts previously exercised by the Department of the Interior. The Justice Department was created to consolidate the various law officers throughout the Executive Branch departments and bring more supervision over all of the attorneys in government, including the district attorneys, under the Office of the Attorney General. The office of the Solicitor of the Treasury was transferred to the Department of Justice and took the lead in supervising the accounts of clerks, district attorneys, marshals, and commissioners, and oversaw procurement services and the preparation of budget estimates for the courts. The Justice Department also employed a small number of examiners tasked with auditing the accounts of court officers for the purpose of detecting fraud.

Beginning in 1870, Congress passed a series of laws designed to give itself greater control over the finances of the courts and executive agencies. The appropriations statute for FY 1871 included two key provisions. First, the statute included what came to be known as the Anti-Deficiency Law, which stated that no government department could spend, or contract to be spent, any more in a fiscal year than was appropriated by Con-

---

2. *Official Opinions of the Attorneys General of the United States* 9 (1858): 176.
3. House Committee on the Judiciary, *Federal Courts—Fees, etc.*, 32d Cong., 1st Sess., 1852, H. Rep. 50.
4. *U.S. Statutes at Large* 10 (1853): 161.

gress. Second, the statute provided that all balances of annual appropriations remaining unexpended at the end of a fiscal year would remain available only to pay expenses incurred during the year for which they were appropriated.[5] Any reimbursement claims for expenses incurred in fiscal years for which the funds had been transferred to the surplus fund had to be reviewed by auditors in the Department of the Treasury and reappropriated by Congress.

The new controls over judicial finances led to the proliferation of appropriation statutes to provide for deficiencies in the funds available for current and previous fiscal years. Each year, when the Attorney General submitted estimates for the annual appropriations of the judiciary, he would also report to Congress how much had been expended from the current year's appropriations and request additional funds for accounts that would likely be, or were already, exhausted. During FY 1873, Attorney General George H. Williams urged Congress to exempt previous years' balances of over $600,000 from the provisions of the 1870 statute limiting the use of funds and asked that all subsequent appropriations from the judiciary be exempted.[6] Congress did not grant the courts an exception.

Throughout the late nineteenth century, the Department of Justice struggled to keep the costs of the courts down. Congressional concern with rising court costs led to the creation in 1874 of a House Committee on Expenditures in the Department of Justice to review the accounts of the Department and the courts, especially the accounts of the district marshals. The Committee on Expenditures investigated the expenses of a number of judicial districts and concluded that "gross frauds" were evident. The committee offered suggestions for decreasing judicial expenditures, including reducing the number of commissioners and assistant district attorneys and a consolidation of recently created judicial districts.[7] In 1875, Congress passed a statute requiring that clerks, marshals, district attorneys, and commissioners prove in open court, under oath and supported by documentation, their claims for reimbursement from the Treasury.[8]

The most important recommendation to emerge out of the work of the committee, which continued its work and held in-depth hearings in 1884, was to convert marshals and district attorneys from fee-based compensation to annual salaries. The committee contended that attorneys and marshals instituted legal proceedings for the "mere sake of personal gain," especially in criminal cases. Examiners in the Department of Justice and investigators for the Committee on Expenditures reported that marshals (or most often, their deputies) collected unwarranted fees and expenses, such as mileage when they had not traveled and per diems when they had not actually attended court. Examinations found that some marshals underreported the extent of the emoluments collected by them that were due the Treasury. Similar complaints were levied against district attorneys and U.S. commissioners. Congress finally passed a law converting marshals and attorneys to

---

5. *U.S. Statutes at Large* 16 (1870): 251.

6. Attorney General George Williams to Chairman of the House Committee on Appropriations, Dec. 2, 1872, printed in *Deficiencies for Expenses of United States Courts*, 42d Cong., 3d Sess., H. Misc. Doc. 23.

7. House Committee on Expenditures in the Department of Justice, *Department of Justice*, 43d Cong., 2d Sess., 1875, H. Rep. 278.

8. *U.S. Statutes at Large* 18 (1875): 333.

the salary system in 1896 and required all fees collected by marshals to be deposited with the district clerks and by them forwarded to the Treasury.[9] The statute also required that marshals and district attorneys obtain prior authorization before incurring certain office expenses, purchasing supplies, or employing deputies and clerical assistants. Clerks of court were converted from fees to salary in 1919 and also required authorization for office expenses and supplies.

Other regulations were put in place to try to limit reliance on deficiency appropriations. The Department of Justice required more frequent, detailed, and uniform estimates and returns from district marshals. Marshals submitted quarterly estimates and requisitions on several forms issued by the Department and dedicated to specific appropriation accounts. In years where the Department of Justice recognized that funds would be exhausted, the Attorney General instructed district marshals to return any funds advanced to them that would not be needed so that they could be redistributed to other districts. In 1906, Congress passed a statute requiring executive agencies to apportion annual appropriations by monthly and other allotments, so as to prevent agencies from requiring deficiency appropriations during the year.[10] Each year, the Department of Justice created a spending plan to allot funds between various categories within the primary appropriation accounts; the spending plans contained instructions to limit expenditures to prescribed amounts each quarter of the year.

1940 to Present

With the creation in 1939 of the Administrative Office of the U.S. Courts (AO), the judiciary took control of formulating its own budget requests. The Director of the Administrative Office compiled expense information from the courts and prepared the budget estimate for the entire judiciary, which was transmitted to Congress through the Bureau of the Budget without any alterations. The AO prepared the budget for the courts of general jurisdiction, while the Supreme Court and other courts of special jurisdiction handled their own budgets separately. After 1958, the Judicial Conference established a standing Budget Committee, which reviewed budget estimates submitted by the AO, as well as estimates from other committees of the Judicial Conference, related to judiciary-wide initiatives and programs.

After 1939, the relationship between judicial expenses and Executive Branch expenses changed in annual appropriations statutes. The salaries of U.S. attorneys and U.S. marshals were incorporated in appropriations for the Department of Justice. The Department of Justice continued to play an important role in the administration of judicial finances, however. United States marshals continued to act as disbursing agents for the individual courts, and officials at the Justice Department retained responsibility for auditing and investigating court accounts. In 1975, the last administrative tasks fulfilled by the Department of Justice were transferred to the AO. The AO took over the role of auditing judicial accounts and established a new Office of the Audit. Also that year, the

---

9. *U.S. Statutes at Large* 29 (1896): 180.
10. *U.S. Statutes at Large* 34 (1906): 48.

clerks of court took over the disbursement functions at the court level and exercised greater management responsibility over finances.

Beginning in 1987, the AO and the Judicial Conference began a movement to decentralize the budgeting and spending processes of the judiciary. Up to that time, the AO handled the administration of payroll, procurement, accounting, and contracting for the courts. The AO staff, following the trend begun by the Department of Justice early in the twentieth century, purchased all equipment and supplies based on requisitions from the individual courts. Under budget decentralization, after funds have been appropriated by Congress, the Executive Committee of the Judicial Conference adopts a National Financial Plan that sets spending priorities for the entire judiciary. The AO is responsible for allotting the funds to the individual courts, which it does according to formulas that consider projections about future caseloads and the staffing needs of the courts. Beginning with fiscal year 1993, Congress has included a provision in the appropriation acts that grants the AO greater authority to transfer funds between appropriation accounts.

Beginning in 1998, the allotments were simplified from 64 separate expense categories to 3 broad classes: salaries, operating expenses, and automation. The individual courts were then responsible for allocating these funds into more specific categories, or "budget object classifications." Courts are required to submit to the AO an organization plan describing the administrative process for budgeting, spending, and accounting as well as detailed spending plans. The courts have the ability to transfer funds among different classifications with the approval of the AO. All transfer of funds must be reported to the AO in quarterly Status of Funds reports; these reports allow the agency to monitor which object classifications have surpluses or deficits and then to adjust the National Financial Plan and budget estimates accordingly. A number of key allotments remained under the central control of the AO, including salaries, travel expenses, training of judges and chamber staff, benefits for judges and court employees, jury fees and expenses, and rent paid to the General Services Administration for courtroom space.

Since 1939, special funds—that is, money received by the government under special authorization of law and which may be expended only for the particular purpose specified—have become more important to the judiciary. In 1946, Congress passed a statute directing that bankruptcy fees be paid into two funds, from which the salaries and expenses of referees in bankruptcy would be appropriated. (The salaries and expenses of bankruptcy courts became a regular appropriation after the reorganization of those courts in 1978.) Beginning in 1986, the federal courts collected into a special fund the fees paid by litigants for filing civil cases. In each annual appropriation statute, Congress authorized monies in the special fund to be used toward the expenses of the operations and maintenance of the courts. In 1990, Congress converted the appropriations from the fund to a permanent, indefinite appropriation that did not need to be renewed each year. The funds were available for expense accounts, as the courts needed, until expended.

In 1990, Congress established another special fund, the Judicial Automation Fund (later renamed the Judicial Information Technology Fund).[11] The fund was designated for expenses related to automation in the collection, management, dissemination, and

---

11. *U.S. Statutes at Large* 103 (1989): 1013.

protection of judicial information. The monies in the Judicial Information Technology Fund carry over automatically from year to year, giving the judiciary the flexibility to plan and budget for multiyear technology projects and investment. Money for the fund is not specified in the appropriations statute but is deposited into the fund based on spending priorities set by the Judicial Conference. Money in the Judicial Information Technology Fund cannot be transferred to other purposes without approval from the AO.

Introduction to Appropriations Tables

These tables present the detailed history of congressional appropriations for the federal judiciary from 1792 to 2010. Each table reports the funds appropriated by Congress through statute for each fiscal year and the citation information for the relevant statutes.

For each fiscal year, the table reports the line-items for judicial funding included in the annual appropriations statute. Each fiscal year also includes any funds appropriated during that fiscal year through so-called deficiency or supplemental appropriation statutes. When Congress passed a deficiency appropriation, it authorized funds to be applied to both the current fiscal year and expenses incurred and outstanding from previous fiscal years. These tables report all deficiency appropriations as part of the fiscal year during which the statute was passed. In some years, Congress passed legislation requiring across-the-board funding rescissions—usually a percentage of all discretionary government spending. These rescissions have not been calculated but are noted when they occurred. At other times, Congress authorized that specific amounts be transferred from one appropriation account to another. These transfers are reported as negative appropriations for the account from which funds were transferred. The table does not include reappropriations of unexpended balances unless those balances were transferred between accounts.

The amounts presented in the table are taken from the portions of annual appropriations statutes that were labeled as "Judicial," "Judiciary," or "United States Courts." What specific objects of funding were considered to be "judicial" or court-related has changed considerably over time. For example, expenses that would today be considered part of the Executive Branch—such as salaries and expenses of the Attorney General's Office and activities of the Department of Justice—were categorized as "judicial" for much of the nation's history. In a few cases, appropriations listed under the executive department charged with supervision of court finances (Department of Interior or Department of Justice) were included in the table if the items were clearly related to the operation of the federal courts.

Whenever possible, the headings, labels, and line-items are organized and presented as they appeared in the statutes. Prior to 1842, however, the statutes included no headings either identifying the judiciary as a distinct entity or for organizing the various line-items that constituted the judiciary's appropriations. In those cases, for organizational clarity, headings—such as "Salaries" and "Court Expenses"—have been added and are set off with brackets. The descriptions of the line-items are summaries and not reproductions of the full details included in the statutes. For clarity, modern language usage has been used. If a category or line-item included detailed appropriations that concluded with a total "in all," the table reports the "in all" figure only. In some cases, Congress appropriated funds without specifying an amount; these are included with the word "indefinite" in place of a dollar amount. The "Total Appropriation" included at the end of each fiscal year is not a total reported in any statute or report, but has been calculated based on the line-items in the statutes listed. Note that the "Total Appropriation" is not the total amount of funds authorized to the judiciary in a given year, since it does not include indefinite appropriations, unexpended balances carried over from previous years, funds that Congress made available for multiple years, or permanent appropriations not reauthorized in each year's statute, such as judiciary filing fees and other special funds.

Between 1791 and 1879, expenses for the operations of the courts were appropriated in a single line-item, which members of Congress and Treasury officials often referred to as "the Judiciary Fund." The line-item for "defraying the expenses of the Supreme, circuit, and district courts" included the fees and expenses of jurors and witnesses, the costs of prosecution of crimes against the United States, and the keeping of prisoners. In 1830, the language for court expenses was expanded to include expenses related to "suits in which the United States are concerned." In 1867, the court expenses were designated also for "defraying the expenses of suits in which the United States are concerned, including legal assistance to the Attorney-General, and other special and extraordinary expenditures, in cases of the Supreme Court of the United States, in which the United States are concerned." The line-item for court expenses specified that these funds were appropriated "in aid of the funds arising from fines, penalties, and forfeitures," which were received by the Treasury and earmarked for court expenses. After 1872, the statutes no longer specified that appropriations for court expenses were "in aid of the funds arising from fines, penalties, and forfeitures." Beginning in 1880, Congress itemized in more detail the various components of the Judiciary Fund, with individual line-items for fees of marshals, clerks, district attorneys, jurors, and witnesses, as well as funds for courtroom rent, support of prisoners, and the cost of transferring prisoners from the District of Columbia to local prisons. A paragraph describing which courts and purposes were designated for "defraying the expenses" preceded the line items. The language of this paragraph changed over the years. For example, from 1872 to 1893, Congress included the costs associated with the enforcement of the voting provisions of the 1871 Force Act, which provided for the appointment of supervisors of congressional elections and gave new responsibilities to district marshals in monitoring elections. After 1913, the statutes no longer included the paragraph describing "the defraying of expenses."

Note for Further Research

The appropriations statutes passed by Congress are just one source for analyzing appropriations throughout the judiciary's history. Since 1826, Congress has after each session published a summary of all the appropriations made during that session, including those for the judiciary. The exact contents and title of this report has changed over the years: "Statement of Appropriations Made" (1826–1840), "Appropriations, New Offices, etc." (1841–1923), and "Appropriations, Budget Estimates, etc." (1924–present). Since 1924, this report has included a comparison between the original estimates submitted to Congress, the amount appropriated during the previous year, and the amount appropriated during that session. Researchers interested in further exploring the legislative history of judicial appropriations can also consult committee hearings on appropriations bills, where representatives of the judiciary explained appropriation requests and discussed changes in statutory language and organization of accounts.

Reports prepared by executive agencies and submitted to congressional committees responsible for appropriations are also an important source. Between 1789 and 1922, the Treasury Department began the appropriations process each year by submitting to Congress estimates of expenditures for the coming fiscal year, which was published as a House Document each year. Beginning with fiscal year 1818, these estimates included a detailed list of all appropriated items, including those for the judiciary. The Treasury estimates at times differed from congressional statutes in terms of organization and categorization of expenses as "judicial." Starting with fiscal year 1836, the Treasury estimates also included a comparison of each estimate with the amount appropriated the previous year. After 1923, the estimates were prepared and submitted to Congress by the Bureau of the Budget (renamed the Office of Management and Budget in 1970) and titled "Budget of the United States Government." Between 1871 and 1939, the Department of Justice also periodically submitted estimates specifically related to court expenses, including estimates of deficiencies expected during the fiscal year.

The Treasury Department has issued reports with information on the expenditures of the Judicial Branch. The Treasury reported to Congress the actual expenditures of the government in its annual report on the "State of the Finances," which included a total expenditure of the judiciary starting with fiscal year 1821. The Treasury reported a more detailed summary of judicial expenditures beginning in 1845 in another annual report titled variously "Receipts and Expenditures," "An Account of the Receipts and Expenditures of the United States," "Receipts and Disbursements," and "Combined Statement of Receipts, Disbursements and Balances of the United States Government." From 1845 to 1890, these reports detailed each disbursement of salaries and reimbursement for fees and expenses to court officers.

The agencies charged with oversight of judicial finances also produced important sources of information. From 1871 to 1939, the *Annual Report of the Attorney General of the United States* included information on appropriations, expenditures, and balances of the various court expense accounts under the control of the Department of Justice. The Attorney General report also included a district-by-district breakdown of expenditures out of the Judiciary Fund. From 1940 to 2001, the *Annual Report of the Director of the Administrative Office of the U.S. Courts* included a summary of appropriations, a breakdown of the allotment of spending within the judiciary, and discussion of the difference between judicial funding requests and final appropriations granted. Since 2002, the director's report has included only a brief overview of the judiciary's appropriations. The reports of the Budget Committee of the Judicial Conference, beginning in 1958, include detailed budget requests and justifications submitted to Congress.

The Government Printing Office (GPO) has published online the complete budget proposals of the federal government since 1996, available at http://www.gpo.gov/fdsys/. The materials include budget appendices that present detailed explanation of objects covered by each appropriation account as well as information on obligations, outlays, and permanent appropriations (such as collected filing fees) not specified in annual appropriation statutes. The GPO also provides access to the Public Budget Database, historical tables presenting budget authority since 1976 and outlays since 1962.

Annual Appropriations, Fiscal Years 1792–2010

1792

Statute (Citation)	Date Passed	Headings	Appropriation	Line-item Details
Ch. 3, 1791 (1 Stat. 226)	December 23, 1791	[Salaries]	$53,000.00	President, Vice President, Chief Justice, associate justices, Attorney General
			$19,800.00	district judges
		[Expenses]	$5,000.00	deficiency for expenses of clerks, jurors, and witnesses
			$4,000.00	keeping of prisoners
		Total	$81,800.00	
Ch. 41, 1792 (1 Stat. 284)	May 8, 1792	[Expenses]	$17,000.00	discharging accounts of officers of the courts of the United States, jurors and witnesses
		TOTAL APPROPRIATION	$98,800.00	

1793

Statute (Citation)	Date Passed	Headings	Appropriation	Line-item Details
Ch. 18, 1792 (1 Stat. 325, 326)	February 28, 1793	[Salaries]	$43,200.00	Chief Justice, associate justices, Attorney General
			$260.82	addition to Attorney General salary, FY 1792
		[Expenses]	$12,000.00	defraying the expense of clerks of court, jurors, and witnesses
			$4,000.00	defraying the expenses of prosecutions for offences against the United States, keeping of prisoners
		TOTAL APPROPRIATION	$59,460.82	

1794

Statute (Citation)	Date Passed	Headings	Appropriation	Line-item Details
Ch. 6, 1794 (1 Stat. 342)	March 14, 1794	[Salaries]	$43,200.00	Chief Justice, associate justices, district judges, and Attorney General
		[Expenses]	$12,000.00	clerks of court, jurors, and witnesses
			$4,000.00	prosecutions for offences against the United States, keeping of prisoners
		TOTAL APPROPRIATION	$59,200.00	

1795

Statute (Citation)	Date Passed	Headings	Appropriation	Line-item Details
Ch. 8, 1795 (1 Stat. 405)	January 2, 1795	[Salaries]	$43,200.00	Chief Justice, associate justices, district judges, and Attorney General
		[Expenses]	$12,000.00	clerks of court, jurors, and witnesses
			$4,000.00	prosecutions for offences against the United States, keeping of prisoners
		TOTAL APPROPRIATION	$59,200.00	

1796

Statute (Citation)	Date Passed	Headings	Appropriation	Line-item Details
Ch. 1, 1796 (1 Stat. 445)	February 5, 1796	[Salaries]	$43,600.00	Chief Justice, associate justices, district judges, and Attorney General
		[Expenses]	$20,000.00	clerks of court, jurors, and witnesses, prosecutions for offences against the United States, keeping of prisoners
			$10,000.00	clerks, jurors, and witnesses, deficiency for FY 1795
		Total	$73,600.00	
Ch. 48, 1796 (1 Stat. 492)	June 1, 1796	[Expenses]	$20,000.00	discharge of incidental demands occasioned by trial of persons for crimes during late insurrection
			$10,000.00	clerks of court, jurors, and witnesses
		TOTAL APPROPRIATION	$103,600.00	

1797

Statute (Citation)	Date Passed	Headings	Appropriation	Line-item Details
Ch. 8, 1797 (1 Stat. 498)	March 3, 1797	[Salaries]	$44,900.00	Chief Justice, associate justices, district judges, and Attorney General
		[Expenses]	$30,000.00	clerks of court, jurors, and witnesses, prosecutions for offences against the United States, keeping of prisoners
		TOTAL APPROPRIATION	$74,900.00	

1798

Statute (Citation)	Date Passed	Headings	Appropriation	Line-item Details
Ch. 18, 1798 (1 Stat. 542)	March 19, 1798	[Salaries]	$44,900.00	Chief Justice, associate justices, district judges, and Attorney General
		[Expenses]	$30,000.00	clerks of court, jurors, and witnesses, prosecutions for offences against the United States, keeping of prisoners
		TOTAL APPROPRIATION	**$74,900.00**	

1799

Statute (Citation)	Date Passed	Headings	Appropriation	Line-item Details
Ch. 25, 1799 (1 Stat. 717)	March 2, 1799	[Salaries]	$47,300.00	Chief Justice, associate justices, district judges, Attorney General, district attorneys, and marshals
		[Expenses]	$30,000.00	clerks of court, jurors, and witnesses, prosecutions for offences against the United States, keeping of prisoners
		TOTAL APPROPRIATION	**$77,300.00**	

1800

Statute (Citation)	Date Passed	Headings	Appropriation	Line-item Details
Ch. 47, 1800 (2 Stat. 62)	May 7, 1800	[Salaries]	$45,500.00	Chief Justice, associate justices, district judges, and Attorney General
		[Expenses]	$33,400.00	compensation for district attorneys, defraying expenses of clerks of court, jurors, and witnesses, prosecutions for offences against the United States, keeping of prisoners
		TOTAL APPROPRIATION	**$78,900.00**	

1801

Statute (Citation)	Date Passed	Headings	Appropriation	Line-item Details
Ch. 27, 1801 (2 Stat. 117, 118)	March 3, 1801	[Salaries]	$83,400.00	judges of the United States, Attorney General, district attorneys, and marshals
		[Expenses]	$30,000.00	defraying expenses of clerks of court, jurors, and witnesses, prosecutions for offences against U.S., keeping of prisoners
		TOTAL APPROPRIATION	**$113,400.00**	

1802

Statute (Citation)	Date Passed	Headings	Appropriation	Line-item Details
Ch. 47, 1802 (2 Stat. 184, 187)	May 1, 1802	[Salaries]	$68,650.00	Chief Justice, associate justices, circuit judges, district judges, including chief justice and 2 associate judges of District of Columbia, Attorney General
			$1,200.00	compensation for marshals of Maine, New Hampshire, Vermont, Kentucky, East and West Tennessee
		[Expenses]	$56,900.00	compensation for district attorneys, defraying the expenses of Supreme, district, and circuit courts, including District of Columbia . . .
		TOTAL APPROPRIATION	**$126,750.00**	

1803

Statute (Citation)	Date Passed	Headings	Appropriation	Line-item Details
Ch. 19, 1803 (2 Stat. 210, 213)	March 2, 1803	[Salaries]	$52,900.00	Chief Justice, associate justices, district judges, including chief justice and 2 associate judges of District of Columbia, Attorney General
			$2,800.00	compensation to the several district attorneys
			$1,400.00	compensation to the marshals for districts of Maine, New Hampshire, Vermont, Kentucky, East and West Tennessee, Ohio
		[Expenses]	$40,000.00	defraying expenses of Supreme, district, and circuit courts, including District of Columbia . . .
			$3,702.66	for constructing a jail in the city of Washington
		TOTAL APPROPRIATION	**$100,802.66**	

1804

Statute (Citation)	Date Passed	Headings	Appropriation	Line-item Details
Ch. 21, 1804 (2 Stat. 264, 267)	March 14, 1804	[Salaries]	$54,900.00	Chief Justice, associate justices, district judges, including chief justice and 2 associate judges of District of Columbia, Attorney General, including $1,000 for district judge of Ohio
			$2,800.00	compensation to the several district attorneys
			$1,400.00	compensation to the marshals for districts of Maine, New Hampshire, Vermont, Kentucky, East and West Tennessee, Ohio

1805

Statute (Citation)	Date Passed	Headings	Appropriation	Line-item Details
Ch. 21, 1805 (2 Stat. 316, 320)	March 1, 1805	[Salaries]	$55,900.00	Chief Justice, associate justices, district judges, including chief justice and 2 associate judges of District of Columbia, Attorney General
			$3,400.00	compensation to the several district attorneys
			$1,600.00	compensation to the marshals for districts of Maine, New Hampshire, Vermont, Kentucky, East and West Tennessee, Ohio, and Orleans
		[Expenses]	$40,000.00	defraying expenses of Supreme, district, and circuit courts, including District of Columbia . . . .
		TOTAL APPROPRIATION	$99,100.00	

1806

Statute (Citation)	Date Passed	Headings	Appropriation	Line-item Details
Ch. 33, 1806 (2 Stat. 384, 388)	April 18, 1806	[Salaries]	$56,400.00	Chief Justice, associate justices, district judges, including chief justice and 2 associate judges of District of Columbia, Attorney General, and district judge of Orleans, including deficiency for his compensation for FY 1804
			$3,400.00	compensation to the several district attorneys
			$1,600.00	compensation to the marshals for districts of Maine, New Hampshire, Vermont, Kentucky, East and West Tennessee, Ohio, Orleans
		[Expenses]	$40,000.00	defraying expenses of Supreme, district, and circuit courts, including District of Columbia . . . .
		TOTAL APPROPRIATION	$101,400.00	

1807

Statute (Citation)	Date Passed	Headings	Appropriation	Line-item Details
Ch. 29, 1807 (2 Stat. 432, 435)	March 3, 1807	[Salaries]	$59,400.00	Chief Justice, associate justices, district judges, including chief justice and 2 associate judges of District of Columbia, Attorney General, and salary of district judge of Orleans
			$3,400.00	compensation to the several district attorneys
			$1,600.00	compensation to the marshals for districts of Maine, New Hampshire, Vermont, Kentucky, East and West Tennessee, Ohio, Orleans
		[Expenses]	$40,000.00	defraying expenses of Supreme, district, and circuit courts, including District of Columbia . . . .
		TOTAL APPROPRIATION	$104,400.00	

1808

Statute (Citation)	Date Passed	Headings	Appropriation	Line-item Details
Ch. 17, 1808 (2 Stat. 462, 465)	February 10, 1808	[Salaries]	$59,400.00	Chief Justice, associate justices, district judges, including chief justice and 2 associate judges of District of Columbia, Attorney General, and salary of district judge of Orleans
			$3,400.00	compensation to the several district attorneys
			$1,600.00	compensation to the marshals for districts of Maine, New Hampshire, Vermont, Kentucky, East and West Tennessee, Ohio, Orleans
		[Expenses]	$40,000.00	defraying expenses of Supreme, district, and circuit courts, including District of Columbia . . . .
		TOTAL APPROPRIATION	$104,400.00	

1809

Statute (Citation)	Date Passed	Headings	Appropriation	Line-item Details
Ch. 18, 1809 (2 Stat. 520, 523)	February 17, 1809	[Salaries]	$59,400.00	Chief Justice, associate justices, district judges, including chief justice and 2 associate judges of District of Columbia, Attorney General, and salary of district judge of Orleans
			$3,400.00	compensation to the several district attorneys

		Headings	Appropriation	Line-item Details
			$2,650.00	compensation to the marshals for districts of Maine, New Hampshire, Vermont, New Jersey, North Carolina, Kentucky, Ohio, East and West Tennessee, Orleans, plus salary for last 3/4 of 1808 for marshals of North Carolina and New Jersey
		[Expenses]	$40,000.00	defraying expenses of Supreme, district, and circuit courts, including District of Columbia . . .
		TOTAL APPROPRIATION	$105,450.00	

1810

Statute (Citation)	Date Passed	Headings	Appropriation	Line-item Details
Ch. 13, 1810 (2 Stat. 552, 560)	February 26, 1810	[Salaries]	$59,400.00	Chief Justice, associate justices, district judges, including chief justice and 2 associate judges of District of Columbia, Attorney General, and salary of district judge of Orleans
			$3,400.00	compensation to the several district attorneys
			$2,200.00	compensation for marshals of Maine, New Hampshire, Vermont, New Jersey, North Carolina, Kentucky, Ohio, East and West Tennessee, Orleans
		[Expenses]	$40,000.00	defraying expenses of Supreme, district, and circuit courts, including District of Columbia . . .
		TOTAL APPROPRIATION	$105,000.00	

1811

Statute (Citation)	Date Passed	Headings	Appropriation	Line-item Details
Ch. 22, 1811 (2 Stat. 643, 646)	February 20, 1811	[Salaries]	$59,400.00	Chief Justice, associate justices, district judges, including chief justice and 2 associate judges of District of Columbia, Attorney General, and salary of district judge of Orleans
			$3,400.00	compensation to the several district attorneys
			$2,200.00	compensation for marshals of Maine, New Hampshire, Vermont, New Jersey, North Carolina, Kentucky, Ohio, East and West Tennessee, Orleans
		[Expenses]	$40,000.00	defraying expenses of Supreme, district, and circuit courts, including District of Columbia . . .
		TOTAL APPROPRIATION	$105,000.00	

1812

Statute (Citation)	Date Passed	Headings	Appropriation	Line-item Details
Ch. 33, 1812 (2 Stat. 686, 690)	February 26, 1812	[Salaries]	$60,950.00	Chief Justice, associate justices, district judges, including chief justice and 2 associate judges of District of Columbia, Attorney General, and salary of district judge of Orleans, including $1,000 for additional 1811 salary of D.C. judges
			$3,400.00	compensation to the several district attorneys
			$2,200.00	compensation for marshals of Maine, New Hampshire, Vermont, New Jersey, North Carolina, Kentucky, Ohio, East and West Tennessee, Orleans
		[Expenses]	$40,000.00	defraying expenses of Supreme, district, and circuit courts, including District of Columbia . . . .
		TOTAL APPROPRIATION	**$106,550.00**	

1813

Statute (Citation)	Date Passed	Headings	Appropriation	Line-item Details
Ch. 58, 1813 (2 Stat. 823, 827)	March 3, 1813	[Salaries]	$65,403.84	Chief Justice, associate justices, district judges, including chief justice and 2 associate judges of District of Columbia, Attorney General, including $953.84 for additional judge for district of New York, and $1,450 for deficiency for Attorney General and district judge of Louisiana
			$3,400.00	compensation to the several district attorneys
			$2,200.00	compensation for marshals of Maine, New Hampshire, Vermont, New Jersey, North Carolina, Kentucky, Ohio, East and West Tennessee, Louisiana
		[Expenses]	$40,000.00	defraying expenses of Supreme, district, and circuit courts, including District of Columbia . . . .
		TOTAL APPROPRIATION	**$111,003.84**	

1814

Statute (Citation)	Date Passed	Headings	Appropriation	Line-item Details
Ch. 28, 1814 (3 Stat. 106, 110)	March 24, 1814	[Salaries]	$62,000.00	Chief Justice, associate justices, district judges, including chief justice and associate judges of District of Columbia, Attorney General
			$4,650.00	compensation for district attorneys of the several districts, including those of the several territories
			$3,200.00	compensation for marshals of Maine, New Hampshire, Vermont, New Jersey, North Carolina, Kentucky, Ohio, East and West Tennessee, and the several territories
		[Expenses]	$40,000.00	defraying expenses of Supreme, district, and circuit courts, including District of Columbia . . . .
		TOTAL APPROPRIATION	$109,850.00	

1815

Statute (Citation)	Date Passed	Headings	Appropriation	Line-item Details
Ch. 44, 1815 (3 Stat. 206, 210)	February 16, 1815	[Salaries]	$64,000.00	Chief Justice, associate justices, district judges, including chief justice and associate judges of District of Columbia, Attorney General, including $1,000 for 1814 salary of district judge of Louisiana
			$7,850.00	compensation of sundry district attorneys and marshals, including those in the several territories
		[Expenses]	$40,000.00	defraying expenses of Supreme, district, and circuit courts, including District of Columbia . . . .
		TOTAL APPROPRIATION	$111,850.00	

1816

Statute (Citation)	Date Passed	Headings	Appropriation	Line-item Details
Ch. 45, 1816 (3 Stat. 277, 282)	April 16, 1816	[Salaries]	$60,000.00	Chief Justice, associate justices, district judges, including chief justice and associate judges of District of Columbia
			$3,000.00	Attorney General
			$7,850.00	compensation of sundry district attorneys and marshals, including those in the several territories

Headings	Line-item Details	Appropriation
[Expenses]	defraying expenses of Supreme, district, and circuit courts, including District of Columbia . . .	$40,000.00
TOTAL APPROPRIATION		$110,850.00

1817

Statute (Citation)	Date Passed	Headings	Line-item Details	Appropriation
Ch. 33, 1817 (3 Stat. 352, 356)	March 3, 1817	[Salaries]	Chief Justice, associate justices, district judges, including chief justice and associate judges of District of Columbia	$61,000.00
			Attorney General	$3,000.00
			compensation of sundry district attorneys and marshals, including those in the several territories	$7,850.00
		[Expenses]	defraying expenses of Supreme, district, and circuit courts, including District of Columbia . . .	$40,000.00
		TOTAL APPROPRIATION		$111,850.00

1818

Statute (Citation)	Date Passed	Headings	Line-item Details	Appropriation
Ch. 45, 1818 (3 Stat. 418, 421)	April 9, 1818	[Salaries]	Chief Justice, associate justices, district judges, including chief justice and associate judges of District of Columbia	$63,000.00
			Attorney General	$3,000.00
			compensation of sundry district attorneys and marshals, including those in the several territories	$8,300.00
			reporter of the decisions of the Supreme Court, for 1817 and 1818	$2,000.00
		TOTAL APPROPRIATION		$76,300.00

1819

Statute (Citation)	Date Passed	Headings	Line-item Details	Appropriation
Ch. 54, 1819 (3 Stat. 496, 500)	March 3, 1819	[Salaries]	Chief Justice, associate justices, district judges, including chief justice and associate judges of District of Columbia	$75,914.28
			Attorney General	$3,500.00
			Attorney General's clerk	$1,000.00
			expenses of Attorney General's Office	$500.00

Line-item Details	Appropriation
compensation of sundry district attorneys and marshals, including those in the several territories	$8,200.00
reporter of the decisions of the Supreme Court	$1,000.00
TOTAL APPROPRIATION	**$90,114.28**

1820

Statute (Citation)	Date Passed	Headings	Line-item Details	Appropriation
Ch. 40, 1820 (3 Stat. 555, 560)	April 11, 1820	[Salaries]	Chief Justice, associate justices, district judges, including chief justice and associate judges of District of Columbia	$77,100.00
			Attorney General	$3,500.00
			Attorney General's clerk	$800.00
			compensation of sundry district attorneys and marshals, including those in the several territories	$9,000.00
			marshal of District of Pennsylvania, for April 1818 to April 1819	$200.00
			district attorney of District of Pennsylvania, for April 1818 to April 1819	$200.00
			reporter of the decisions of the Supreme Court	$1,000.00
			TOTAL APPROPRIATION	**$91,800.00**

1821

Statute (Citation)	Date Passed	Headings	Line-item Details	Appropriation
Ch. 34, 1821 (3 Stat. 628, 632)	March 3, 1821	[Salaries]	Chief Justice, associate justices, district judges, including chief justice and associate judges of District of Columbia	$78,200.00
			Attorney General	$3,500.00
			Attorney General's clerk	$800.00
			compensation of messenger and contingent expenses of Attorney General's Office	$500.00
			reporter of decisions of the Supreme Court	$1,000.00
			compensation of sundry district attorneys and marshals, including those in the several territories	$8,950.00
			TOTAL APPROPRIATION	**$92,950.00**

1822

Statute (Citation)	Date Passed	Headings	Line-item Details	Appropriation
Ch. 41, 1822 (3 Stat. 668, 672)	April 30, 1822	[Salaries]	Chief Justice, associate justices, district judges, including chief justice and associate judges of District of Columbia	$78,200.00
			Attorney General	$3,500.00
			Attorney General's clerk	$800.00
			reporter of the decisions of the Supreme Court	$1,000.00
			compensation of sundry district attorneys and marshals, including those in the several territories	$8,950.00
		[Expenses]	defraying expenses of Supreme, district, and circuit courts, including District of Columbia	$30,000.00
			TOTAL APPROPRIATION	**$122,450.00**

1823

Statute (Citation)	Date Passed	Headings	Line-item Details	Appropriation
Ch. 31, 1823 (3 Stat. 757, 762)	March 3, 1823	[Salaries]	Chief Justice, associate justices, district judges, including chief justice and associate judges of District of Columbia	$78,400.00
			Attorney General	$3,500.00
			Attorney General's clerk	$800.00
			reporter of the decisions of the Supreme Court	$1,000.00
			compensation of sundry district attorneys and marshals, including those in the several territories	$9,973.63
		[Expenses]	defraying expenses of Supreme, district, and circuit courts, including District of Columbia	$65,000.00
			TOTAL APPROPRIATION	**$158,673.63**

1824

Statute (Citation)	Date Passed	Headings	Line-item Details	Appropriation
Ch. 32, 1824 (4 Stat. 11, 15)	April 2, 1824	[Salaries]	Chief Justice, associate justices, district judges, including chief justice and associate judges of District of Columbia	$78,400.00
			Attorney General	$3,500.00
			Attorney General's clerk	$800.00

			Line-item Details	Appropriation
			reporter of the decisions of the Supreme Court	$1,000.00
			compensation of sundry district attorneys and marshals, including those in the several territories	$10,100.00
		[Expenses]	defraying expenses of Supreme, district, and circuit courts, including District of Columbia . . .	$60,000.00
		TOTAL APPROPRIATION		$153,800.00

1825

Statute (Citation)	Date Passed	Headings	Line-item Details	Appropriation
Ch. 13, 1825 (4 Stat. 85, 89)	February 25, 1825	[Salaries]	Chief Justice, associate justices, district judges, including chief justice and associate judges of District of Columbia	$79,200.00
			Attorney General	$3,500.00
			Attorney General's clerk	$800.00
			reporter of the decisions of the Supreme Court	$1,000.00
			compensation of sundry district attorneys and marshals, including those in the several territories	$10,500.00
		[Expenses]	defraying expenses of Supreme, district, and circuit courts, including District of Columbia . . .	$200,000.00
		TOTAL APPROPRIATION		$295,000.00

1826

Statute (Citation)	Date Passed	Headings	Line-item Details	Appropriation
Ch. 13, 1826 (4 Stat. 142, 146)	March 14, 1826	[Salaries]	Chief Justice, associate justices, district judges, including chief justice and associate judges of District of Columbia	$79,200.00
			Attorney General	$3,500.00
			Attorney General's clerk	$800.00
			compensation of sundry district attorneys and marshals, including those in the several territories	$10,900.00
		[Expenses]	defraying expenses of Supreme, district, and circuit courts, including District of Columbia . . .	$150,000.00
		TOTAL APPROPRIATION		$244,400.00

1827

Statute (Citation)	Date Passed	Headings	Line-item Details	Appropriation
Ch. 23, 1827 (4 Stat. 208, 213)	March 2, 1827	[Salaries]	Chief Justice, associate justices, district judges, including chief justice and associate judges of District of Columbia	$78,711.42
			reporter of the decisions of the Supreme Court, for 1826 and 1827	$2,000.00
			Attorney General	$3,500.00
			Attorney General's clerk	$800.00
			compensation of sundry district attorneys and marshals, including those in the several territories	$10,900.00
		[Expenses]	defraying expenses of Supreme, district, and circuit courts, including District of Columbia	$150,000.00
		TOTAL APPROPRIATION		$245,911.42

1828

Statute (Citation)	Date Passed	Headings	Line-item Details	Appropriation
Ch. 6, 1828 (4 Stat. 247, 252)	February 12, 1828	[Salaries]	Chief Justice, associate justices, district judges, including chief justice and associate judges of District of Columbia, including additional compensation to district judge of Missouri	$79,200.00
			reporter of the decisions of the Supreme Court	$1,000.00
			Attorney General	$3,500.00
			Attorney General's clerk	$800.00
			compensation of sundry district attorneys and marshals, including those in the several territories	$10,900.00
		[Expenses]	defraying expenses of Supreme, district, and circuit courts, including District of Columbia . . .	$150,000.00
		TOTAL APPROPRIATION		$245,400.00

1829

Statute (Citation)	Date Passed	Headings	Line-item Details	Appropriation
Ch. 1, 1829 (4 Stat. 323, 328) – First Quarter of the Year	January 6, 1829	[Salaries]	Chief Justice, associate justices, district judges, including chief justice and associate judges of District of Columbia	$19,600.00
			Attorney General	$875.00

Statute (Citation)	Date Passed	Headings	Line-item Details	Appropriation
			Attorney General's clerk	$200.00
			reporter of the decisions of the Supreme Court	$250.00
			compensation of district attorneys and marshals, including those in the several territories	$2,725.00
		[Expenses]	defraying expenses of Supreme, district, and circuit courts, including District of Columbia . . .	$37,500.00
		Total		$61,150.00
Ch. 24, 1829 (4 Stat. 336, 342) – Remainder of Year	March 2, 1829	[Salaries]	Chief Justice, associate justices, district judges, including chief justice and associate judges of District of Columbia, and additional compensation to district judge of Missouri	$59,600.00
			Attorney General	$2,625.00
			Attorney General's clerk	$600.00
			reporter of the decisions of the Supreme Court	$750.00
			compensation of district attorneys and marshals, including those in the several territories	$8,575.00
			compensation for marshal of Northern District of Alabama for 1824 and 1825	$300.00
		[Expenses]	defraying expenses of Supreme, district, and circuit courts, including District of Columbia . . .	$112,500.00
		Total		$184,950.00
		TOTAL APPROPRIATION		**$246,100.00**

1830

Statute (Citation)	Date Passed	Headings	Line-item Details	Appropriation
Ch. 33, 1830 (4 Stat. 377, 380)	March 18, 1830	[Salaries]	Chief Justice, associate justices, district judges, including chief justice and associate judges of District of Columbia, including additional compensation to district judge of Missouri	$78,723.00
			Attorney General	$3,500.00
			Attorney General's clerk	$800.00
			reporter of the decisions of the Supreme Court	$1,000.00
			compensation of district attorneys and marshals, including those in the several territories	$11,300.00
		[Expenses]	defraying expenses of Supreme, district, and circuit courts, including District of Columbia . . .	$150,000.00
		TOTAL APPROPRIATION		**$245,323.00**

1831

Statute (Citation)	Date Passed	Headings	Line-item Details	Appropriation
Ch. 55, 1831 (4 Stat. 452, 457)	March 2, 1831	[Judges' Salaries]	Chief Justice, associate justices, district judges, including arrearages for district judge salary increases under Ch. 213, 1830	$87,720.18
			chief justice and associate judges of District of Columbia, and judges of the orphans' court	$9,500.00
			compensation to William Cranch for preparation of civil and criminal code, done under Ch. 143, 1816	$1,000.00
		[Attorney General]	salary of the Attorney General	$4,000.00
			salary of the Attorney General's clerk	$800.00
			contingencies of Attorney General's Office	$500.00
			salary of the messenger in Attorney General's Office	$500.00
			purchase of books for Attorney General's Office	$500.00
			"expenses already incurred in fitting up the office of the Attorney General"	$733.00
		[Supreme Court Reporter]	salary of the reporter of the decisions of the Supreme Court	$1,000.00
		[Attorneys and Marshals]	compensation of district attorneys and marshals, including those in the several territories	$11,300.00
		[Court Expenses]	defraying expenses of Supreme, district, and circuit courts, including District of Columbia . . .	$190,000.00
		TOTAL APPROPRIATION		**$307,553.18**

1832

Statute (Citation)	Date Passed	Headings	Line-item Details	Appropriation
Ch. 74, 1832 (4 Stat. 506, 511)	May 5, 1832	[Judges' Salaries]	Chief Justice, associate justices, district judges	$81,400.00
			chief justice and associate judges of District of Columbia, and judges of the orphans' court	$9,500.00
		[Attorney General]	salary of the Attorney General	$4,000.00
			salary of the Attorney General's clerk	$800.00
			salary of the messenger in Attorney General's Office	$500.00
			contingent expenses, Attorney General's Office	$500.00
		[Supreme Court Reporter]	salary of the reporter of the decisions of the Supreme Court	$1,000.00
		[Attorneys and Marshals]	compensation of district attorneys and marshals, including those in the several territories	$11,300.00

1833

Statute (Citation)	Date Passed	Headings	Appropriation	Line-item Details
		[Court Expenses]	$7,500.00	compensation of assistant counsel and district attorneys, supplementary to several acts providing for settlement of private land claims in Florida, under Ch. 70, 1828
			$190,000.00	defraying expenses of Supreme, district, and circuit courts, including District of Columbia . . . .
		TOTAL APPROPRIATION	**$306,500.00**	
Ch. 1, 1833 (4 Stat. 609)	January 14, 1833	[Court Expenses]	$51,655.00	defraying expenses of several courts of the United States, jurors and witnesses, expenses of suits in which the U.S. is concerned, prosecutions for offences against U.S., keeping of prisoners
Ch. 54, 1833 (4 Stat. 619, 624)	March 2, 1833	[Judges' Salaries]	$81,400.00	Chief Justice, associate justices, district judges
			$9,500.00	chief justice and associate judges of District of Columbia, and judges of the orphans' court
		[Attorney General]	$4,000.00	salary of the Attorney General
			$800.00	salary of the Attorney General's clerk
			$500.00	salary of the messenger in Attorney General's Office
			$500.00	contingent expenses, Attorney General's Office
		[Supreme Court Reporter]	$1,000.00	salary of the reporter of the decisions of the Supreme Court
		[Attorneys and Marshals]	$12,700.00	compensation of district attorneys and marshals, including those in the several territories
		[Court Expenses]	$225,000.00	defraying expenses of Supreme, district, and circuit courts, including District of Columbia . . . .
		TOTAL APPROPRIATION	**$387,055.00**	

1834

Statute (Citation)	Date Passed	Headings	Appropriation	Line-item Details
Ch. 92, 1834 (4 Stat. 689, 695)	June 27, 1834	[Judges' Salaries]	$81,400.00	Chief Justice, associate justices, district judges
			$9,500.00	chief justice and associate judges of District of Columbia, and judges of the orphans' court
		[Attorney General]	$4,000.00	salary of the Attorney General
			$800.00	salary of the Attorney General's clerk

Headings	Appropriation	Line-item Details
	$500.00	salary of the messenger in Attorney General's Office
	$500.00	contingent expenses, Attorney General's Office
[Supreme Court Reporter]	$1,000.00	salary of the reporter of the decisions of the Supreme Court
	$3,000.00	for printing the records of the Supreme Court
[Attorneys and Marshals]	$12,700.00	compensation of district attorneys and marshals, including those in the several territories
[Court Expenses]	$260,000.00	defraying expenses of Supreme, district, and circuit courts, including District of Columbia . . . .
TOTAL APPROPRIATION	$373,400.00	

1835

Statute (Citation)	Date Passed	Headings	Appropriation	Line-item Details
Ch. 30, 1835 (4 Stat. 760, 767)	March 3, 1835	[Judges' Salaries]	$81,400.00	Chief Justice, associate justices, district judges
			$9,500.00	chief justice and associate judges of District of Columbia, and judges of the orphans' court
		[Attorney General]	$4,000.00	salary of the Attorney General
			$800.00	salary of the Attorney General's clerk
			$500.00	salary of the messenger in Attorney General's Office
			$500.00	contingent expenses, Attorney General's Office
		[Supreme Court Reporter]	$1,000.00	salary of the reporter of the decisions of the Supreme Court
			$3,000.00	for printing the records of the Supreme Court
		[Attorneys and Marshals]	$15,875.00	compensation of district attorneys and marshals, including those in the several territories, including $3,175 deficiency for fourth quarter of 1834
		[Court Expenses]	$300,000.00	defraying expenses of Supreme, district, and circuit courts, including District of Columbia . . . .
		TOTAL APPROPRIATION	$416,575.00	

1836

Statute (Citation)	Date Passed	Headings	Appropriation	Line-item Details
Ch. 59, 1836 (5 Stat. 17, 22)	May 9, 1836	[Judges' Salaries]	$81,400.00	Chief Justice, associate justices, district judges
			$9,500.00	chief justice and associate judges of District of Columbia, and judges of the orphans' court
		[Attorney General]	$4,000.00	salary of the Attorney General

			$800.00	salary of the Attorney General's clerk
			$500.00	salary of the messenger in Attorney General's Office
			$500.00	contingent expenses, Attorney General's Office
		[Supreme Court Reporter]	$1,000.00	salary of the reporter of the decisions of the Supreme Court
			$3,000.00	for printing the records of the Supreme Court
		[Attorneys and Marshals]	$12,900.00	compensation of district attorneys and marshals, including those in the several territories
		[Court Expenses]	$345,000.00	defraying expenses of Supreme, district, and circuit courts, including District of Columbia . . .
		TOTAL APPROPRIATION	**$458,600.00**	

1837

Statute (Citation)	Date Passed	Headings	Appropriation	Line-item Details
Ch. 33, 1837 (5 Stat. 163, 168)	March 3, 1837	[Judges' Salaries]	$84,900.00	Chief Justice, associate justices, district judges
			$9,500.00	chief justice and associate judges of District of Columbia, and judges of the orphans' court
		[Attorney General]	$4,000.00	salary of the Attorney General
			$1,300.00	salaries of the Attorney General's clerk and messenger
			$500.00	contingent expenses, Attorney General's Office
		[Supreme Court Reporter]	$1,000.00	salary of the reporter of the decisions of the Supreme Court
			$3,000.00	for printing the records of the Supreme Court
		[Attorneys and Marshals]	$13,250.00	compensation of district attorneys and marshals, including those in the several territories
		[Court Expenses]	$330,000.00	defraying expenses of Supreme, district, and circuit courts, including District of Columbia . . .
		TOTAL APPROPRIATION	**$447,450.00**	

1838

Statute (Citation)	Date Passed	Headings	Appropriation	Line-item Details
Ch. 54, 1838 (5 Stat. 216, 221)	April 6, 1838	[Judges' Salaries]	$101,400.00	Chief Justice, associate justices, district judges
			$9,500.00	chief justice and associate judges of District of Columbia, and judges of the orphans' court
		[Attorney General]	$4,000.00	salary of the Attorney General

Headings	Line-item Details	Appropriation
	salaries of the Attorney General's clerk and messenger	$1,300.00
	contingent expenses, Attorney General's Office	$500.00
[Supreme Court Reporter]	salary of the reporter of the decisions of the Supreme Court	$1,000.00
	for printing the records of the Supreme Court	$3,000.00
[Attorneys and Marshals]	compensation of district attorneys and marshals, including those in the several territories	$13,250.00
[Court Expenses]	defraying expenses of Supreme, district, and circuit courts, including District of Columbia	$350,000.00
TOTAL APPROPRIATION		**$483,950.00**

1839

Statute (Citation)	Date Passed	Headings	Line-item Details	Appropriation
Ch. 82, 1839 (5 Stat. 339, 344)	March 3, 1839	[Judges' Salaries]	Chief Justice, associate justices, district judges	$93,900.00
			chief justice and associate judges of District of Columbia, and judges of the criminal and orphans' courts	$12,700.00
		[Attorney General]	salary of the Attorney General	$4,000.00
			salaries of the Attorney General's clerk and messenger	$1,300.00
			contingent expenses, Attorney General's Office	$500.00
		[Supreme Court Reporter]	salary of the reporter of the decisions of the Supreme Court	$1,000.00
		[Attorneys and Marshals]	compensation of district attorneys and marshals, including those in the several territories (including arrearages)	$14,842.00
		[Court Expenses]	defraying expenses of Supreme, district, and circuit courts, including District of Columbia	$128,000.00
		TOTAL APPROPRIATION		**$256,242.00**

1840

Statute (Citation)	Date Passed	Headings	Line-item Details	Appropriation
Ch. 22, 1840 (5 Stat. 371, 377)	May 8, 1840	[Judges' Salaries]	Chief Justice, associate justices, district judges	$93,900.00
			chief justice and associate judges of District of Columbia, and judges of the criminal and orphans' courts	$12,700.00
		[Attorney General]	salary of the Attorney General	$4,000.00
			salaries of the Attorney General's clerk and messenger	$1,500.00
			contingent expenses, Attorney General's Office	$500.00
			purchasing of law books	$1,000.00

Headings	Appropriation	Line-item Details
[Supreme Court Reporter]	$1,000.00	salary of the reporter of the decisions of the Supreme Court
[Attorneys and Marshals]	$14,450.00	compensation of district attorneys and marshals, including those in the several territories
[Court Expenses]	$300,000.00	defraying expenses of Supreme, district, and circuit courts, including District of Columbia . . .
TOTAL APPROPRIATION	$429,050.00	

1841

Statute (Citation)	Date Passed	Headings	Appropriation	Line-item Details
Ch. 35, 1841 (5 Stat. 421, 427)	March 3, 1841	[Judges' Salaries]	$93,900.00	Chief Justice, associate justices, district judges
			$12,700.00	chief justice and associate judges of District of Columbia, and judges of the criminal and orphans' courts
		[Attorney General]	$4,000.00	salary of the Attorney General
			$1,500.00	salaries of the Attorney General's clerk and messenger
			$500.00	contingent expenses, Attorney General's Office
		[Supreme Court Reporter]	$1,000.00	salary of the reporter of the decisions of the Supreme Court
		[Attorneys and Marshals]	$14,450.00	compensation of district attorneys and marshals, including those in the several territories
		[Court Expenses]	$325,000.00	defraying expenses of Supreme, district, and circuit courts, including District of Columbia . . .
		TOTAL APPROPRIATION	$453,050.00	

1842

Statute (Citation)	Date Passed	Headings	Appropriation	Line-item Details
Ch. 29, 1842 (5 Stat. 475, 481)	May 18, 1842	Judiciary	$5,000.00	salary of the Chief Justice of the Supreme Court
			$36,000.00	salaries of the associate justices of the Supreme Court
			$52,900.00	salaries of district judges (these are itemized by district in the statute)
			$2,700.00	salary of the chief justice of the District of Columbia
			$5,000.00	salary of the 2 associate judges of the District of Columbia
			$2,000.00	salary of the judge of the criminal court, District of Columbia
			$1,000.00	salary of the judge of the orphans' court, Washington County (D.C.)
			$1,000.00	salary of the judge of the orphans' court, Alexandria County (D.C.)

Appropriation	Line-item Details
$4,000.00	salary of the Attorney General
$1,500.00	salaries of the Attorney General's clerk and messenger
$6,800.00	compensation for district attorneys
$366.11	compensation for district attorney, South Carolina, April 27, 1841, to December 31, 1842
$600.00	compensation for district attorney, Eastern District of Louisiana
$250.00	compensation for district attorney, Wisconsin
$6,800.00	compensation for marshals
$400.00	compensation for marshal, North Carolina
$375,000.00	[Court Expenses] defraying expenses of Supreme, district, and circuit courts, including District of Columbia . . .

TOTAL APPROPRIATION $501,316.11

1843

Statute (Citation)	Date Passed	Headings	Appropriation	Line-item Details
Ch. 2, 1842 (5 Stat. 586, 592) First Half of 1843	December 24, 1842	Judiciary	$2,500.00	salary of the Chief Justice of the Supreme Court
			$18,000.00	salaries of associate justices of the Supreme Court
			$26,450.00	salaries of district judges (itemized in statute)
			$1,350.00	salary of chief justice of the District of Columbia
			$2,500.00	salaries of 2 associate judges of the District of Columbia
			$1,000.00	salary of judge of the Criminal Court of D.C.
			$500.00	salary of judge of orphans' court, Washington County (D.C.)
			$500.00	salary of judge of orphans' court, Alexandria County (D.C.)
			$3,000.00	salary of Attorney General, his clerk and messenger, and expenses of office
			$650.00	salary of the reporter of decisions of the Supreme Court
			$4,225.00	compensation of district attorneys (itemized in statute)
			$3,600.00	compensation of marshals (itemized in statute)
		[Court Expenses]	$238,000.00	defraying expenses of Supreme, district, and circuit courts, including District of Columbia . . .

TOTAL APPROPRIATION $302,275.00

1844

Statute (Citation)	Date Passed	Headings	Appropriation	Line-item Details
Ch. 100, 1843 (5 Stat. 630, 639)	March 3, 1843	Judiciary	$93,900.00	salaries of the Chief Justice and associate justices of the Supreme Court of the United States, and district judges
			$5,500.00	salaries of Attorney General, his clerk and messenger
			$500.00	contingent expenses, Attorney General's Office
			$11,700.00	salaries of the chief justice, associate judges, judges of criminal and orphans' courts, District of Columbia
			$1,350.00	salary of the reporter of the decisions of the Supreme Court, including arrears for 1842
			$8,450.00	salaries of district attorneys
			$400.00	arrears for salaries of district attorneys of Maryland and Massachusetts for 1842
			$7,200.00	salaries of marshals
		[Court Expenses]	$373,000.00	defraying expenses of Supreme, district, and circuit courts, including District of Columbia....
		TOTAL APPROPRIATION	**$502,000.00**	

1845

Statute (Citation)	Date Passed	Headings	Appropriation	Line-item Details
Ch. 105, 1844 (5 Stat. 681, 689)	June 17, 1844	Judiciary	$41,000.00	salaries of the Chief Justice and associate justices of the Supreme Court of the United States
			$52,900.00	salaries of district judges
			$11,700.00	salaries of the chief justice, associate judges, judges of criminal and orphans' courts, District of Columbia
			$5,500.00	salaries of the Attorney General, his clerk and messenger
			$500.00	contingent expenses, Attorney General's Office
			$1,300.00	salary of the reporter of the decisions of the Supreme Court
			$8,000.00	compensation for district attorneys
			$7,200.00	compensation for marshals
		[Court Expenses]	$400,000.00	defraying expenses of Supreme, district, and circuit courts, including District of Columbia....
		TOTAL APPROPRIATION	**$528,100.00**	

1846

Statute (Citation)	Date Passed	Headings	Appropriation	Line-item Details
Ch. 71, 1845 (5 Stat. 752, 760)	March 3, 1845	Judiciary	$41,000.00	salaries of the Chief Justice and associate justices of the Supreme Court of the United States
			$52,900.00	salaries of district judges
			$11,700.00	salaries of the chief justice, associate judges, judges of criminal and orphans' courts, District of Columbia
			$5,000.00	salaries of the Attorney General and clerk in his office
			$500.00	contingent expenses, Attorney General's Office
			$1,300.00	salary of the reporter of the decisions of the Supreme Court
			$8,000.00	compensation of district attorneys
			$7,200.00	compensation of marshals
		[Court Expenses]	$400,000.00	defraying expenses of Supreme, district, and circuit courts, including District of Columbia . . .
			$5,000.00	for employing additional counsel to represent U.S. in land claims arising under Act of June 17, 1844, Ch. 95
		Total	$532,600.00	
Ch. 14, 1846 (9 Stat. 6, 7)	May 8, 1846		$2,394.97	additional salary for district judges of Ohio, Indiana, Illinois, Missouri, from March 3, 1845
			$150,000.00	defraying expenses of Supreme, district, and circuit courts, including District of Columbia . . .
		Total	$1,106,994.97	
		TOTAL APPROPRIATION	$1,639,594.97	

1847

Statute (Citation)	Date Passed	Headings	Appropriation	Line-item Details
Ch. 175, 1846 (9 Stat. 85, 91)	August 10, 1846	Judiciary	$41,000.00	salaries of the Chief Justice and associate justices of the Supreme Court of the United States
			$56,700.00	salaries of district judges
			$4,000.00	additional salary for district judges of Missouri, Arkansas, Louisiana, Mississippi, and Alabama, under Ch. 95, 1844, section (a)
			$11,700.00	salaries of the chief justice, associate judges, judges of criminal and orphans' courts, District of Columbia

	Line-item Details	Appropriation
	salary of Attorney General, his clerk and messenger	$5,500.00
	contingent expenses, Attorney General's Office	$500.00
	salary of the reporter of the decisions of the Supreme Court	$1,300.00
	compensation of district attorneys	$7,000.00
	compensation of marshals	$6,200.00
[Court Expenses]	defraying expenses of Supreme, district, and circuit courts, including District of Columbia . . .	$439,000.00
TOTAL APPROPRIATION		**$572,900.00**

1848

Statute (Citation)	Date Passed	Headings	Line-item Details	Appropriation
Ch. 47, 1847 (9 Stat. 155, 161, 167)	March 3, 1847	Judiciary	salaries of the Chief Justice and associate justices of the Supreme Court of the United States	$41,000.00
			salaries of district judges	$61,700.00
			additional salary for district judges of Missouri, Arkansas, Louisiana, Mississippi, and Alabama, under Ch. 95, 1844, section (a)	$1,000.00
			salaries of the chief justice, associate judges, judges of criminal and orphans' courts, District of Columbia	$10,700.00
			salary of Attorney General, his clerk and messenger	$6,700.00
			contingent expenses, Attorney General's Office	$500.00
			salary of the reporter of the decisions of the Supreme Court	$1,300.00
			compensation of district attorneys (including territory of Wisconsin)	$7,200.00
			compensation of marshals (including territory of Wisconsin)	$6,400.00
		[Court Expenses]	defraying expenses of Supreme, district, and circuit courts, including District of Columbia	$435,000.00
			additional salary for district judge of Texas for May 1846 to June 1847	$2,180.30
			additional salary for district attorney and marshal of Texas for May 1846 to June 1847	$436.26
		Total		$574,116.56

Statute (Citation)	Date Passed		Line-item Details	Appropriation
Ch. 23, 1848 (9 Stat. 215)	March 27, 1848		for judge of Southern District of Florida, under Ch. 20, 1847	$2,661.12
			compensation of district attorney and marshal of Southern District of Florida, under Ch. 20, 1847	$532.22
		Total		$3,193.34
		TOTAL APPROPRIATION		**$577,309.90**

1849

Statute (Citation)	Date Passed	Headings	Line-item Details	Appropriation
Ch. 166, 1848 (9 Stat. 284, 292)	August 12, 1848	Judiciary	salaries of the Chief Justice and associate justices of the Supreme Court of the United States	$41,000.00
			salaries of district judges	$63,700.00
			salaries of the chief justice, associate judges, judges of criminal and orphans' courts, District of Columbia	$10,700.00
			salary of Attorney General, his clerk and messenger	$6,100.00
			contingent expenses, Attorney General's Office	$500.00
			salary of the reporter of the decisions of the Supreme Court	$1,300.00
			compensation of district attorneys	$7,400.00
			compensation of marshals	$6,600.00
		[Court Expenses]	defraying expenses of Supreme, district, and circuit courts, including District of Columbia . . .	$443,000.00
			repairs of the United States courthouse at Detroit	indefinite
		TOTAL APPROPRIATION		**$580,300.00**

1850

Statute (Citation)	Date Passed	Headings	Line-item Details	Appropriation
Ch. 100, 1849 (9 Stat. 354, 361)	March 3, 1849	Judiciary	salaries of the Chief Justice and associate justices of the Supreme Court of the United States	$41,000.00
			salaries of district judges	$63,700.00
			salaries of the chief justice, associate judges, judges of criminal and orphans' courts, District of Columbia	$10,700.00
			additional salary for district judge of Louisiana for FYE 1848 and 1849	$1,400.00
			salary of Attorney General, his clerk and messenger	$6,100.00
			contingent expenses, Attorney General's Office	$500.00

Statute (Citation)	Date Passed	Headings	Line-item Details	Appropriation
			purchase of books and bookcases for Attorney General's Office	$2,000.00
			salary of the reporter of the decisions of the Supreme Court	$1,300.00
			compensation of district attorneys	$7,400.00
			compensation of marshals	$6,800.00
		[Court Expenses]	defraying expenses of Supreme, district, and circuit courts, including District of Columbia . . .	$443,000.00
		TOTAL APPROPRIATION		$583,900.00

1851

Statute (Citation)	Date Passed	Headings	Line-item Details	Appropriation
Ch. 90, 1850 (9 Stat. 523, 532)	September 30, 1850	Judiciary	salaries of the Chief Justice and associate justices of the Supreme Court of the United States	$41,000.00
			salaries of district judges	$63,700.00
			salaries of the chief justice, associate judges, judges of criminal and orphans' courts, District of Columbia	$10,700.00
			additional salary of judge of D.C. orphans' court	$500.00
			salary of Attorney General, his clerk and messenger	$8,300.00
			additional clerk in Attorney General's Office	$2,000.00
			contingent expenses, Attorney General's Office	$500.00
			purchase of law books for Attorney General's Office	$1,500.00
			reimbursement to former-Attorney General Reverdy Johnson, for compensation of use of a clerk	$866.59
			salary of the reporter of the decisions of the Supreme Court (plus $1,300 for each additional volume)	$1,300.00
			compensation of district attorneys	$8,400.00
			compensation of marshals	$7,000.00
		[Court Expenses]	defraying expenses of Supreme, district, and circuit courts, including District of Columbia . . .	$557,537.00
			clerk of district judge of Florida	$900.00
		Total		$704,203.59
Ch. 12, 1851 (9 Stat. 570)	February 27, 1851		judges for the Northern and Southern Districts of California	$3,250.00
		TOTAL APPROPRIATION		$707,453.59

1852

Statute (Citation)	Date Passed	Headings	Appropriation	Line-item Details
Ch. 32, 1851 (9 Stat. 598, 607)	March 3, 1851	Judiciary	$41,000.00	salaries of the Chief Justice and associate justices of the Supreme Court of the United States
			$70,000.00	salaries of district judges
			$11,200.00	salaries of the chief justice, associate judges, judges of criminal and orphans' courts, District of Columbia
			$10,300.00	salaries of the Attorney General, clerk, and messenger
			$500.00	contingent expenses, Attorney General's Office
			$1,300.00	salary of the reporter of the decisions of the Supreme Court (plus $1,300 for each additional volume)
			$8,800.00	compensation of district attorneys
			$7,400.00	compensation of marshals
		[Court Expenses]	$592,747.00	defraying expenses of Supreme, district, and circuit courts, including District of Columbia . . . .
		TOTAL APPROPRIATION	**$743,247.00**	

1853

Statute (Citation)	Date Passed	Headings	Appropriation	Line-item Details
Ch. 66, 1852 (10 Stat. 15, 22)	July 21, 1852	Court Expenses	$90,000.00	defraying expenses of Supreme, district, and circuit courts, including District of Columbia . . . .
Ch. 108, 1852 (10 Stat. 76, 84)	August 31, 1852	Judiciary	$41,000.00	salaries of the Chief Justice and associate justices of the Supreme Court of the United States
			$72,000.00	salaries of district judges
			$11,200.00	salaries of the chief justice, associate judges, judges of criminal and orphans' courts, District of Columbia
			$10,300.00	salaries of the Attorney General, clerk, and messenger
			$500.00	contingent expenses, Attorney General's Office
			$1,300.00	salary of the reporter of the decisions of the Supreme Court (plus $1,300 for each additional volume)
			$8,800.00	compensation of district attorneys
			$7,400.00	compensation of marshals

			Appropriation	Line-item Details
[Court Expenses]			$630,000.00	defraying expenses of Supreme, district, and circuit courts, including District of Columbia . . .
Total			$782,500.00	
TOTAL APPROPRIATION			$872,500.00	

1854

Statute (Citation)	Date Passed	Headings	Appropriation	Line-item Details
Ch. 97, 1853 (10 Stat. 189, 198)	March 3, 1853	Judiciary	$41,000.00	salaries of the Chief Justice and associate justices of the Supreme Court of the United States
			$70,700.00	salaries of district judges
			$11,700.00	salaries of the chief justice, associate judges, judges of criminal and orphans' courts, District of Columbia
			$10,300.00	salaries of the Attorney General, clerk, and messenger
			$500.00	contingent expenses, Attorney General's Office
			$1,300.00	salary of the reporter of the decisions of the Supreme Court
			$8,800.00	compensation of district attorneys
			$7,400.00	compensation of marshals
		[Court Expenses]	$672,900.00	defraying expenses of Supreme, district, and circuit courts, including District of Columbia . . . .
			$14,400.00	for district court in Iowa, reimbursement of Lee County for expenses prior to statehood
			$20,000.00	Washington Infirmary, for benefit of sick transient paupers
TOTAL APPROPRIATION			$859,000.00	

1855

Statute (Citation)	Date Passed	Headings	Appropriation	Line-item Details
Ch. 242, 1854 (10 Stat. 546, 557, 567)	August 4, 1854	Judiciary	$41,000.00	salaries of the Chief Justice and associate justices of the Supreme Court of the United States
			$70,700.00	salaries of district judges
			$4,028.88	additional compensation to judge of Southern District of California for 1854
			$11,700.00	salaries of the chief justice, associate judges, judges of criminal and orphans' courts, District of Columbia
			$12,300.00	salaries of the Attorney General, clerk, and messenger

Line-item Details	Appropriation
contingent expenses, Attorney General's Office	$500.00
purchase of books for Attorney General's Office	$1,500.00
salary of the reporter of the decisions of the Supreme Court	$1,300.00
compensation of district attorneys	$9,400.00
compensation of marshals	$8,200.00
[Court Expenses] defraying expenses of Supreme, district, and circuit courts, including District of Columbia....	$700,000.00
rent to city of Norfolk for use of rooms in City Hall for District Court of Eastern District of Virginia	$900.00
TOTAL APPROPRIATION	**$861,528.88**

1856

Statute (Citation)	Date Passed	Headings	Line-item Details	Appropriation
Ch. 175, 1855 (10 Stat. 643, 655, 662)	March 3, 1855	Judiciary	salaries of the Chief Justice and associate justices of the Supreme Court of the United States	$54,500.00
			salary of the circuit judge of California	$4,500.00
			salaries of district judges, including deficiencies for FY ending 1855	$111,668.00
			salaries of the chief justice, associate judges, judges of criminal and orphans' courts, District of Columbia	$11,700.00
			salaries of the Attorney General, clerk, and messenger	$18,040.00
			contingent expenses, Attorney General's Office	$1,000.00
			purchase of law books for Attorney General's Office	$1,500.00
			salary of the reporter of the decisions of the Supreme Court	$1,300.00
			150 copies of Vol. 16 of Howard's Reports of the Decisions of the Supreme Court for the State Department	$1,300.00
			compensation of district attorneys	$10,150.00
			compensation of marshals	$8,600.00
			for repairs of courtrooms and offices from fire in Southern District of New York	$7,148.81
		[Court Expenses]	defraying expenses of Supreme, district, and circuit courts, including District of Columbia....	$800,000.00
		Total		$1,031,406.81

Statute (Citation)	Date Passed	Headings	Line-item Details	Appropriation
Ch. 29, 1856 (11 Stat. 10, 12, 14)	May 15, 1856	[Salaries]	salaries of the Chief Justice and associate justices of the Supreme Court of the United States	$1,444.81
			salary of the circuit judge of California	$1,487.50
			compensation of district attorneys	$4,696.86
			compensation of marshals	$5,150.99
		[Court Expenses]	defraying expenses of Supreme, district, and circuit courts, including District of Columbia . . .	$200,000.00
		Total		$212,780.16
		TOTAL APPROPRIATION		**$1,244,186.97**

1857

Statute (Citation)	Date Passed	Headings	Line-item Details	Appropriation
Ch. 162, 1856 (11 Stat. 102, 114)	August 18, 1856	Judiciary	salaries of the Chief Justice and associate justices of the Supreme Court of the United States	$54,500.00
			salary of the circuit judge of California	$4,500.00
			salaries of district judges	$101,250.00
			salaries of the chief justice, associate judges, judges of criminal and orphans' courts, District of Columbia	$11,700.00
		Office of Attorney General	salaries of the Attorney General, clerks, and messengers	$18,040.00
			contingent expenses	$1,500.00
			legal assistance and other expenditures in disposal of private land claims in California	$12,000.00
			purchase of law books	$1,500.00
			purchase of Mexican and Spanish law books	$500.00
			fuel and labor for the office	$500.00
			furniture and bookcases	$500.00
			contingent expenses for codifying laws of D.C.	$600.00
			compensation of district attorneys	$11,350.00
			compensation of marshals	$9,800.00
			salary of the reporter of decisions of the Supreme Court	$1,300.00
			salaries of 2 commissioners to codify laws of D.C.	$6,000.00
		Court of Claims	salaries of 3 judges, solicitor, assistant solicitor, deputy, clerk, assistant clerks, messenger	$27,000.00
			stationery, fuel, gas, labor, printing, miscellaneous items	$3,000.00
			fees of witnesses on behalf of government and attorneys appointed to take depositions	$1,500.00

			Line-item Details	
		[Court Expenses]	defraying expenses of Supreme, district, and circuit courts, including District of Columbia . . .	$1,000,000.00
		TOTAL APPROPRIATION		**$1,267,040.00**

1858

Statute (Citation)	Date Passed	Headings	Line-item Details	Appropriation
Ch. 107, 1857 (11 Stat. 206, 217, 219)	March 3, 1857	Judiciary	salaries of the Chief Justice and associate justices of the Supreme Court of the United States	$54,500.00
			salaries of district judges	$101,250.00
			salary of the salary of the circuit judge of California	$6,000.00
			salaries of the chief justice, associate judges, judges of criminal and orphans' courts, District of Columbia	$11,700.00
		Office of Attorney General	salaries of the Attorney General, clerks, and messengers	$18,100.00
			contingent expenses	$1,500.00
			purchase of law books	$1,500.00
			purchase of deficient state reports and statutes	$1,500.00
			fuel and labor	$500.00
			furniture and bookcases	$500.00
			salaries of 2 commissioners to codify laws of D.C.	$2,500.00
			salary of the reporter of decisions of the Supreme Court	$1,300.00
			compensation of district attorneys	$11,550.00
			compensation of marshals	$10,000.00
		[Court Expenses]	defraying expenses of Supreme, district, and circuit courts, including District of Columbia . . .	$1,000,000.00
		TOTAL APPROPRIATION		**$1,222,400.00**

1859

Statute (Citation)	Date Passed	Headings	Line-item Details	Appropriation
Ch. 82, 1858 (11 Stat. 295, 306, 307)	June 2, 1858	Judiciary	salaries of the Chief Justice and associate justices of the Supreme Court of the United States	$54,500.00
			salaries of district judges	$108,750.00
			salary of the circuit judge of California	$6,000.00
			salaries of the chief justice, associate judges, judges of criminal and orphans' courts, District of Columbia	$15,750.00

Headings	Line-item Details	Appropriation
Office of Attorney General	salaries of the Attorney General, clerks, and messengers	$18,100.00
	contingent expenses	$2,500.00
	purchase of books	$1,000.00
	purchase of deficient state reports and statutes	$1,000.00
	fuel and labor	$1,000.00
	furniture and bookcases	$1,000.00
	legal assistance and other expenditures in disposal of private land claims in California	$12,000.00
	services of special counsel and other extraordinary expenses, defending title of U.S. to public property in California	$40,000.00
	compensation, clerks for district attorney of Northern District of California, transcription of records in land cases appealed to the Supreme Court	indefinite
	salary of the reporter of decisions of the Supreme Court	$1,300.00
	compensation of district attorneys	$11,750.00
	compensation of marshals	$10,400.00
[Court Expenses]	defraying expenses of Supreme, district, and circuit courts, including District of Columbia . . .	$1,000,000.00
	TOTAL APPROPRIATION	**$1,285,050.00**

1860

Statute (Citation)	Date Passed	Headings	Line-item Details	Appropriation
Ch. 80, 1859 (11 Stat. 410, 419)	March 3, 1859	Judiciary	salaries of the Chief Justice and associate justices of the Supreme Court of the United States	$54,500.00
			salaries of district judges	$110,750.00
			salary of the circuit judge of California	$6,000.00
			salaries of the chief justice, associate judges, judges of criminal and orphans' courts, District of Columbia	$15,750.00
		Office of Attorney General	salaries of the Attorney General, assistant, clerks, and messenger	$14,367.00
			contingent expenses	$2,000.00
			purchase of law books	$800.00
			fuel and labor	$500.00
			furniture and bookcases	$500.00
			purchase of deficient state reports	$800.00
			legal assistance and expenditures in disposal of private land claims in California	$10,000.00

1861

Statute (Citation)	Date Passed	Headings	Appropriation	Line-item Details
			$40,000.00	special and extraordinary expenses of California land claims
			$1,300.00	salary of the reporter of decisions of the Supreme Court
			$11,700.00	compensation of district attorneys
			$10,400.00	compensation of marshals
		[Court Expenses]	$785,000.00	defraying expenses of Supreme, district, and circuit courts, including District of Columbia . . .
		TOTAL APPROPRIATION	**$1,064,367.00**	
Ch. 205, 1860 (12 Stat. 91, 101)	June 23, 1860	Judiciary	$54,500.00	salaries of the Chief Justice and associate justices of the Supreme Court of the United States
			$113,250.00	salaries of district judges
			$6,000.00	salary of the circuit judge of California
			$15,750.00	salaries of the chief justice, associate judges, judges of criminal and orphans' courts, District of Columbia
		Office of Attorney General	$17,500.00	salaries of the Attorney General, assistant attorney general, clerks, and messenger
			$2,000.00	contingent expenses
			$500.00	purchase of law books
			$500.00	purchase of deficient state reports and statutes
			$500.00	fuel and labor
			$300.00	furniture
			$10,000.00	legal assistance and expenditures in disposal of private land claims in California
			$20,000.00	special and extraordinary expenses of California land claims
			$1,300.00	salary of the reporter of decisions of the Supreme Court
			$750.00	purchase of Howard's Reports of Supreme Court for distribution to the State Department
			$10,000.00	prosecution of counterfeiters
			$11,850.00	compensation of district attorneys
			$10,400.00	compensation of marshals
		[Court Expenses]	$1,000,000.00	defraying expenses of Supreme, district, and circuit courts, including District of Columbia . . .
		TOTAL APPROPRIATION	**$1,275,100.00**	

1862

Statute (Citation)	Date Passed	Headings	Line-item Details	Appropriation
Ch. 44, 1861 (12 Stat. 133, 142)	February 20, 1861	Judiciary	salaries of the Chief Justice and associate justices of the Supreme Court of the United States	$54,500.00
			salaries of district judges	$115,184.06
			salary of the circuit judge of California	$6,000.00
			salaries of the chief justice, associate judges, judges of criminal and orphans' courts, District of Columbia	$15,750.00
		Office of the Attorney General	salaries of the Attorney General, assistant attorney general, clerks, and messenger	$17,500.00
			contingent expenses	$1,700.00
			purchase of law books	$500.00
			furniture and bookcases	$300.00
			legal assistance and expenditures in disposal of private land claims in California	$10,000.00
			special and extraordinary expenses of California land claims	$20,000.00
			salary of the reporter of decisions of the Supreme Court	$1,300.00
			compensation of district attorneys	$11,850.00
			compensation of marshals	$10,400.00
		[Court Expenses]	defraying expenses of Supreme, district, and circuit courts, including District of Columbia. . . .	$1,000,000.00
		TOTAL APPROPRIATION		**$1,264,984.06**

1863

Statute (Citation)	Date Passed	Headings	Line-item Details	Appropriation
Ch. 41, 1862 (12 Stat. 355, 365)	March 14, 1862	Judiciary	salaries of the Chief Justice and associate justices of the Supreme Court of the United States	$54,500.00
			salaries of district judges	$115,750.00
			salary of the circuit judge of California	$6,000.00
			salaries of the chief justice, associate judges, judges of criminal and orphans' courts, District of Columbia	$15,750.00
		Office of the Attorney General	salaries of the Attorney General, assistant attorney general, clerks, and messenger	$20,300.00
			fuel and labor	$3,000.00

Appropriation	Line-item Details
$250.00	purchase of law books
$10,000.00	legal assistance and expenditures in disposal of private land claims in California
$20,000.00	special and extraordinary expenses of California land claims
$1,300.00	salary of the reporter of decisions of the Supreme Court
$18,550.00	compensation of district attorneys
$11,000.00	compensation of marshals
$1,000,000.00	[Court Expenses] defraying expenses of Supreme, district, and circuit courts, including District of Columbia . . . .
TOTAL APPROPRIATION $1,276,400.00	

1864

Statute (Citation)	Date Passed	Headings	Appropriation	Line-item Details
Ch. 59, 1863 (12 Stat. 682, 693)	February 25, 1863	Judiciary	$30,000.00	salaries of the Chief Justice and associate justices of the Supreme Court of the United States
			$30,000.00	salaries of district judges
			$6,000.00	salary of the circuit judge of California
			$15,750.00	salaries of the chief justice, associate judges, judges of criminal and orphans' courts, District of Columbia
		Office of the Attorney General	$20,300.00	salaries of the Attorney General, assistant attorney general, clerks, and messenger
			$3,000.00	fuel and labor
			$250.00	purchase of law books
			$10,000.00	legal assistance and expenditures in disposal of private land claims in California
			$10,000.00	special and extraordinary expenses of California land claims
			$1,300.00	salary of the reporter of decisions of the Supreme Court
			$0.00	compensation of district attorneys
			$0.00	compensation of marshals
		Expenses of Courts of the United States	$1,000,000.00	defraying expenses of Supreme, district, and circuit courts, including District of Columbia . . . .
		TOTAL APPROPRIATION	$1,126,600.00	

1865

Statute (Citation)	Date Passed	Headings	Appropriation	Line-item Details
Ch. 147, 1864 (13 Stat. 145, 152, 157)	June 25, 1864	Office of the Attorney General	$20,300.00	salaries of the Attorney General, assistant attorney general, clerks, and messenger
			$3,000.00	fuel and labor
			$250.00	purchase of law books
			$10,000.00	legal assistance and expenditures in disposal of private land claims in California
			$10,000.00	special and extraordinary expenses of California land claims
		Justices of the Supreme Court of the United States	$60,500.00	salaries of the Chief Justice and associate justices of the Supreme Court of the United States
			$1,000.00	traveling expenses of the judge assigned to Tenth Circuit for attending session of Supreme Court
			$118,750.00	salaries of district judges
			$14,500.00	salaries of the chief justice, associate judges, judge of orphans' court, District of Columbia
			$1,300.00	salary of the reporter of the decisions of the Supreme Court
			$19,250.00	compensation of district attorneys
			$11,600.00	compensation of marshals
		Expenses of Courts of the United States	$500,000.00	defraying expenses of Supreme, district, and circuit courts, including District of Columbia . . . (listed under Dept. of Interior)
		TOTAL APPROPRIATION	**$770,450.00**	

1866

Statute (Citation)	Date Passed	Headings	Appropriation	Line-item Details
Ch. 73, 1865 (13 Stat. 445, 452, 457)	March 2, 1865	Office of the Attorney General	$20,400.00	salaries of the Attorney General, assistant attorney general, clerks, and messenger
			$3,500.00	fuel, labor, furniture, stationery, and miscellaneous items
			$500.00	purchase of books
			$10,000.00	legal assistance and expenditures in disposal of private land claims in California
		Justices of the Supreme Court of the United States	$60,500.00	salaries of the Chief Justice and associate justices of the Supreme Court of the United States
			$2,000.00	traveling expenses of the judge assigned to Tenth Circuit for attending session of Supreme Court

Headings	Line-item Details	Appropriation
	salaries of district judges	$118,750.00
	salaries of the chief justice, associate judges, judge of orphans' court, District of Columbia	$14,500.00
	salary of the reporter of the decisions of the Supreme Court	$1,300.00
	compensation of district attorneys	$19,100.00
	compensation of marshals	$12,000.00
Expenses of Courts of the United States	defraying expenses of Supreme, district, and circuit courts, including District of Columbia . . . (listed under Dept. of Interior)	$700,000.00
TOTAL APPROPRIATION		**$962,550.00**

1867

Statute (Citation)	Date Passed	Headings	Line-item Details	Appropriation
Ch. 208, 1866 (14 Stat. 191, 198, 205)	July 23, 1866	Office of the Attorney General	salaries of the Attorney General, assistant attorney general, clerks, and messenger	$23,700.00
			fuel, labor, furniture, stationery, and miscellaneous items	$4,000.00
			purchase of books	$500.00
			legal assistance and expenditures in disposal of private land claims in California	$5,000.00
		Justices of the Supreme Court of the United States	salaries of the Chief Justice and associate justices of the Supreme Court of the United States	$60,500.00
			traveling expenses of the judge assigned to Tenth Circuit for attending session of Supreme Court	$1,000.00
			salaries of district judges	$126,000.00
			salaries of the chief justice, associate judges, judges of criminal and orphans' courts, District of Columbia	$19,000.00
			salary of the reporter of the decisions of the Supreme Court	$2,500.00
			additional compensation to clerks of Attorney General's Office for services under amnesty proclamation	$2,000.00
			compensation of district attorneys	$19,250.00
			compensation of marshals	$12,000.00
		Expenses of Courts of the United States	defraying expenses of Supreme, district, and circuit courts, including District of Columbia . . . including $4,000 credited back for expenditures for New Orleans customs house (listed under Dept. of Interior)	$304,000.00
TOTAL APPROPRIATION				**$579,450.00**

1868

Statute (Citation)	Date Passed	Headings	Appropriation	Line-item Details
Ch. 166, 1867 (14 Stat. 440, 448, 455)	March 2, 1867	Office of the Attorney General	$27,500.00	salaries of the Attorney General, assistant attorney general, law clerk, chief clerk, clerks, and messenger
			$100.00	additional compensation to one messenger
			$7,000.00	fuel, labor, furniture, stationery, and miscellaneous items
			$1,000.00	purchase of books
			$1,000.00	for purchase of reports of the Supreme Court for Department of State
		Justices of the Supreme Court of the United States	$48,500.00	salaries of the Chief Justice and 7 associate justices of the Supreme Court of the United States
			$6,000.00	salary of 1 associate justice
			$1,000.00	traveling expenses of the judge assigned to Ninth Circuit for attending session of Supreme Court
			$121,500.00	salaries of district judges
			$19,000.00	salaries of the chief justice, associate judges, judges of criminal and orphans' courts, District of Columbia
			$2,500.00	salary of the reporter of the decisions of the Supreme Court
			$18,550.00	compensation of district attorneys
			$11,300.00	compensation of marshals
		Expenses of Courts of the United States	$1,300,000.00	defraying expenses of Supreme, district, and circuit courts, including District of Columbia . . . (listed under Dept. of Interior)
		TOTAL APPROPRIATION	**$1,564,950.00**	

1869

Statute (Citation)	Date Passed	Headings	Appropriation	Line-item Details
Ch. 176, 1868 (15 Stat. 92, 101, 109)	July 20, 1868	Office of the Attorney General	$25,200.00	salaries of the Attorney General, assistant attorney general, clerks, and messenger
			$5,000.00	fuel, labor, furniture, stationery, and miscellaneous items
			$1,000.00	purchase of books
		Justices of the Supreme Court of the United States	$42,500.00	salaries of the Chief Justice and 6 associate justices of the Supreme Court of the United States
			$6,000.00	salary of 1 associate justice
			$1,000.00	traveling expenses of justice assigned to Tenth Circuit

Appropriation	Line-item Details
$165,000.00	salaries of district judges
$19,000.00	salaries of the chief justice, associate judges, judges of criminal and orphans' courts, District of Columbia
$2,500.00	salary of the reporter of the decisions of the Supreme Court
$12,500.00	compensation of district attorneys
$14,600.00	compensation of marshals
Expenses of Courts of the United States $1,000,000.00	defraying expenses of Supreme, district, and circuit courts, including District of Columbia . . . (listed under Dept. of Interior)
TOTAL APPROPRIATION $1,294,300.00	

1870

Statute (Citation)	Date Passed	Headings	Appropriation	Line-item Details
Ch. 121, 1869 (15 Stat. 283, 294, 300)	March 3, 1869	Justices of the Supreme Court of the United States	$42,500.00	salaries of the Chief Justice and 6 associate justices of the Supreme Court of the United States
			$6,000.00	salary of 1 associate justice
			$1,000.00	traveling expenses for judge assigned to Tenth Circuit for attending session of Supreme Court
			$165,000.00	salaries of district judges
			$19,000.00	salaries of the chief justice, associate judges, judges of criminal and orphans' courts, District of Columbia
			$2,500.00	salary of the reporter of the decisions of the Supreme Court
			$12,500.00	compensation of district attorneys
			$14,800.00	compensation of marshals
		Office of the Attorney General	$25,200.00	salaries of Attorney General, law clerk, chief clerk, other clerks, messenger
			$8,000.00	salaries of 2 assistant attorneys general
			$2,000.00	salary of 1 clerk
			$3,600.00	salary of 2 class four clerks
			$10,000.00	fuel, labor, furniture, stationery, and miscellaneous items
			$1,000.00	purchase of law books
		Expenses of Courts of the United States	$1,500,000.00	defraying expenses of Supreme, district, and circuit courts, including District of Columbia . . . (listed under Dept. of Interior)
		TOTAL APPROPRIATION	$1,813,100.00	

1871

Statute (Citation)	Date Passed	Headings	Appropriation	Line-item Details
Ch. 251, 1870 (16 Stat. 230, 249)	July 12, 1870	Office of the Attorney General	$34,540.00	salaries for Attorney General, assistant attorney generals, clerks, and messengers
			$2,000.00	salary for 1 clerk
			$10,000.00	contingent expenses for fuel, labor, furniture, stationery, and miscellaneous items
			$1,000.00	purchase of books
		Supreme Court of the United States	$60,500.00	salaries of the Chief Justice and 9 associate or retired justices of the Supreme Court of the United States
			$3,500.00	salary of the marshal of the Supreme Court
			$2,500.00	salary of the reporter of the decisions of the Supreme Court
			$1,000.00	traveling expenses for judge assigned to Tenth Circuit for attending session of Supreme Court
			$45,000.00	salaries of 9 circuit judges
			$168,500.00	salaries of district judges
			$19,000.00	salaries of the chief justice, associate judges, judges of criminal and orphans' courts, District of Columbia
			$2,000.00	salary of the warden of the jail, District of Columbia
			$18,550.00	compensation of district attorneys
			$11,300.00	compensation of marshals
		Total	$379,390.00	
Ch. 292, 1870 (16 Stat. 291, 308)	July 15, 1870	[Court Expenses]	$1,200,000.00	defraying expenses of Supreme, district, and circuit courts, including District of Columbia . . . (listed under Dept. of Interior)
		TOTAL APPROPRIATION	$1,579,390.00	

1872

Statute (Citation)	Date Passed	Headings	Appropriation	Line-item Details
Ch. 113, 1871 (16 Stat. 475, 493)	March 3, 1871	Supreme Court of the United States	$72,500.00	salaries of the Chief Justice and 8 associate or retired justices of Supreme Court of the United States
			$54,000.00	salaries of circuit judges
			$2,500.00	salary of the reporter of the decisions of the Supreme Court
			$3,500.00	salary of the marshal of the Supreme Court

Statute (Citation)	Date Passed	Headings	Line-item Details	Appropriation
			salaries of district judges	$175,500.00
			salaries of the chief justice and 4 associate judges of the Supreme Court of the District of Columbia	$20,500.00
			salary of the warden of the jail, District of Columbia	$2,000.00
			compensation of district attorneys	$18,750.00
			compensation of marshals	$11,500.00
		Total		$360,750.00
Ch. 114, 1871 (16 Stat. 495, 498)	March 3, 1871	United States Courts	defraying expenses of Supreme, district, and circuit courts, including District of Columbia . . .	$2,000,000.00
			support of convicts transferred from District of Columbia	$10,000.00
		Total		$2,010,000.00
Ch. 172, 1872 (17 Stat. 122, 133)	May 18, 1872	District Courts of the United States	salaries for district judges for FY 1872	$14,325.00
			for defraying the expenses of the courts of the United States, including enforcement of Voting Rights Act (Ch. 99, 1871)	$1,000,000.00
			expenses, commission on revision of the statutes	$9,000.00
			fees of attorneys, marshals, and commissioners, Court of Claims	$800.00
			fees of attorneys and commissioners, Court of Claims, FY 1870	$341.14
			books for the Department of Justice	$2,500.00
			reimburse marshal for Eastern District of Texas for travel of Judge Thomas Duval	$825.75
		Total		$1,027,791.89
Ch. 415, 1872 (17 Stat. 347, 348)	June 10, 1872	Judiciary	defraying expenses of the courts of the United States, including the District of Columbia . . .	$200,000.00
		TOTAL APPROPRIATION		**$3,587,940.69**

1873

Statute (Citation)	Date Passed	Headings	Line-item Details	Appropriation
Ch. 140, 1872 (17 Stat. 61, 81)	May 8, 1872	United States Courts	salaries of the Chief Justice and 8 associate and retired justices of Supreme Court of the United States	$72,500.00
			salaries of 9 circuit judges	$54,000.00
			salary of the reporter of the decisions of the Supreme Court	$2,500.00
			salary of the marshal of the Supreme Court	$3,500.00

Appropriation	Line-item Details
$189,500.00	salary of district judges, including retired judges · · ·
$20,500.00	salaries of the chief justice and 4 associate judges of the Supreme Court of the District of Columbia
$2,000.00	salary of the warden of the jail, District of Columbia
$19,150.00	compensation of district attorneys
$11,700.00	compensation of marshals
$27,340.00	salaries of judges, clerks, bailiff, messenger
$3,000.00	contingent expenses
$1,000.00	reporting decisions
$400,000.00	to pay judgments of the Court of Claims

Court of Claims

$806,690.00	**Total**

Ch. 415, 1872 (17 Stat. 347, 348) June 10, 1872 Judiciary

Appropriation	Line-item Details
$3,000,000.00	defraying expenses of the courts of the United States, including the District of Columbia, and including enforcement of Voting Rights Act (Ch. 99, 1871)
$10,000.00	support of convicts transferred from District of Columbia
$25,000.00	compensation and fees, American and British Claims Commission
$10,000.00	defending claims under convention with Mexico
$30,000.00	defending claims against the United States
$50,000.00	detection and prosecution of crimes
$25,000.00	prosecution and collection of claims due the United States
$150,000.00	collection of captured and abandoned property

$3,300,000.00	**Total**
$4,106,690.00	**TOTAL APPROPRIATION**

1874

Statute (Citation)	Date Passed	Headings	Appropriation	Line-item Details
Ch. 226, 1873 (17 Stat. 485, 507)	March 3, 1873	United States Courts	$72,500.00	salaries of the Chief Justice and 8 associate justices of the Supreme Court of the United States
			$8,000.00	salary of 1 retired justice of the Supreme Court
			$54,000.00	salaries of 9 circuit judges
			$2,500.00	salary of the reporter of the decisions of the Supreme Court
			$3,500.00	salary of the marshal of the Supreme Court
			$193,000.00	salaries of district judges, including retired judges

Date	Citation	Category	Purpose	Amount
			salaries of the chief justice and 4 associate judges of the Supreme Court of the District of Columbia	$20,500.00
			salary of the warden of the jail, District of Columbia	$2,000.00
			compensation of district attorneys	$19,350.00
			compensation of marshals	$11,700.00
			salaries of judges, clerks, bailiff, messenger	$29,840.00
			contingent expenses	$3,000.00
			reporting of decisions	$1,000.00
		Court of Claims	to pay judgments of the Court of Claims	$400,000.00
		Total		$820,890.00
March 3, 1873	Ch. 227, 1873 (17 Stat. 510, 512)	Judiciary	defraying expenses of the courts of the United States, including the District of Columbia, including enforcement of Voting Rights Act (Ch. 99, 1871)	$3,000,000.00
			purchase of published case reports for distribution to the courts	$12,500.00
			purchase of volumes of U.S. Statutes at Large	$7,000.00
			support of convicts transferred from District of Columbia	$10,000.00
			defending claims under convention with Mexico	$10,000.00
			defending claims against the United States	$30,000.00
			detection and prosecution of crimes	$50,000.00
			prosecution and collection of claims due the United States	$15,000.00
			detecting and punishing violation of the intercourse acts	$10,000.00
			completing revision of statutes	$12,000.00
			repairs to City Hall building occupied by Supreme Court of the District of Columbia	$2,500.00
		Total		$3,159,000.00
June 22, 1874	Ch. 388, 1874 (18 Stat. 133, 144)	Judicial	defraying the expenses of the Supreme, circuit, and district courts, FY 1873	$350,000.00
			defraying the expenses of the Supreme, circuit, and district courts, FY 1872	$20,000.00
			salary, assistant Attorney General of the Post Office Department, FY 1873	$670.33
			salaries of district judges, to pay audited and certified accounts, FY 1873	$2,875.00
			pay to late district attorney, Colorado Territory, FY 1873	$35.71
			pay to district attorney, Eastern District of Pennsylvania, FY 1873	$39.90

			Appropriation	Line-item Details
			$33.52	pay to marshal, Wyoming, FY 1872
			$1,750.00	salary of late judge, Eastern District of Wisconsin
			$417.00	pay to telegraph operator
		Total	$375,821.46	
		TOTAL APPROPRIATION	$4,355,711.46	

1875

Statute (Citation)	Date Passed	Headings	Appropriation	Line-item Details
Ch. 328, 1874 (18 Stat. 85, 108)	June 20, 1874	United States Courts	$90,500.00	salaries of the Chief Justice and 8 associate or retired justices of the Supreme Court of the United States
			$54,000.00	salaries of 9 circuit judges
			$2,500.00	salary of the reporter of the decisions of the Supreme Court
			$3,500.00	salary of the marshal of the Supreme Court
			$193,000.00	salaries of district judges, including retired judges . . .
			$20,500.00	salaries of the chief justice and 4 associate judges of the Supreme Court of the District of Columbia
			$19,350.00	compensation of district attorneys
			$11,900.00	compensation of marshals
			$2,000.00	salary of the warden of the jail, District of Columbia
		Court of Claims	$29,840.00	salaries of judges, clerks, bailiff, messenger
			$3,000.00	contingent expenses
			$1,000.00	reporting of decisions
			$1,000.00	furniture and repairs of clerk's office and courtroom
			$1,000,000.00	to pay judgments of the Court of Claims
		Total	$1,432,090.00	
Ch. 455, 1874 (18 Stat. 204, 206)	June 23, 1874	Judiciary	$3,000,000.00	defraying expenses of the courts of the United States, including the District of Columbia, including enforcement of Voting Rights Act (Ch. 99, 1871)
			$10,000.00	support of convicts transferred from District of Columbia
			$30,000.00	defending claims against the United States
			$25,000.00	detection and prosecution of crimes
			$10,000.00	prosecution and collection of claims due the United States
			$10,000.00	expenses of defending claims under convention with Mexico
			$10,000.00	detecting and punishing violation of the intercourse acts

			Line-item Details	Appropriation
			penitentiary at Deer Lodge, Montana	$6,020.00
			publishing of opinions of the Attorneys General	$1,000.00
			repairs to penitentiary at Steilacoom, Washington Territory	$7,271.00
		Total		$3,109,291.00
Ch. 131, 1875 (18 Stat. 402, 418)	March 3, 1875	Department of Justice	for unsettled claims before Department of Justice for defraying the expenses of the courts	$20,000.00
		TOTAL APPROPRIATION		$4,561,381.00

1876

Statute (Citation)	Date Passed	Headings	Line-item Details	Appropriation
Ch. 129, 1875 (18 Stat. 343, 368)	March 3, 1875	United States Courts	salaries of the Chief Justice and 8 associate or retired justices of the Supreme Court of the United States	$90,500.00
			salaries of 9 circuit judges	$54,000.00
			salary of the reporter of the decisions of the Supreme Court	$2,500.00
			salary of the marshal of the Supreme Court	$3,500.00
			salaries of district judges, including retired judges . . .	$193,000.00
			salaries of the chief justice and 4 associate judges of the Supreme Court of the District of Columbia	$20,500.00
			compensation of district attorneys	$19,350.00
			compensation of marshals	$11,900.00
			salary of the warden of the jail, District of Columbia	$2,000.00
		Court of Claims	salaries of judges, clerks, bailiff, messenger	$29,840.00
			contingent expenses	$3,000.00
			reporting of decisions	$1,000.00
			digest of decisions	$1,000.00
			repairs	$550.00
			to pay judgments of the Court of Claims	$400,000.00
		Total		$832,640.00
Ch. 130, 1875 (18 Stat. 371, 373)	March 3, 1875	Judiciary	defraying expenses of the Supreme, district, and circuit courts, including the District of Columbia, and including enforcement of Voting Rights Act (Ch. 99, 1871)	$3,000,000.00
			support of convicts transferred from District of Columbia	$8,000.00
			defending claims against the United States	$50,000.00

Statute (Citation)	Date Passed	Headings	Line-item Details	Appropriation
			prosecution and collection of claims due the United States	$5,000.00
			expenses of defending claims under convention with Mexico	$5,000.00
			detecting and punishing violation of the intercourse acts	$8,000.00
			detection and prosecution of crimes	$25,000.00
			penitentiary, Territory of Montana	$1,200.00
			repair of the courthouse building, City of Washington (D.C.)	$3,000.00
		Total		$3,105,200.00
Ch. 88, 1876 (19 Stat. 41, 46)	May 1, 1876	Judicial	defraying expenses of Supreme, district, and circuit courts, including District of Columbia	$65,000.00
			defraying expenses of marshal of Territory of Utah	$6,000.00
		Total		$71,000.00
		TOTAL APPROPRIATION		$4,008,840.00

1877

Statute (Citation)	Date Passed	Headings	Line-item Details	Appropriation
Ch. 246, 1876 (19 Stat. 102, 107)	July 31, 1876	Judiciary	defraying expenses of Supreme, district, and circuit courts, including District of Columbia, and including enforcement of Voting Rights Act (Ch. 99, 1871)	$2,500,000.00
			support of convicts transferred from District of Columbia	$8,000.00
			expenses of marshal of Territory of Utah	$20,000.00
			prosecution and collection of claims due the United States	$2,500.00
			detecting and punishing violation of the intercourse acts	$8,000.00
			detection and prosecution of crimes	$25,000.00
			defending claims against the United States	$25,000.00
		Total		$2,588,500.00
Ch. 287, 1876 (19 Stat. 143, 167)	August 15, 1876	United States Courts	salaries of the Chief Justice and 8 associate justices of the Supreme Court of the United States	$90,500.00
			salaries of 9 circuit judges	$54,000.00
			salary of the reporter of the decisions of the Supreme Court	$2,500.00
			salary of the marshal of the Supreme Court	$3,500.00
			salaries of 52 district judges	$182,500.00
			salaries of the chief justice and 4 associate judges of the Supreme Court of the District of Columbia	$20,500.00

		Line-item Details	Appropriation
			compensation of district attorneys	$19,350.00
			compensation of marshals	$12,100.00
			salary of the warden of the jail, District of Columbia	$2,000.00
			purchase of books for the Supreme Court by Library of Congress	$2,000.00
		Court of Claims	salaries of judges, clerks, bailiff, messenger	$29,840.00
			expenses	$3,000.00
		Office of the Attorney General	salaries	$72,440.00
			horses and wagons	$1,000.00
			rent	$14,000.00
		Office of Solicitor of the Treasury	salaries	$24,800.00
		Total		$534,030.00
Ch. 106, 1877 (19 Stat. 363, 369)	March 3, 1877	Expenses of the United States Courts	safekeeping of prisoners, FY 1876	$5,243.55
			for district judge for Eastern District of Arkansas, expenses of holding court in Western District of Arkansas	$650.00
			expenses of whisky, cotton, and Credit Mobilier prosecutions	$69,755.00
			pay to James St. C. Boal, special counsel, legal services	$400.00
			pay to W.A. Britton, late marshal, Western District of Arkansas	$8,912.07
			defraying expenses of Supreme, district, and circuit courts, including District of Columbia . . . , FY 1877	$300,000.00
			pay, district judge, Eastern District of Arkansas, expenses of court in Western District of Arkansas	$650.00
			expenses of defending suits against Secretary of the Treasury, defense of U.S. in Court of Claims, FY 1877	$15,000.00
			costs in case of Milliken v. Spooner	$772.15
		Total		$401,382.77
		TOTAL APPROPRIATION		$3,523,912.77

1878

Statute (Citation)	Date Passed	Headings	Line-item Details	Appropriation
Ch. 102, 1877 (19 Stat. 294, 318)	March 3, 1877	United States Courts	salaries of the Chief Justice and 8 associate justices of the Supreme Court of the United States	$90,500.00
			salary of the marshal of the Supreme Court	$3,000.00
			purchase of books for the Supreme Court by Library of Congress	$2,000.00

		Description	Amount
		salaries of 9 circuit judges	$54,000.00
		salary of the reporter of the decisions of the Supreme Court	$2,500.00
		salaries of 51 district judges	$186,000.00
		salary of Wilson McCandless, retired judge of Western District of Pennsylvania	$4,000.00
		salaries of the chief justice and 4 associate judges of the Supreme Court of the District of Columbia	$20,500.00
		compensation of district attorneys	$19,300.00
		compensation of marshals	$12,100.00
		contingent expenses for Territory of Utah	$20,000.00
	Office of the Attorney General	salaries	$77,140.00
		contingent expenses	$13,200.00
		horses and wagons	$750.00
		rent	$14,000.00
	Court of Claims	salaries of judges, clerks, bailiff, messenger	$29,840.00
		expenses	$3,500.00
	Office of Solicitor of the Treasury	salaries	$24,800.00
	Total		$577,130.00
Ch. 105, 1877 (19 Stat. 344, 346)	March 3, 1877	Judiciary	
		defraying expenses of Supreme, district, and circuit courts, including District of Columbia . . . including enforcement of voting rights act (Ch. 99, 1871)	$2,650,000.00
		support of convicts transferred from District of Columbia	$4,000.00
		detecting and punishing violation of the intercourse acts	$8,000.00
		detection and prosecution of crimes	$25,000.00
		defending claims against the United States	$25,000.00
		for summary report of disallowed claims	$1,000.00
	Reform School, District of Columbia	salaries and expenses	$10,000.00
		improvements and repairs	$5,000.00
	Metropolitan Police	salaries and expenses	$150,000.00
	Total		$2,878,000.00

Statute (Citation)	Date Passed	Headings	Line-item Details	Appropriation
Ch. 2, 1877 (20 Stat. 4)	November 21, 1877	Judicial	salaries of 5 district judges for second quarter of FY 1877	$4,230.89
			defraying expenses of Supreme, district, and circuit courts, including District of Columbia . . .	$208,057.50
			support of convicts transferred from District of Columbia	$2,304.33
			Total	$214,592.72
Ch. 191, 1878 (20 Stat. 115, 121)	June 14, 1878	Judicial	defraying expenses of Supreme, district, and circuit courts, including District of Columbia, and including enforcement of Voting Rights Act (Ch. 99, 1871)	$120,000.00
			rent for courtrooms in Covington, Ky.	$200.00
			support of convicts transferred from District of Columbia	$6,000.00
			expenses of courts of Territory of Utah	$7,000.00
			Total	$133,200.00
Ch. 359, 1878 (20 Stat. 206, 235)	June 20, 1878	United States Courts	defraying expenses of Supreme, district, and circuit courts, including District of Columbia . . .	$150,000.00
			support of convicts transferred from District of Columbia and other districts, collection of criminal statistics	$15,000.00
			Total	$165,000.00
			TOTAL APPROPRIATION	$3,967,922.72

1879

Statute (Citation)	Date Passed	Headings	Line-item Details	Appropriation
Ch. 329, 1878 (20 Stat. 178, 204)	June 19, 1878	United States Courts	salaries of the Chief Justice and 8 associate justices of the Supreme Court of the United States	$90,500.00
			salary of the marshal of the Supreme Court	$3,000.00
			purchase of books for the Supreme Court by Library of Congress	$3,500.00
			salaries of 9 circuit judges	$54,000.00
			salary of the reporter of the decisions of the Supreme Court	$2,500.00
			salaries of 51 district judges	$190,000.00
			salaries of retired judges	indefinite
			salaries of the chief justice and 4 associate judges of the Supreme Court of the District of Columbia	$20,500.00
			compensation of district attorneys	$19,300.00
			compensation of marshals	$12,100.00
			salary of the warden of the jail, District of Columbia	$1,800.00

Citation	Date	Agency	Purpose	Amount
			salaries of the Southern Claims Commission	$16,500.00
			expenses of the Southern Claims Commission	$30,000.00
		Office of the Attorney General	salaries	$73,280.00
			contingent expenses	$10,000.00
			books for Solicitor of the Treasury	$500.00
			horses and wagons	$1,200.00
			rent	$10,000.00
			salaries	$28,080.00
		Office of Solicitor of the Treasury / Court of Claims	salaries of judges, clerks, bailiff, messenger	$29,840.00
			expenses	$3,000.00
		Total		$599,600.00
Ch. 359, 1878 (20 Stat. 206, 235)	June 20, 1878	United States Courts	defraying expenses of Supreme, district, and circuit courts, including District of Columbia, and including enforcement of Voting Rights Act (Ch. 99, 1871)	$2,750,000.00
			support of convicts transferred from District of Columbia and other districts, collection of criminal statistics	$15,000.00
			pay to Judge Elmer S. Dundy, District of Nebraska, travel expenses	$400.00
			pay to district attorney pro tempore Dewitt Stearns, Northern District of Mississippi	$321.00
			pay to district attorney pro tempore Henry B. Whitfield, Northern District of Mississippi	$150.00
			pay to late marshal of Territory of Utah, George R. Maxwell	$25,000.00
		Total		$2,790,871.00
Ch. 183, 1879 (20 Stat. 410, 415, 422)	March 3, 1879	Southern Claims Commission		$6,477.74
		Department of Justice	defraying expenses of Supreme, district, and circuit courts, including District of Columbia . . .	$50,000.00
			salaries for district marshals, FY 1877	$185.18
			for expenses of United States courts, FY 1878	$110,000.00
			expenses of Territory of Utah	$6,000.00
			marshals and court expenses	$1,544.08
		Total		$167,729.26
		TOTAL APPROPRIATION		$3,558,200.26

1880

Statute (Citation)	Date Passed	Headings	Line-item Details	Appropriation
Ch. 34, 1879 (21 Stat. 23)	June 21, 1879	United States Courts	salaries of the Chief Justice and 8 associate justices of the Supreme Court of the United States	$90,500.00
			salary of the marshal of the Supreme Court	$3,000.00
			purchase of books for the Supreme Court by Library of Congress	$3,500.00
			salaries of 9 circuit judges	$54,000.00
			salary of the reporter of the decisions of the Supreme Court	$2,500.00
			salaries of 51 district judges	$190,000.00
			salaries of retired judges	indefinite
			salaries of the chief justice and 4 associate judges of the Supreme Court of the District of Columbia	$20,500.00
			compensation of district attorneys	$19,300.00
			compensation of marshals	$12,100.00
			salary of the warden of the jail, District of Columbia	$1,800.00
		Judicial	salary of associate judge of District of Columbia	$4,000.00
			salary of the district judge for Northern District of Texas	$3,500.00
		Office of the Attorney General	salaries	$73,280.00
			contingent expenses	$10,000.00
			books for Solicitor of the Treasury	$500.00
			horses and wagons	$1,200.00
			rent	$10,000.00
		Office of Solicitor of the Treasury	salaries	$28,080.00
		Court of Claims	salaries of judges, clerks, bailiff, messenger	$29,840.00
			expenses	$3,000.00
		Total		$560,600.00
Ch. 52, 1879 (21 Stat. 43)	June 30, 1879	"... Certain Judicial Expenses ..."	payment of district attorneys and their assistants	$300,000.00
			fees of clerks	$160,000.00
			fees of United States commissioners	$140,000.00
			fees of jurors	$400,000.00
			fees of witnesses	$550,000.00
			support of United States prisoners	$193,000.00

			$67,000.00	rent for court rooms
			$280,000.00	for miscellaneous expenditures (see statute for detailed list)
		Total	$2,090,000.00	
		TOTAL APPROPRIATION	**$2,650,600.00**	

1881

Statute (Citation)	Date Passed	Headings	Appropriation	Line-item Details
Ch. 225, 1880 (21 Stat. 210, 235)	June 15, 1880	United States Courts	$90,500.00	salaries of the Chief Justice and 8 associate justices of the Supreme Court of the United States
			$3,000.00	salary of the marshal of the Supreme Court
			$54,000.00	salaries of 9 circuit judges
			$2,500.00	salary of the reporter of the decisions of the Supreme Court
			$193,000.00	salaries of 53 district judges
			indefinite	salaries of retired judges
			$24,500.00	salaries of the chief justice and 5 associate judges of the Supreme Court of the District of Columbia
			$19,500.00	compensation of district attorneys
			$12,300.00	compensation of marshals
			$1,800.00	salary of the warden of the jail, District of Columbia
		Office of the Attorney General	$73,600.00	salaries
			$10,000.00	contingent expenses
			$1,000.00	preparation of volumes of Attorney General decisions
			$1,200.00	horses and wagons
			$10,000.00	rent
		Office of Solicitor of the Treasury	$28,080.00	salaries
			$500.00	books
		Court of Claims	$29,840.00	salaries of judges, clerks, bailiff, messenger
			$3,500.00	expenses
		Total	$558,820.00	
Ch. 235, 1880 (21 Stat. 259, 277)	June 16, 1880	United States Courts	$650,000.00	payment of marshals and their deputies
			$350,000.00	payment of district attorneys and their assistants
			$160,000.00	fees of clerks
			$140,000.00	fees of United States commissioners

Appropriation	Line-item Details
$400,000.00	fees of jurors
$550,000.00	fees of witnesses
$200,000.00	support of United States prisoners
$75,000.00	rent for courtrooms
$2,500.00	repair and furniture for U.S. Courthouse in Charleston, S.C.
$300,000.00	expenses of bailiffs, other miscellaneous expenses
$25,000.00	support of convicts transferred from D.C. and other districts
$20,000.00	expenses of courts in Territory of Utah
$2,872,500.00	Total
$3,431,320.00	**TOTAL APPROPRIATION**

1882

Statute (Citation)	Date Passed	Headings	Appropriation	Line-item Details
Ch. 130, 1881 (21 Stat. 385, 412)	March 3, 1881	United States Courts	$90,500.00	salaries of the Chief Justice and 8 associate justices of the Supreme Court of the United States
			$3,000.00	salary for the marshal of the Supreme Court
			$54,000.00	salaries of 9 circuit judges
			$2,500.00	salary of the reporter of the decisions of the Supreme Court
			$193,000.00	salaries of 53 district judges
			indefinite	salaries of retired judges
			$24,500.00	salaries of the chief justice and 5 associate judges of the Supreme Court of the District of Columbia
			$19,500.00	compensation of district attorneys
			$12,300.00	compensation of marshals
		Office of the Attorney General	$73,600.00	salaries
			$10,000.00	contingent expenses
			$1,200.00	horses and wagons
			$12,000.00	rent
		Office of Solicitor of the Treasury	$28,080.00	salaries
		Court of Claims	$500.00	books
			$29,840.00	salaries of judges, clerks, bailiff, messenger
			$3,000.00	expenses
			$1,000.00	reporting decisions
		Total	$558,520.00	

Statute (Citation)	Date Passed	Headings	Line-item Details	Appropriation
Ch. 133, 1881 (21 Stat. 435, 454)	March 3, 1881	United States Courts	payment of marshals and their deputies	$600,000.00
			payment of district attorneys and their assistants	$325,000.00
			fees of clerks	$150,000.00
			fees of United States commissioners	$100,000.00
			fees of jurors	$450,000.00
			fees of witnesses	$600,000.00
			support of United States prisoners	$325,000.00
			rent for court rooms	$75,000.00
			expenses and fees of bailiffs, expenses of district judges sent to other districts, other miscellaneous expenses	$325,000.00
			preservation of records of district court of Frankfurt, Ky.	$1,000.00
			for publishing reports of Supreme Court of Territory of Wyoming	$1,000.00
			support of convicts transferred from D.C. and other districts	$25,000.00
			providing judges and attorneys with copies of Supreme Court Reports and Statutes at Large	indefinite
		Total		$2,977,000.00
		TOTAL APPROPRIATION		$3,535,520.00

1883

Statute (Citation)	Date Passed	Headings	Line-item Details	Appropriation
Ch. 389, 1882 (22 Stat. 219, 253)	August 5, 1882	Office of the Attorney General	salaries	$85,410.00
			salaries of assistant attorneys, and others	$18,320.00
			clerks	$3,000.00
			contingent expenses	$11,160.00
			horses and wagons	$1,200.00
		Office of Solicitor of the Treasury	salaries	$28,080.00
			books	$500.00
			salary of the warden of the jail, District of Columbia	$1,800.00
		United States Courts	salaries of the Chief Justice and 8 associate justices of the Supreme Court of the United States	$90,500.00
			salaries of 9 circuit judges	$54,000.00
			salary of the reporter of the decisions of the Supreme Court; entitled to $1,200 for additional volume	$4,500.00

		salary of clerk and expenses of Supreme Court reporter	$1,800.00
		salary of the marshal of the Supreme Court	$3,000.00
		salaries of 54 district judges	$196,500.00
		salaries of retired judges	indefinite
		salaries of the chief justice and 5 associate judges of the Supreme Court of the District of Columbia	$24,500.00
		compensation of district attorneys	$19,700.00
		compensation of marshals	$12,500.00
Court of Claims		salaries of judges, clerks, bailiff, messenger	$29,840.00
		expenses	$3,000.00
		reporting decisions	$1,000.00
Total			$590,310.00
United States Courts	Ch. 433, 1882 (22 Stat. 302, 335) August 7, 1882	payments of district attorneys and their assistants	$325,000.00
		fees of clerks	$160,000.00
		fees of United States commissioners	$130,000.00
		fees of jurors	$450,000.00
		fees of witnesses	$600,000.00
		support of prisoners	$325,000.00
		rent of courtrooms	$70,000.00
		fees and expenses of marshals	$600,000.00
		fees and expenses of bailiffs, expenses of district judges sent out of their districts, and other miscellaneous expenses	$325,000.00
		salaries for district judge, attorney, and marshal for Northern District of Iowa	$3,900.00
		for support and transport of convicts transferred from D.C., and gathering of criminal statistics	$13,400.00
		provide district judges, attorneys, and clerks with copies of Revised Statutes and U.S. Statutes at Large	indefinite
Total			$3,002,300.00
TOTAL APPROPRIATION			**$3,592,610.00**

1884

Statute (Citation)	Date Passed	Headings	Appropriation	Line-item Details
Ch. 128, 1883 (22 Stat. 531, 562)	March 3, 1883	Office of the Attorney General	$110,310.00	salaries
			$11,160.00	contingent expenses
			$1,200.00	horses and wagons
			$9,840.00	care and protection of courthouse, District of Columbia
			$3,280.00	care and protection of courthouse, District of Columbia, FY 1883
		Office of Solicitor of the Treasury	$28,080.00	salaries
			$500.00	books
			$1,800.00	salary of the warden of the jail, District of Columbia
		United States Courts	$90,500.00	salaries of the Chief Justice and 8 associate justices of the Supreme Court of the United States
			$54,000.00	salaries of 9 circuit judges
			$3,000.00	salary of the marshal of the Supreme Court
			$203,500.00	salaries of 56 district judges
			indefinite	salaries of retired judges
			$24,500.00	salaries of the chief justice and 5 associate judges of the Supreme Court of the District of Columbia
			$20,100.00	compensation of district attorneys
			$12,700.00	compensation of marshals
		Court of Claims	$29,840.00	salaries of judges, clerks, bailiff, messenger
			$3,000.00	expenses
			$1,000.00	reporting decisions
		Total	$608,310.00	
Ch. 143, 1883 (22 Stat. 603, 630)	March 3, 1883	United States Courts	$600,000.00	fees and expenses of marshals and deputies
			$325,000.00	payments of district attorneys and their assistants
			$160,000.00	fees of clerks
			$130,000.00	fees of commissioners
			$450,000.00	fees of jurors
			$600,000.00	fees of witnesses
			$300,000.00	support of prisoners
			$50,000.00	rent of courtrooms

		Appropriation	Line-item Details
		$310,000.00	fees and expenses of bailiffs, expenses of district judges sent out of their districts, and other miscellaneous expenses
		$10,000.00	for support and transport of convicts transferred from D.C., and gathering of criminal statistics
	Total	$2,935,000.00	
	TOTAL APPROPRIATION	**$3,543,310.00**	

1885

Statute (Citation)	Date Passed	Headings	Appropriation	Line-item Details
Ch. 331, 1884 (23 Stat. 159, 192)	July 7, 1884	Office of the Attorney General	$112,110.00	salaries
			$12,060.00	contingent expenses
			$1,600.00	horses and wagons
			$10,500.00	building maintenance and repairs
			$11,760.00	care and protection of courthouse, District of Columbia
		Office of Solicitor of the Treasury	$28,080.00	salaries
			$500.00	books
			$1,800.00	salary of the warden of the jail, District of Columbia
		United States Courts	$90,500.00	salaries of Chief Justice and 8 associate justices of the Supreme Court of the United States
			$54,000.00	salaries of 9 circuit judges
			$3,000.00	salary of the marshal of the Supreme Court
			$203,500.00	salaries of 56 district judges
			indefinite	salaries of retired judges
			$24,500.00	salaries of the chief justice and 5 associate judges of the Supreme Court of the District of Columbia
		Court of Claims	$29,840.00	salaries of judges, clerks, bailiff, messenger
			$3,000.00	expenses
			$1,000.00	reporting decisions
		Total	$587,750.00	
Ch. 332, 1884 (23 Stat. 194, 224)	July 7, 1884	United States Courts	$600,000.00	payment of fees and expenses of marshals and deputies
			$12,700.00	compensation of marshals
			$325,000.00	payments of district attorneys and their assistants
			$20,100.00	compensation of district attorneys

Statute (Citation)	Date Passed	Headings	Line-item Details	Appropriation
			fees of clerks	$160,000.00
			fees of U.S. commissioners	$100,000.00
			fees of jurors	$400,000.00
			fees of witnesses	$500,000.00
			support of U.S. prisoners	$300,000.00
			rent of courtrooms	$50,000.00
			pay of bailiffs and criers, expenses of district judges sent out of their district, and other miscellaneous expenses	$325,000.00
			for support and transport of convicts transferred from D.C., and gathering of criminal statistics	$10,000.00
			for providing a uniform system of bookkeeping for court officials	$10,000.00
			Total	$2,812,800.00
Ch. 334, 1884 (23 Stat. 236, 249)	July 7, 1884	Judicial	fees of United States attorneys	$70,000.00
			fees of clerks	$50,000.00
			fees of jurors	$60,000.00
			fees of witnesses	$60,000.00
			fees of marshals	$40,000.00
			miscellaneous expenses of courts	$15,000.00
			expenses of territorial courts of Utah	$6,000.00
			fees of district attorneys, FY 1882	$2,370.37
			payment of district attorneys and assistants, FY 1883	$115,000.00
			fees of clerks, FY 1883	$60,000.00
			fees of commissioners, FY 1883	$17,000.00
			pay to J.D. Rouse, defending suits in claims against U.S., FY 1874	$87.80
			Total	$495,458.17
			TOTAL APPROPRIATION	$3,896,008.17

1886

Statute (Citation)	Date Passed	Headings	Line-item Details	Appropriation
Ch. 343, 1885 (23 Stat. 388, 424)	March 3, 1885	Office of the Attorney General	salaries	$112,110.00
			contingent expenses	$10,660.00
			horses and wagons	$1,600.00
			care and protection of courthouse, District of Columbia	$11,760.00

Office of Solicitor of the Treasury	salaries	$28,080.00	
	books	$500.00	
	stationery	$400.00	
	salary of the warden of the jail, District of Columbia	$1,800.00	
United States Courts	salaries of Chief Justice and 8 associate justices of the Supreme Court of the United States	$90,500.00	
	salaries of 9 circuit judges	$54,000.00	
	salary of the marshal of the Supreme Court	$3,000.00	
	salaries of 56 district judges	$203,500.00	
	salaries of retired judges	indefinite	
	salaries of the chief justice and 5 associate judges of the Supreme Court of the District of Columbia	$24,500.00	
	compensation of district attorneys	$20,100.00	
	compensation of marshals	$12,700.00	
Court of Claims	salaries of judges, clerks, bailiff, messenger	$29,840.00	
	expenses	$3,000.00	
	reporting decisions	$1,000.00	
Total		$609,050.00	
March 3, 1885 Ch. 360, 1885 (23 Stat. 478, 511)			
United States Courts	payment of fees and expenses of marshals and deputies	$675,000.00	
	payments of district attorneys and their assistants	$350,000.00	
	fees of clerks	$175,000.00	
	fees of U.S. commissioners	$100,000.00	
	fees of jurors	$450,000.00	
	fees of witnesses	$550,000.00	
	support of U.S. prisoners	$250,000.00	
	rent of courtrooms	$50,000.00	
	pay of bailiffs and criers, expenses of district judges sent out of their district, and other miscellaneous expenses	$300,000.00	
Total		$2,900,000.00	
TOTAL APPROPRIATION		$3,509,050.00	

1887

Statute (Citation)	Date Passed	Headings	Line-item Details	Appropriation
Ch. 827, 1886 (24 Stat. 172, 207)	July 31, 1886	Office of the Attorney General	salaries	$112,610.00
			contingent expenses	$11,160.00
			postage	$100.00
			official transportation	$500.00
			care and protection of courthouse, District of Columbia	$11,760.00
		Office of Solicitor of the Treasury	salaries	$27,580.00
			books	$500.00
			stationery	$400.00
			salary of the warden of the jail, District of Columbia	$1,800.00
		United States Courts	salaries of Chief Justice and 8 associate justices of the Supreme Court of the United States	$90,500.00
			salaries of 9 circuit judges	$54,000.00
			salary of the marshal of the Supreme Court	$3,000.00
			salaries of 56 district judges	$203,500.00
			salary, additional justice of Supreme Court of Territory of Montana	$3,000.00
			salaries of retired judges	indefinite
			salaries of the chief justice and 5 associate judges of the Supreme Court of the District of Columbia	$24,500.00
			compensation of district attorneys	$20,100.00
			compensation of marshals	$12,700.00
		Court of Claims	salaries of judges, clerks, bailiff, messenger	$29,840.00
			expenses	$3,000.00
			reporting decisions	$1,000.00
		Total		$611,550.00
Ch. 902, 1886 (24 Stat. 222, 253)	August 4, 1886	United States Courts	payment of fees and expenses of marshals and deputies	$675,000.00
			payments of district attorneys and their assistants	$350,000.00
			fees of clerks	$175,000.00
			fees of U.S. commissioners	$100,000.00
			fees of jurors	$450,000.00
			fees of witnesses	$550,000.00

Federal Judiciary Appropriations: 1792–2010

Statute (Citation)	Date Passed	Headings	Line-item Details	Appropriation
			support of U.S. prisoners	$240,000.00
			rent of courtrooms	$50,000.00
			pay of bailiffs and criers, expenses of district judges sent out of their district, and other miscellaneous expenses	$314,400.00
			clerical services, Court of Claims, for French spoliation claims	$1,200.00
		Total		$2,905,600.00
Ch. 903, 1886 (24 Stat. 256, 274)	August 4, 1886	Fees and Expenses of Marshals	fees and expenses of marshals, FY 1886	$20,000.00
			fees and expenses of marshals, FY 1885	$24,447.47
			fees and expenses of marshals, FY 1884	$10,753.17
			pay to legal representative of Thomas Simons, services in Choctaw Nation v. United States	$2,500.00
			pay to William Rush, Jr., assistant U.S. attorney, Western District of Missouri	$875.00
		Fees of Clerks	fees of clerks, FY 1885	$32,043.53
		Fees of Commissioners	fees of commissioners, FY 1886	$50,000.00
			fees of commissioners, FY 1885	$24,856.22
		Fees of Witnesses	fees of witnesses, FY 1886	$50,000.00
			fees of witnesses, FY 1885	$4,440.00
		Fees of Jurors	fees of jurors, FY 1886	$25,000.00
		Rent of United States Courtrooms	rent of courtrooms, FY 1885	$6,942.70
			rent of courtrooms, FY 1884	$19,430.00
		Miscellaneous Expenses	miscellaneous expenses, FY 1886	$10,000.00
		Territorial Courts in Utah	FY 1886	$4,000.00
			FY 1885	$2,033.15
		Support of Insane Convicts	pay to state asylum, Auburn, N.Y., care and support of U.S. convicts	$773.29
			pay to Henry Fink, late U.S. marshal, Eastern District of Wisconsin	$95.80
		Total		$288,190.33
		TOTAL APPROPRIATION		$3,805,340.33

1888

Statute (Citation)	Date Passed	Headings	Line-item Details	Appropriation
Ch. 362, 1887 (24 Stat. 509, 541)	March 3, 1887	United States Courts	payment of fees and expenses of marshals and deputies	$675,000.00
			payment of district attorneys	$225,000.00
			payment to assistants to district attorneys	$100,000.00

Citation	Date	Category	Item	Amount
			fees of clerks	$175,000.00
			fees of U.S. commissioners	$50,000.00
			fees of jurors	$450,000.00
			fees of witnesses	$550,000.00
			support of U.S. prisoners	$250,000.00
			rent of courtrooms	$60,000.00
			pay of bailiffs and criers, expenses of judges sent outside their districts, jury commissioners, stenographic clerks for Supreme Court justices, etc.	$100,000.00
			miscellaneous expenses	$214,400.00
		Total		$2,849,400.00
Ch. 392, 1887 (24 Stat. 594, 630)	March 3, 1887	Office of the Attorney General	salaries	$112,610.00
			contingent expenses	$11,160.00
			postage	$100.00
			official transportation	$500.00
			care and protection of courthouse, District of Columbia	$11,760.00
		Office of Solicitor of the Treasury	salaries	$26,600.00
			books	$500.00
			stationery	$400.00
			salary of the warden of the jail, District of Columbia	$1,800.00
		United States Courts	salaries of Chief Justice and 8 associate justices of the Supreme Court of the United States	$90,500.00
			salaries of 9 circuit judges	$54,000.00
			salary of the marshal of the Supreme Court	$3,000.00
			salaries of 58 district judges	$211,000.00
			salaries of retired judges	indefinite
			salaries of the chief justice and 5 associate judges of the Supreme Court of the District of Columbia	$24,500.00
			compensation of district attorneys	$20,300.00
			compensation of marshals	$12,900.00
		Court of Claims	salaries of judges, clerks, bailiff, messenger	$32,240.00
			expenses	$2,500.00
			reporting decisions	$1,000.00
		Total		$617,370.00

Statute (Citation)	Date Passed	Headings	Appropriation	Line-item Details
Ch. 47, 1888 (25 Stat. 47, 57)	March 30, 1888	Fees of Jurors, United States Courts	$150,000.00	FY 1888
		Fees of Witnesses, United States Courts	$300,000.00	FY 1888
			$321.50	FY 1884
			$5,080.00	FY 1883
		Pay of Bailiffs and Criers	$75,000.00	bailiffs, criers, etc.
		Support of United States Prisoners	$90,000.00	
		Fees and Expenses of Marshals	$20,000.00	FY 1887
		Fees of Commissioners	$10,000.00	FY 1886
		Salary of Circuit Judge	$10,000.00	FY 1886
			$6,000.00	
		Total	$666,401.50	
		TOTAL APPROPRIATION	**$4,133,171.50**	

1889

Statute (Citation)	Date Passed	Headings	Appropriation	Line-item Details
Ch. 615, 1888 (25 Stat. 256, 293)	July 11, 1888	Office of the Attorney General	$115,890.00	salaries
			$1,000.00	furniture and repairs
			$1,500.00	books for library of Department of Justice
			$1,000.00	purchase of laws and statutes of states and territories
			$1,500.00	stationery
			$7,160.00	miscellaneous expenses
			$500.00	official transportation
			$100.00	postage
			$11,760.00	care and protection of courthouse, District of Columbia
		Office of Solicitor of the Treasury	$26,680.00	salaries
			$500.00	books
			$400.00	stationery
		United States Courts	$1,800.00	salary of the warden of the jail, District of Columbia
			$90,500.00	salaries of Chief Justice and 8 associate justices of the Supreme Court of the United States

			Description	Amount
			salaries of 10 circuit judges	$60,000.00
			salary of the marshal of the Supreme Court	$3,000.00
			salaries of 58 district judges	$211,000.00
			salaries of retired judges	indefinite
			salaries of the chief justice and 5 associate judges of the Supreme Court of the District of Columbia	$24,500.00
			compensation of district attorneys	$20,300.00
			compensation of marshals	$12,900.00
			salaries of judges, clerks, bailiff, messenger	$32,240.00
			expenses	$3,000.00
			reporting decisions	$1,000.00
		Court of Claims		
		Total		$628,230.00
Ch. 1069, 1888 (25 Stat. 505, 544)	October 2, 1888	Expenses of the United States Courts	payment of fees and expenses of marshals and deputies	$675,000.00
			payment of district attorneys	$225,000.00
			payment to assistants to district attorneys	$105,000.00
			payment to special assistant district attorneys	$20,000.00
			payment of district attorneys for services not covered by salaries or fees	$5,000.00
			fees of clerks	$175,000.00
			fees of U.S. commissioners	$100,000.00
			fees of jurors	$650,000.00
			fees of witnesses	$900,000.00
			support of prisoners	$300,000.00
			rent of courtrooms	$75,000.00
			pay of bailiffs and criers, jury commissioners, meals for jurors, expenses of judges sent outside their districts	$135,600.00
			stenographic clerks for Chief Justice and associate justices, Supreme Court	$14,400.00
			miscellaneous expenses	$140,000.00
		Total		$3,520,000.00
Ch. 1210, 1888 (25 Stat. 565, 582)	October 19, 1888	Fees and Expenses of Marshals	fees and expenses of marshals, FY 1887	$50,000.00
			fees and expenses of marshals, FY 1886	$40,000.00
		Fees of District Attorneys	fees of district attorneys . . . for official services of district attorneys, FY 1888	$37,367.41

		$42,526.28	fees of district attorneys . . . for official services of district attorneys, FY 1887
		$300.00	fees of district attorneys . . . for official services of district attorneys, FY 1886
		$1,500.00	payment to Joseph Campbell for assistance in prosecuting Apache Indian on murder charge
	Pay of Assistant Attorneys	$40,550.00	payment to regular assistant district attorneys, reimbursement of 20% in compensation made in FY 1888
	Fees of Clerks	$7,500.00	fees for clerks, FY 1886
	Fees of Commissioners	$52,498.72	fees of commissioners, FY 1888
		$19,757.35	fees of commissioners, FY 1887
	Rent of Courtrooms	$11,310.00	rent of courtrooms, FY 1888
	Pay of Bailiffs	$25,000.00	expenses of bailiffs and criers, etc. . . . FY 1888
	Pay of District Attorneys and Assistants	$8,030.80	payment to district attorneys for unofficial services for FY 1886–1888
		$8,986.82	payment to special district attorneys, FY 1886–1888
		$4,153.70	payment of claims for fees of district attorneys, FY 1886–1888
	Territorial Courts in Utah	$15,000.00	expenses, including penitentiary
		$10,016.81	expenses, including penitentiary, FY 1887
		$2,866.67	expenses, support and care of penitentiary, FY 1886
	Total	$377,364.56	
Ch. 410, 1889 (25 Stat. 905, 923) March 2, 1889	Fees and Expenses of Marshals	$124,000.00	payment to special deputy marshals at congressional elections, 1889
		$50,000.00	fees and expenses of marshals, FY 1888
	Support of Prisoners	$50,000.00	support of prisoners
		$32,583.11	support of prisoners, FY 1880–1888
	Fees of Jurors	$2,039.30	fees of jurors, FY 1885–1886
	Fees of Witnesses	$2,622.20	fees of witnesses, FY 1877, 1879–1880, 1883–1886
	Miscellaneous Expenses	$61.78	miscellaneous expenses, FY 1887
		$10,000.00	miscellaneous expenses, FY 1889
	Expenses of Territorial Courts, Utah	$6,402.55	FY 1887–1888
	Fees of District Attorneys	$15,000.00	regular fees for official services of district attorneys
		$15,000.00	regular fees for official services of district attorneys, FY 1888
		$600.00	regular fees for official services of district attorneys, FY 1887
		$1,000.00	A.L. Rhodes, special counsel in Mare Islands case, FY 1888

A.J. Fountain, special assistant U.S. attorney, Territory of New Mexico, FY 1887	$500.00
J.C. Baird, services as assistant U.S. attorney, Territory of Wyoming, FY 1888	$134.00
Solomon Claypool, services as assistant U.S. attorney, District of Indiana, FY 1888	$2,250.00
S.G. Hilburn, services in Mare Islands case	$3,750.00
D.H. Murphy, services as assistant to district attorney, Alaska, FY 1887–1888	$1,000.00
J.E. Bruce, assistant district attorney, Southern District of Ohio, FY 1888	$84.66
unofficial fees of district attorneys, FY 1882, 1885–1888	$6,141.72
Robert F. Arnold, services in prosecution, FY 1888	$1,000.00
William Ewing, district attorney, Northern District of Illinois	$300.00
Graham H. Harris, services in prosecution, services rendered in 1888	$325.00
salaries of judge and expenses, U.S. court in Indian Territory	$10,000.00
fees for clerks, FY 1888	$10,000.00
fees of commissioners, FY 1888	$15,000.00
Fees of Clerks	
Fees of Commissioners	
Total	$359,794.32
TOTAL APPROPRIATION	**$4,885,388.88**

1890

Statute (Citation)	Date Passed	Headings	Line-item Details	Appropriation
Ch. 279, 1889 (25 Stat. 705, 744)	February 26, 1889	United States Courts	salaries of the Chief Justice and 8 associate justices of the Supreme Court of the United States	$90,500.00
			salaries of 10 circuit judges	$60,000.00
			salaries of the marshal of the Supreme Court	$3,000.00
			salaries of stenographic clerks for Supreme Court justices	$14,400.00
			salaries of 58 district judges	$211,000.00
			salaries of retired judges	indefinite
			salaries of the chief justice and 5 associate judges of the Supreme Court of the District of Columbia	$24,500.00
			compensation of district attorneys	$20,300.00
			compensation of marshals	$12,900.00

	Court of Claims	salaries of judges, clerks, bailiff, messenger	$32,240.00
		expenses	$3,000.00
		reporting decisions	$1,000.00
	Total		$472,840.00
Ch. 411, 1889 (25 Stat. 939, 977)	Expenses of the United States Courts	fees and expenses of marshals	$675,000.00
March 2, 1889		payment of district attorneys	$255,000.00
		special compensation of district attorneys for services not covered by salaries or fees	$5,000.00
		payment of regular assistants to district attorneys	$105,000.00
		payment of special assistants to district attorneys	$20,000.00
		fees of clerks	$175,000.00
		fees of commissioners	$100,000.00
		fees of jurors	$650,000.00
		fees of witnesses	$900,000.00
		support of prisoners	$350,000.00
		rent of courtrooms	$65,000.00
		pay of bailiffs, criers, jury commissioners, meals for jurors, expenses of judges sent outside their districts	$135,600.00
		miscellaneous expenses	$140,000.00
	Total		$3,575,600.00
Ch. 63, 1890 (26 Stat. 34, 41)	District Judges	salary, district judges for North Dakota, South Dakota, Montana, and Washington	indefinite
April 4, 1890	District Attorneys	salary, district attorney, Indian Territory	$250.00
		salary, district attorneys for North Dakota, South Dakota, Montana, and Washington	indefinite
	District Marshals	salary, marshal, Indian Territory	$250.00
		salary, marshals for North Dakota, South Dakota, Montana, and Washington	indefinite
	United States Courts	fees of witnesses	$200,000.00
	Total		$200,500.00
	TOTAL APPROPRIATION		**$4,248,940.00**

1891

Statute (Citation)	Date Passed	Headings	Line-item Details	Appropriation
Ch. 667, 1890 (26 Stat. 228, 267)	July 11, 1890	United States Courts	salaries of Chief Justice and 8 associate justices of the Supreme Court of the United States	$90,500.00
			salaries of 10 circuit judges	$60,000.00
			salary of the marshal of the Supreme Court	$3,000.00
			salaries of stenographic clerks for Supreme Court justices	$14,400.00
			salaries of 63 district judges	$228,500.00
			salaries of retired judges	indefinite
			salaries of the chief justice and 5 associate judges of the Supreme Court of the District of Columbia	$24,500.00
			compensation of district attorneys	$20,800.00
			compensation of marshals	$13,500.00
		Court of Claims	salaries of judges, clerks, bailiff, messenger	$32,240.00
			expenses	$3,000.00
			reporting decisions	$1,000.00
		Total		$491,440.00
Ch. 837, 1890 (26 Stat. 371, 409)	August 30, 1890	Expenses of the United States Courts	fees and expenses of marshals	$675,000.00
			payment of district attorneys	$255,000.00
			special compensation of district attorneys for services not covered by salaries or fees	$5,000.00
			payment of regular assistants to district attorneys	$115,000.00
			payment of special assistants to district attorneys	$30,000.00
			special counsel, equity suit in Supreme Court regarding Territory of Oklahoma, fees and expenses	$10,000.00
			salaries of district judges, attorneys, marshals in Idaho and Wyoming	indefinite
			fees of clerks	$175,000.00
			fees of commissioners	$100,000.00
			fees of jurors	$650,000.00
			fees of witnesses	$900,000.00
			support of prisoners	$375,000.00
			rent of courtrooms	$50,000.00

Chapter	Date	Category	Description	Amount
			pay of bailiffs, criers, jury commissioners, meals for jurors, expenses of judges sent outside their districts	$135,600.00
			miscellaneous expenses	$140,000.00
			expenses of transportation and per diem of jurors and witnesses in district court of Alaska	$1,000.00
			oil portrait of Chief Justice John Marshall for Supreme Court	$1,000.00
		Total		$3,617,600.00
Ch. 1126, 1890 (26 Stat. 504, 527)	September 30, 1890	United States Court in Alaska	payment to late Judge Dawson, FY 1886	$246.60
		Fees and Expenses of Marshals	fees of marshals, FY 1888–1890	$196,469.03
			special deputy marshals at congressional elections, FY 1889	$34,745.00
			pay of widow of late deputy marshal, Oklahoma, FY 1889	$300.00
			pay to Daniel F. Wyatt, deputy marshal, Indian Territory, FY 1889	$198.00
		Fees of Jurors	fees of jurors, FY 1890	$65,000.00
		Fees of Witnesses	fees of witnesses, FY 1887–1890	$101,356.87
		Total		$398,315.50
Ch. 540, 1891 (26 Stat. 862, 881)	March 3, 1891	Fees of Marshals	fees and expenses of marshals, FY 1891	$400,000.00
			fees and expenses of marshals, FY 1890	$214,327.74
		Fees of District Attorneys	fees of district attorneys, FY 1891	$25,000.00
			fees of district attorneys, FY 1890	$8,061.94
			fees of district attorneys, FY 1889	$1,464.48
		Pay of Special Assistant Attorneys	pay of special assistant attorneys, 1890	$8,674.24
			pay of special assistant attorneys, FY 1889	$2,261.86
		Fees of Clerks	fees for clerks, FY 1891	$45,000.00
			fees for clerks, FY 1890	$23,255.30
			fees for clerks, FY 1889	$2,474.58
		Fees of Commissioners	fees for commissioners, FY 1891	$45,000.00
			fees for commissioners, FY 1890	$32,988.19
			fees for commissioners, FY 1889	$2,515.40
		Fees of Witnesses	fees for witnesses, FY 1891	$300,000.00
			fees for witnesses, FY 1890	$108,090.56
			fees for witnesses, FY 1889	$9,500.00
			fees for witnesses, FY 1888	$802.20
			fees for witnesses, FY 1887	$539.60

	$435.10	fees for witnesses, FY 1886
	$200.00	fees for witnesses, FY 1885
	$200.00	fees for witnesses, FY 1884
	$800.00	fees for witnesses, FY 1883
Support of Prisoners	$7,063.47	support of prisoners, FY 1890
	$6,418.89	support of prisoners, FY 1889
	$45.65	support of prisoners, FY 1888
	$11.15	support of prisoners, FY 1887
	$81.75	support of prisoners, FY 1885
Pay of Bailiffs	$3,552.90	pay of bailiffs and criers, etc., FY 1889
	$89.90	pay of bailiffs and criers, etc., FY 1888
Miscellaneous Expenses	$25,000.00	miscellaneous expenses, FY 1891
	$65.70	miscellaneous expenses, FY 1888
Rent of courtrooms	$15,000.00	rent of courtrooms, 1891
[Court of Private Land Claims]	$15,000.00	salaries and expenses related to establishment of court of private land claims, FY 1891
	$40,000.00	salaries and expenses related to establishment of court of private land claims, FY 1892
Expenses of Territorial Courts, Utah	$10,987.60	expenses of territorial courts, Territory of Utah, FY 1890
	$11,000.00	expenses of territorial courts, Territory of Utah, FY 1889
	$3,500.00	expenses of territorial courts, Territory of Utah, FY 1888
Rent and Incidental Expenses, Alaska	$500.00	rent and expenses, Territory of Alaska, FY 1891
	$100.00	rent and expenses, Territory of Alaska, FY 1890
	$16.00	rent and expenses, Territory of Alaska, FY 1885
	$7,550.00	transport of witnesses and arrests of murderers
Support of Convicts	$846.10	support of convicts of D.C. in penitentiaries of New York, FY 1890
	$258.70	support of D.C. convicts in penitentiaries in Albany, N.Y., FY 1889
[Circuit Court of Appeals]	$60,000.00	salaries and expenses related to establishment of circuit courts of appeals
Total	$1,438,679.00	
TOTAL APPROPRIATION	$5,946,034.50	

1892

Statute (Citation)	Date Passed	Headings	Line-item Details	Appropriation
Ch. 541, 1891 (26 Stat. 908, 947)	March 3, 1891	United States Courts	salaries of the Chief Justice and 8 associate justices of the Supreme Court of the United States	$90,500.00
			salaries of 10 circuit judges	$60,000.00
			salary of the marshal of the Supreme Court	$3,000.00
			salaries of stenographic clerks for Supreme Court justices	$14,400.00
			salaries of 64 district judges	$320,000.00
			salaries of retired judges	indefinite
			salary of the judge of the U.S. court in Indian Territory	$3,500.00
			salaries of the chief justice and 5 associate judges of the Supreme Court of the District of Columbia	$30,000.00
			compensation of district attorneys	$20,700.00
			compensation of marshals	$13,500.00
		Court of Claims	salaries of judges, clerks, bailiff, messenger	$33,440.00
			expenses	$3,000.00
			reporting decisions	$1,000.00
		Total		$593,040.00
Ch. 542, 1891 (26 Stat. 948, 986)	March 3, 1891	Expenses of the United States Courts	fees and expenses of marshals	$675,000.00
			payment of district attorneys	$255,000.00
			special compensation of district attorneys for services not covered by salaries or fees	$5,000.00
			payment of regular assistants to district attorneys	$125,000.00
			payment of special assistants to district attorneys	$35,000.00
			special counsel, equity suit in Supreme Court regarding Territory of Oklahoma, fees and expenses	$5,000.00
			salary of special counsel to assist in United States v. Des Moines Navigation Railway Co.	$2,500.00
			fees of clerks	$175,000.00
			fees of commissioners	$100,000.00
			fees of jurors	$650,000.00
			fees of witnesses	$1,000,000.00
			support of prisoners	$375,000.00

Line-item Details	Appropriation
rent of courtrooms	$50,000.00
pay of bailiffs, criers, jury commissioners, meals for jurors, expenses of judges sent outside their districts	$135,600.00
miscellaneous expenses	$150,000.00
expenses of transportation and per diem of jurors and witnesses in district court of Alaska	$1,000.00
Total	$3,739,100.00
TOTAL APPROPRIATION	**$4,332,140.00**

1893

Statute (Citation)	Date Passed	Headings	Line-item Details	Appropriation
Ch. 196, 1892 (27 Stat. 183, 222)	July 16, 1892	Supreme Court	salaries of the Chief Justice and 8 associate justices of the Supreme Court of the United States	$90,500.00
			salaries of 10 circuit judges	$60,000.00
			salary of the marshal of the Supreme Court	$3,000.00
			salaries of stenographic clerks for Supreme Court justices	$14,400.00
		Circuit Courts of Appeals	salaries of 9 circuit judges, 9 clerks	$81,000.00
		Court of Private Land Claims	salaries of justices, clerk, stenographer, attorney, interpreter	$33,500.00
			salaries of deputy clerks	indefinite
		District Courts	salaries of 64 district judges, judge of U.S. court of Indian Territory	$323,500.00
			salaries of retired judges	indefinite
		Supreme Court, District of Columbia	salaries of the chief justice and 5 associate judges of the Supreme Court of the District of Columbia	$24,500.00
		District Attorneys	salaries of district attorneys	$20,700.00
		Marshals	salaries of marshals	$13,500.00
		Court of Claims	salaries of judges, clerks, bailiff, messenger	$34,640.00
			expenses	$3,000.00
			reporting decisions	$1,000.00
		Total		$703,240.00
Ch. 380, 1892 (27 Stat. 349, 385)	August 5, 1892	Expenses of the United States Courts	fees and expenses of marshals	$675,000.00
			payment of district attorneys	$250,000.00
			special compensation of district attorneys for services not covered by salaries or fees	$5,000.00

Date	Citation	Category	Description	Amount
			payment of regular assistants to district attorneys	$100,000.00
			payment of special assistants to district attorneys	$20,000.00
			fees of clerks	$175,000.00
			fees of commissioners	$100,000.00
			fees of jurors	$600,000.00
			fees of witnesses	$750,000.00
			support of prisoners	$300,000.00
			rent of courtrooms	$50,000.00
			pay of bailiffs, criers, jury commissioners, meals for jurors, expenses of judges sent outside their districts	$135,600.00
			miscellaneous expenses	$170,000.00
		Total		$3,330,600.00
July 28, 1892	Ch. 311, 1892 (27 Stat. 282, 297)	Fees for Marshals	fees and expenses of marshals, FY 1892	$250,000.00
			fees and expenses of marshals, FY 1891	$175,201.07
			fees and expenses of marshals, FY 1890	$1,000.00
			special deputies for congressional elections, FY 1891	$130.00
			special deputies for congressional elections, FY 1889	$25.00
		Fees of Witnesses	fees of witnesses, FY 1889	$1,000.00
		Fees of District Attorneys	fees of district attorneys, FY 1892	$65,000.00
			fees of district attorneys, FY 1890	$1,916.27
			fees of district attorneys, FY 1891	$47,894.95
			special compensation, FY 1892	$3,563.86
			special compensation, FY 1891	$7,461.76
			special compensation, FY 1890	$1,815.09
		Pay of Special Assistant Attorneys	pay of special assistant attorneys, FY 1891	$24,990.47
			pay of special assistant attorneys, FY 1890	$14,360.00
		Fees of Clerks	fees of clerks, FY 1892	$45,000.00
			fees of clerks, FY 1891	$53,969.85
		Fees of Commissioners	fees of commissioners, FY 1892	$91,196.43
			fees of commissioners, FY 1891	$62,363.15
			fees of commissioners, FY 1890	$7,212.83
		Support of Prisoners	support of prisoners, FY 1892	$125,000.00
			support of prisoners, FY 1891	$99,768.28
		Pay of Bailiffs	pay of bailiffs and criers, etc., FY 1890	$62,077.87

	pay of bailiffs and criers, etc., FY 1892	$27,000.00
	pay of bailiffs and criers, etc, FY 1891	$37,137.27
	pay of bailiffs and criers, etc., FY 1890	$1,155.50
	pay of bailiffs and criers, etc., FY 1889	$162.00
Miscellaneous Expenses	miscellaneous expenses, FY 1892	$33,000.00
	miscellaneous expenses, FY 1891	$36,636.49
	miscellaneous expenses, FY 1890	$518.75
Rent of Courtrooms	rent of courtrooms, FY 1892	$20,000.00
	rent of courtrooms, FY 1891	$20,825.45
Expenses of Territorial Courts, Utah	expenses of territorial courts in Utah, FY 1892	$25,000.00
	expenses of territorial courts in Utah, FY 1891	$22,547.54
	expenses of territorial courts in Utah, FY 1890	$750.00
	expenses of territorial courts in Utah, FY 1889	$2,770.51
	expenses of territorial courts in Utah, FY 1887	$652.10
Rent and Incidental Expenses, Territory of Alaska	rent and expenses of marshals, district attorney, and commissioner, FY 1892	$697.27
	rent and expenses of marshals, district attorney, and commissioner, FY 1890	$304.05
Defending Suits in Claims Against the U.S.	expenses in claims against the U.S. and defending suits in the Court of Claims, FY 1892	$1,321.80
	expenses in claims against the U.S. and defending suits in the Court of Claims, FY 1891	$433.80
	expenses in claims against the U.S. and defending suits in the Court of Claims, FY 1888	$10.00
	expenses in claims against the U.S. and defending suits in the Court of Claims, FY 1885	$200.25
Circuit Courts of Appeals	salaries and expenses, FY 1892	$30,080.50
Court of Private Land Claims	salaries and expenses, FY 1892	$11,294.30
	publishing notice of organization of the court	$28,036.46
Expenses, U.S. Courts, Indian Territory	travel and other expenses of judge, Indian Territory, FY 1891–1892	$901.95
Deputy Marshals in Oklahoma	investigation and payment of sums owed to deputy marshals, FY 1889–1890	$21,000.00
	expenses of apportionment of territory	$1,000.00
Judicial	difference in salary of district judges prior to Act of February 24, 1891	$30,800.00
Total		$1,495,182.87

Ch. 210 (27 Stat. 646, 661)	March 3, 1893	Fees of Marshals	fees and expenses of marshals, FY 1893	$775,000.00

Statute	Date	Category	Description	Amount
Ch. 210 (27 Stat. 646, 661)	March 3, 1893	Fees of Marshals	fees and expenses of marshals, FY 1893	$775,000.00
			fees and expenses of marshals, FY 1892	$286,925.00
		Fees of Witnesses	fees of witnesses, FY 1893	$400,000.00
		Fees of District Attorneys	fees of district attorneys, FY 1893	$75,000.00
			fees of district attorneys, FY 1892	$30,000.00
			special compensation, district attorneys, FY 1893	$4,307.95
			special compensation, district attorneys, FY 1892	$5,000.00
			special compensation, district attorneys, FY 1891	$100.00
			special compensation, district attorneys, FY 1890	$150.00
			pay of regular assistant attorneys, FY 1893	$21,000.00
			pay of special assistant attorneys, FY 1893	$7,937.00
			pay of special assistant attorneys, FY 1892	$8,477.23
			pay of special assistant attorneys, FY 1891	$1,650.00
			"payment of certain legal counsel" named in House Ex. Doc. 193, 52d Cong., 2d Sess.	$3,500.00
		Fees of Clerks	fees of clerks, FY 1893	$93,000.00
			fees of clerks, FY 1892	$50,000.00
		Fees of Commissioners	fees of commissioners, FY 1893	$165,000.00
			fees of commissioners, FY 1892	$65,000.00
		Fees of Jurors	fees of jurors, FY 1893	$25,000.00
		Support of Prisoners	support of prisoners, FY 1893	$165,000.00
			support of prisoners, FY 1892	$61,357.83
			support of prisoners, FY 1890	$18.47
			support of prisoners, FY 1889	$83.50
			support of prisoners, FY 1888	$129.00
			support of prisoners, FY 1887	$28.20
			support of prisoners, FY 1886	$57.55
		Pay of Bailiffs	pay of bailiffs, etc., FY 1893	$40,000.00
		Miscellaneous Expenses	miscellaneous expenses, FY 1893	$55,000.00
			miscellaneous expenses, FY 1876	$41.00
			miscellaneous expenses, FY 1875	$709.00
			miscellaneous expenses, FY 1873	$40.00
			miscellaneous expenses, FY 1872	$42.50
			miscellaneous expenses, FY 1871	$14.50

			Appropriation	
			$42.50	miscellaneous expenses, FY 1870
		Rent of Courtrooms	$35,000.00	rent of courtrooms FY 1893
			$16,000.00	rent of courtrooms, FY 1892
		Total	$2,390,611.23	
		TOTAL APPROPRIATION	**$7,919,634.10**	

1894

Statute (Citation)	Date Passed	Headings	Appropriation	Line-item Details
Ch. 208, 1893 (27 Stat. 572, 608)	March 3, 1893	Expenses of the United States Courts	$675,000.00	fees and expenses of marshals
			$250,000.00	payment of district attorneys
			$5,000.00	special compensation of district attorneys for services not covered by salaries or fees
			$100,000.00	payment of regular assistants to district attorneys
			$20,000.00	payment of special assistants to district attorneys
			$175,000.00	fees of clerks
			$100,000.00	fees of commissioners
			$600,000.00	fees of jurors
			$750,000.00	fees of witnesses
			$300,000.00	support of prisoners
			$50,000.00	rent of courtrooms
			$150,000.00	pay of bailiffs, criers, jury commissioners, meals for jurors, expenses of judges sent outside their districts
			$170,000.00	miscellaneous expenses
		Total	$3,345,000.00	
Ch. 211, 1893 (27 Stat. 675, 713)	March 3, 1893	Supreme Court	$90,500.00	salaries of the Chief Justice and 8 associate justices of the Supreme Court of the United States
			$60,000.00	salaries of 10 circuit judges
			$3,000.00	salary of the marshal of the Supreme Court
			$14,400.00	salaries of stenographic clerks for Supreme Court justices
		Circuit Courts of Appeals	$81,000.00	salaries of 9 circuit judges, 9 clerks
		Court of Private Land Claims	$33,500.00	salaries of justices, clerk, stenographer, attorney, interpreter
			indefinite	salaries of deputy clerks
		District Courts	$323,500.00	salaries of 64 district judges, judge of U.S. court in Indian Territory

Statute (Citation)	Date Passed	Headings	Line-item Details	Appropriation
		Court of Appeals, District of Columbia	salaries of retired judges	indefinite
			salaries of chief justice and 2 associate justices of D.C. Court of Appeals	$18,500.00
			salary and expenses of clerk for D.C. Court of Appeals	$4,000.00
		Supreme Court, District of Columbia	salaries for chief justice and 5 associate judges of Supreme Court of District of Columbia	$30,500.00
		District Attorneys	salaries	$20,700.00
		Marshals	salaries	$13,500.00
		Court of Claims	salaries of judges, clerks, bailiff, messenger	$34,640.00
			expenses	$3,000.00
			furnishing clerk's office	$250.00
			reporting decisions	$1,000.00
			Total	$693,100.00
Ch. 61, 1894 (28 Stat. 58, 61)	April 21, 1894	Fees of Marshals	fees and expenses of marshals, FY 1894	$350,000.00
		Fees of Jurors	fees of jurors, FY 1894	$50,000.00
		Fees of Witnesses	fees of witnesses, FY 1894	$200,000.00
		District Attorneys	fees of district attorneys, FY 1894	$101,000.00
			special compensation of district attorneys, FY 1894	$10,000.00
			regular assistant attorneys, FY 1894	$21,000.00
			special assistant attorneys, FY 1894	$30,000.00
			special assistant attorneys, FY 1892–1893	$10,340.00
		Fees of Clerks	fees of clerks, FY 1894	$116,000.00
		Fees of Commissioners	fees of commissioners, FY 1894	$187,200.00
		Rent of Courtrooms	rent of courtrooms, FY 1894	$42,000.00
		Support of Prisoners	support of prisoners, FY 1894	$275,000.00
			Total	$1,392,540.00
			TOTAL APPROPRIATION	$5,430,640.00

1895

Statute (Citation)	Date Passed	Headings	Line-item Details	Appropriation
Ch. 174, 1894 (28 Stat. 162, 203)	July 31, 1894	Supreme Court	salaries of the Chief Justice and 8 associate justices of the Supreme Court of the United States	$90,500.00
			salary of the marshal of the Supreme Court	$3,000.00
			salaries of stenographic clerks for Supreme Court justices	$14,400.00

			Circuit Courts	salaries of 10 circuit judges	$60,000.00
			Circuit Court of Appeals	salaries of 9 circuit judges, 9 clerks	$81,000.00
			Salary, Clerk, Northern District of Illinois	salary	$3,000.00
			Court of Private Land Claims	salaries of justices, clerk, stenographer, attorney, interpreter	$33,500.00
				expenses	$16,000.00
			District Courts	salaries of 64 district judges, judge of U.S. court, Indian Territory	$323,500.00
				salaries of retired judges	indefinite
			Court of Appeals, District of Columbia	salaries of chief justice, associate justices, clerk, messenger, expenses	$24,220.00
			Supreme Court, District of Columbia	salaries of chief justice, 5 associate judges	$30,000.00
			District Attorneys	salaries	$20,900.00
			Marshals	salaries	$13,700.00
			Court of Claims	salaries of judges, clerks, bailiff, messenger	$35,840.00
				expenses	$3,000.00
				reporting decisions	$1,000.00
			Total		$713,720.00
Ch. 301, 1894 (28 Stat. 372, 415)	August 18, 1894		Expenses of the United States Courts	fees and expenses of marshals	$675,000.00
				expenses of marshals in executing orders protecting property in hands of receivers, FY 1894–1895	$250,000.00
				regular fees of district attorneys	$250,000.00
				special compensation of district attorneys	$5,000.00
				salary of regular assistant attorneys	$100,000.00
				payment of special assistant attorneys	$20,000.00
				fees of clerks	$175,000.00
				fees of commissioners	$100,000.00
				fees of jurors	$600,000.00
				fees of witnesses	$750,000.00
				support of prisoners	$300,000.00
				rent of courtrooms	$50,000.00
				pay of bailiffs, criers, jury commissioners, meals for jurors, expenses of judges sent outside their districts	$150,000.00
				miscellaneous expenses	$170,000.00
				salary of additional circuit judge for Eighth Circuit	$6,000.00

			assistant clerk for court of appeals of D.C.	$2,000.00
			expenses of clerk for court of appeals of D.C.	$500.00
			for Attorney General for cases involving Pacific railroads	$30,000.00
			pay to supervisors of elections	$500.00
		Total		$3,634,000.00
Ch. 307, 1894 (28 Stat. 424, 442)	August 23, 1894	Judicial	salary, district attorney, Middle District of Alabama	$200.00
			salary, marshal, Middle District of Alabama	$200.00
			expenses of judge, Indian Territory	$500.00
		Expenses United States Courts		
		Fees of Marshals	for expenses in executing orders for the protection of property in receivership, FY 1894	$125,000.00
			fees and expenses, FY 1894	$250,000.00
		Fees of District Attorneys	fees of district attorneys, FY 1893	$26,288.32
			fees of district attorneys, FY 1892	$904.00
		[Special Compensation for District Attorneys]	special compensation, FY 1893	$5,000.00
			special compensation, FY 1892	$1,500.00
		[Special Assistant Attorneys]	pay of special assistant attorneys, FY 1893	$22,000.00
			pay of special assistant attorneys, FY 1892	$4,000.00
			pay of Alexander Chalmers, Arizona Territory, for defense of Indians	$2,000.00
			pay of Richard W. Young and C.S. Varian for services related to indictment for homicide	$2,000.00
		Fees of Clerks	fees of clerks, FY 1893	$23,130.48
		Fees of Commissioners	fees of commissioners, FY 1893	$28,072.37
			fees of commissioners, FY 1892	$7,764.56
		Fees of Jurors	fees of jurors, FY 1894	$80,000.00
			fees of jurors, FY 1893	$20,384.12
			fees of jurors, FY 1890	$6.00
			fees of jurors, FY 1887	$12.00
			fees of jurors, FY 1873	$506.50
		Fees of Witnesses	fees of witnesses, FY 1894	$150,000.00
			fees of witnesses, FY 1893	$16,492.35
			fees of witnesses, FY 1891	$343.10
			fees of witnesses, FY 1890	$370.40

	fees of witnesses, FY 1889	$874.40
	fees of witnesses, FY 1888	$645.60
	fees of witnesses, FY 1887	$235.80
	fees of witnesses, FY 1886	$253.35
	fees of witnesses, FY 1885	$44.70
Support of Prisoners	support of prisoners, FY 1894	$65,000.00
	support of prisoners, FY 1893	$140,834.37
	support of prisoners, FY 1892	$93.00
	support of prisoners, FY 1891	$950.57
	support of prisoners, FY 1890	$499.79
	support of prisoners, FY 1889	$159.79
	support of prisoners, FY 1888	$114.55
	support of prisoners, FY 1885	$44.00
Rent of Courtrooms	rent of courtrooms, FY 1892	$744.77
Pay of Bailiffs	pay of bailiffs and criers, etc, FY 1894	$20,000.00
	pay of bailiffs and criers, etc, FY 1892	$1,019.00
	pay of bailiffs and criers, etc, FY 1889	$80.00
	pay of bailiffs and criers, etc., FY 1888	$114.50
	pay of bailiffs and criers, etc., FY 1887	$60.00
Miscellaneous Expenses	miscellaneous expenses, FY 1894	$20,000.00
	miscellaneous expenses, FY 1893	$5,034.52
	miscellaneous expenses, FY 1891	$255.00
	miscellaneous expenses, FY 1885	$106.20
	for select deputy marshals, Georgia, FY 1879–1881	$4,370.38
	pay to Edwin Walker, for service in specific case, FY 1893	$500.00
	pay to Patrick Winston, legal services rendered, FY 1892	$600.00
Total		$1,029,308.49

January 25, 1895	Ch. 43, 1895 (28 Stat. 636, 639)	United States Courts	
		fees of jurors, FY 1895	$130,000.00
		fees of witnesses, FY 1895	$500,000.00
		support of prisoners	$340,000.00
		Total	$970,000.00
March 2, 1895	Ch. 187, 1895 (28 Stat. 843, 860)	Fees of Marshals	
		fees and expenses of marshals, FY 1895	$713,000.00
		fees and expenses of marshals, FY 1894	$195,450.00

	$28,159.58	fees and expenses of marshals, FY 1893
	$140,000.00	marshal's expenses for protecting property in receivership, FY 1894–1895
Fees of Jurors	$100,000.00	fees of jurors, FY 1895
	$11,000.00	fees of jurors, FY 1893
	$401.65	fees of jurors, FY 1892
	$8.00	fees of jurors, FY 1891
	$13.00	fees of jurors, FY 1890
	$20.00	fees of jurors, FY 1887
	$10.00	fees of jurors, FY 1885
	$506.50	fees of jurors, FY 1872
Fees of Witnesses	$80,000.00	fees of witnesses, FY 1895
	$82,800.00	fees of witnesses, FY 1894
	$1,506.36	fees of witnesses, FY 1892
	$18.30	fees of witnesses, FY 1891
	$61.70	fees of witnesses, FY 1890
	$2.50	fees of witnesses, FY 1888
	$256.35	fees of witnesses, FY 1886
	$105.00	fees of witnesses, FY 1883
Support of Prisoners	$50,000.00	support of prisoners, FY 1895
	$78,000.00	support of prisoners, FY 1894
	$1,000.77	support of prisoners, FY 1892
	$190.22	support of prisoners, FY 1891
	$609.67	support of prisoners, FY 1890
	$75.60	support of prisoners, FY 1889
	$3.00	support of prisoners, FY 1887
Pay of Bailiffs	$45,000.00	pay of bailiffs and criers, etc., FY 1895
	$5,838.55	pay of bailiffs and criers, etc., FY 1894
	$15.00	pay of bailiffs and criers, etc., FY 1892
	$54.00	pay of bailiffs and criers, etc., FY 1888
Miscellaneous Expenses	$70,000.00	miscellaneous expenses, FY 1895
	$5.00	miscellaneous expenses, FY 1891
	$7.25	miscellaneous expenses, FY 1889
	$41.20	miscellaneous expenses, FY 1888
	$18.50	miscellaneous expenses, FY 1887

1896 — (continued)

Headings	Appropriation	Line-item Details
Fees of District Attorneys	$100,000.00	fees of district attorneys, FY 1895
	$54,281.10	fees of district attorneys, FY 1894
	$30,000.00	pay of special assistant attorneys, FY 1895
	$25,652.49	pay of special assistant attorneys, FY 1894
	$1,209.36	pay of special assistant attorneys, FY 1893
Fees of Clerks	$120,000.00	fees of clerks, FY 1895
	$4,000.00	fees of clerks, FY 1894
Fees of Commissioners	$187,200.00	fees of commissioners, FY 1895
	$40,181.55	fees of commissioners, FY 1894
	$3,000.00	fees of commissioners, FY 1893
Rent of Courtrooms	$62,000.00	rent of courtrooms, FY 1895
Refund, Noble Butler, Clerk, United States Court	$49.30	
Total	$2,231,751.50	
TOTAL APPROPRIATION	**$8,578,779.99**	

1896

Statute (Citation)	Date Passed	Headings	Appropriation	Line-item Details
Ch. 177, 1895 (28 Stat. 764, 805)	March 2, 1895	Supreme Court	$107,900.00	salaries of Chief Justice, associate justices, marshal, stenographic clerks
		Circuit Courts	$60,000.00	salaries of 10 circuit judges
		Circuit Court of Appeals	$99,000.00	salaries of 12 additional circuit judges, 9 clerks
		Court of Private Land Claims	$33,500.00	salaries of justices, clerk, stenographer, attorney, interpreter
		District Courts	$323,500.00	salaries of 64 district judges, judge of U.S. court, Indian Territory
			indefinite	salaries of retired judges
		Court of Appeals, District of Columbia	$24,720.00	salaries of chief justice, associate justices, clerk, messenger, expenses
		Supreme Court, District of Columbia	$30,000.00	salaries of chief justice, 5 associate judges
			$18,500.00	salaries of chief justice and 2 associate justices of D.C. Court of Appeals
		Clerk, District Court, Northern District of Illinois	$3,000.00	
		District Attorneys	$20,900.00	
		Marshals	$13,700.00	

Citation	Date	Category	Amount	Purpose
		Court of Claims	$35,840.00	salaries of judges, clerks, bailiff, messenger
			$3,000.00	expenses
			$1,000.00	reporting decisions
		Total	$734,720.00	
Ch. 189, 1895 (28 Stat. 910, 956)	March 2, 1895	Expenses of the United States Courts	$675,000.00	fees and expenses of marshals
			indefinite	settle account of D.T. Guyton, marshal, Northern District of Mississippi
			$250,000.00	payment of district attorneys for official services
			$5,000.00	special compensation of district attorneys
			$100,000.00	payment of regular assistant attorneys
			$25,000.00	payment of special assistant attorneys
			$175,000.00	fees of clerks
			$100,000.00	fees of commissioners
			$600,000.00	fees of jurors
			$750,000.00	fees of witnesses
			$400,000.00	support of prisoners
			$5,600.00	purchase of land and building for jail at Guthrie, Oklahoma Territory
			$50,000.00	rent of courtrooms
			$150,000.00	pay of bailiffs, criers, jury commissioners, meals for jurors, expenses of judges sent outside their districts
			$170,000.00	miscellaneous expenses
		Total	$3,455,600.00	
Ch. 33, 1896 (29 Stat. 17, 24)	February 26, 1896	[District Court of Indian Territory] United States Courts	$210,000.00	salaries and expenses of judges, marshals, district attorneys, etc.
		[Fees of Marshals]	$960,000.00	fees and expenses of marshals, FY 1896
			$230,573.34	fees and expenses of marshals, FY 1895
		[Fees of District Attorneys]	$160,000.00	fees of district attorneys, FY 1896
			$72,461.07	fees of district attorneys, FY 1895
		[Fees of Clerks]	$155,000.00	fees of clerks, FY 1896
			$58,513.87	fees of clerks, FY 1895
			$10,179.36	fees of clerks, FY 1894

Category	Description	Amount
[Fees of Commissioners]	fees of commissioners, FY 1896	$240,000.00
	fees of commissioners, FY 1895	$75,836.93
	fees of commissioners, FY 1894	$11,653.20
[Fees of Jurors]	fees of jurors, FY 1896	$200,000.00
	fees of jurors, FY 1895	$103.45
[Fees of Witnesses]	fees of witnesses, FY 1896	$750,000.00
	fees of witnesses, FY 1895	$30,722.38
[Support of Prisoners]	support of prisoners, FY 1896	$365,000.00
[Rent of Courtrooms]	rent of courtrooms, FY 1896	$50,000.00
[Pay of Bailiffs]	pay of bailiffs and criers, etc., FY 1896	$70,000.00
	pay of bailiffs and criers, etc., FY 1895	$1,698.46
[Miscellaneous Expenses]	miscellaneous expenses, FY 1896	$25,000.00
[Pay of Special Assistant Attorneys]	pay of special assistant attorneys, FY 1895	$10,067.81
	pay of special assistant attorneys, FY 1894	$14,004.65
[Pay of Regular Assistant Attorneys]	pay of regular assistant attorneys, FY 1896	$31,000.00
[Pay of Assistants to Attorney General]	for services and expenses in cases appealed from Court of Private Land Claims, FY 1896	$10,000.00
[Protecting Property in Receivership]	FY 1894–1895	$20,506.86
Total		$3,762,321.38

Ch. 373, 1896 (29 Stat. 267, 297)	June 8, 1896		
	Salaries, Circuit Courts	for salary of additional circuit judge for Seventh Circuit, for March to June 1895	$1,533.33
		for salary of additional circuit judge for Ninth Circuit, March to June 1895	$1,950.00
	Salaries, District Judges	for salary of district judge for District of Utah, FY 1896	$2,032.94
	Salaries, District Attorneys	for salary of district attorney for District of Utah, FY 1896	$81.29
	Salaries, District Marshals	salary of marshal for District of Utah, FY 1896	$81.29
	United States Courts		
	Special Assistant Attorneys	payment of special assistant attorneys, FY 1896	$30,000.00
		payment of special assistant attorneys, FY 1895	$4,820.00
		payment of special assistant attorneys, FY 1894	$3,200.00
	Fees of Clerks	fees of clerks, FY 1894	$191.35
	Fees of Commissioners	fees of commissioners, FY 1895	$6,809.75
		fees of commissioners, FY 1894	$1,807.62

Headings	Appropriation	Line-item Details
Fees of Jurors	$25.20	fees of jurors, FY 1892
	$17.30	fees of jurors, FY 1889
	$698.80	fees of jurors, FY 1888
Fees of Witnesses	$100,000.00	fees of witnesses, FY 1896
	$91,431.74	fees of witnesses, FY 1895
Support of Prisoners	$77,056.64	support of prisoners, FY 1895
	$50,000.00	support of prisoners, FY 1896
	$7,766.73	support of prisoners, FY 1895
	$6,754.58	accounts reported by Attorney General, FY 1895
	$1,461.75	for Southern District of New York, FY 1893
Bailiffs and Criers	$10,000.00	pay of bailiffs and criers, etc., FY 1896
	$15,375.73	pay of bailiffs and criers, etc., FY 1895
	$30.00	pay of bailiffs and criers, etc., FY 1894
	$280.00	pay of bailiffs and criers, etc., FY 1893
	$35.00	pay of bailiffs and criers, etc., FY 1892
Miscellaneous Expenses	$50.00	miscellaneous expenses, FY 1892
	$25,000.00	miscellaneous expenses, FY 1896
Protecting Property in Hands of Receiver	$25,176.82	FY 1894–1895
	$4,365.00	FY 1894
Total	$468,032.86	
TOTAL APPROPRIATION	**$8,420,674.24**	

1897

Statute (Citation)	Date Passed	Headings	Appropriation	Line-item Details
Ch. 252, 1896 (29 Stat. 140, 177)	May 28, 1896	Supreme Court	$107,900.00	salaries of Chief Justice, associate justices, marshal, stenographic clerks
		Circuit Courts	$132,000.00	salaries of 22 circuit judges
			$27,000.00	9 clerks for circuit courts of appeals
			$2,000.00	salary of messenger/librarian, Eighth Circuit Court of Appeals
		Court of Private Land Claims	$33,500.00	salaries of justices, clerk, stenographer, attorney, interpreter
			indefinite	deputy clerks, Court of Private Land Claims
		District Courts	$325,000.00	salaries of 65 district judges
		United States Courts, Indian Territory	$175,000.00	salaries and expenses of district court in Indian Territory

Statute	Date	Item	Amount	Description
		Retired Judges	indefinite	salaries
		Court of Appeals, District of Columbia	$25,720.00	salaries of chief justice, associate justices, clerk, deputy clerk, messenger, expenses
		Supreme Court, District of Columbia	$30,000.00	salaries of chief justice, 5 associate judges
		Clerk of District Court, Northern District of Illinois	$3,000.00	
		Commissioner, Yellowstone Park	$1,000.00	salary
		Court of Claims	$35,840.00	salaries of judges, clerks, bailiff, messenger
			$3,000.00	expenses
			$1,000.00	reporting decisions
		Total	$862,120.00	
Ch. 420, 1896 (29 Stat. 413, 449)	June 11, 1896	Expenses of the United States Courts	$1,000,000.00	salaries, fees, expenses of marshals and deputies
			$275,000.00	salaries of district attorneys and expenses of district attorneys and regular assistants
			$85,000.00	salaries of regular assistant attorneys
			$25,000.00	pay of special assistant attorneys
			$225,000.00	commissioners
			$220,000.00	fees of clerks
			$533,000.00	fees of jurors
			$1,066,000.00	fees of witnesses
			$460,000.00	support of prisoners
			$131,212.00	support of Leavenworth Penitentiary
			$80,000.00	rent of courtrooms
			$110,000.00	pay of bailiffs, criers, jury commissioners, meals for jurors, expenses of judges sent outside their districts, expenses of judges in circuit courts of appeals
			$150,000.00	miscellaneous expenses
		Total	$4,360,212.00	
		TOTAL APPROPRIATION	**$5,222,332.00**	

1898

Statute (Citation)	Date Passed	Headings	Appropriation	Line-item Details
Ch. 265, 1897 (29 Stat. 538, 576)	February 19, 1897	Supreme Court	$107,900.00	salaries of Chief Justice, associate justices, marshal, stenographic clerks
		Circuit Courts	$132,000.00	salaries of 22 circuit judges
			$27,000.00	9 clerks for circuit courts of appeals
			$2,000.00	salary of messenger/librarian, Eighth Circuit Court of Appeals
		Court of Private Land Claims	$33,500.00	salaries of justices, clerk, stenographer, attorney, interpreter
			indefinite	deputy clerks, Court of Private Land Claims
		District Courts	$325,000.00	salaries of 65 district judges
		Retired Judges	indefinite	salaries
		United States Courts, Indian Territory	$15,000.00	salaries of United States courts, Indian Territory
		Court of Appeals, District of Columbia	$25,720.00	salaries of chief justice, associate justices, clerk, deputy clerk, messenger, expenses
		Supreme Court, District of Columbia	$30,000.00	salaries of chief justice, 5 associate judges
		Clerk of District Court, Northern District of Illinois	$3,000.00	salary
		Commissioner, Yellowstone Park	$1,000.00	salary
		Court of Claims	$35,840.00	salaries of judges, clerks, bailiff, messenger
			$3,000.00	expenses
			$1,000.00	reporting decisions
		Total	$741,960.00	
Ch. 2, 1897 (30 Stat. 11, 56)	June 4, 1897	Expenses of the United States Courts	$1,200,000.00	salaries, fees, and expenses of marshals
			$360,000.00	salaries and expenses of district attorneys
			$23,800.00	fees of district attorney for the District of Columbia
			$140,000.00	salaries of regular assistant attorneys
			$50,000.00	payment of special assistant attorneys
			$350,000.00	fees of clerks
			$300,000.00	fees of commissioners
			$500,000.00	fees of jurors
			$750,000.00	fees of witnesses

Citation	Date	Category	Amount	Description
			$700,000.00	support of prisoners
			$130,712.00	support for Leavenworth Penitentiary
			$50,000.00	establish site for erection of new penitentiary, Leavenworth, under act 29 Stat. 380
			$90,000.00	rent of courtrooms
			$150,000.00	pay of bailiffs, criers, jury commissioners, meals for jurors, expenses of judges sent outside their districts, expenses of judges in circuit courts of appeals
			$15,000.00	salary and expenses of 3 commissioners appointed to codify criminal laws
			$200,000.00	miscellaneous expenses
			$75,000.00	salaries and expenses for court of Indian Territory
		Total	$5,084,512.00	
Ch. 9, 1897 (30 Stat. 105, 131)	July 19, 1897	United States Court, Indian Territory	$45,000.00	salaries and expenses, FY 1897
			$5,000.00	salary of additional judge
			$8,100.00	pay for deputy clerks, FY 1895–1897
			$947.00	reimbursement of clerk, FY 1895
		United States Courts		
		[Salaries and Expenses of Marshals]	$200,000.00	salaries and expenses of marshals, FY 1897
		[Fees of D.C. District Attorney]	$1,200.00	fees of district attorney, District of Columbia, FY 1897
		[Salaries and Expenses of District Attorneys]	$75,000.00	salaries of district attorneys, expenses of district attorneys and regular assistants, FY 1897
		[Fees of District Attorneys]	$65,145.11	fees of district attorneys, FY 1896
		[Regular Assistant Attorneys]	$55,000.00	pay of regular assistant attorneys, FY 1897
		[Special Assistant Attorneys]	$25,000.00	pay of special assistant attorneys, FY 1897
			$29,758.20	pay of special assistant attorneys, FY 1896
			$9,828.15	pay of special assistant attorneys, FY 1895
			$6,500.00	pay to special assistant attorney Baxter, FY 1886, 1893–1895
			$500.00	pay to special assistant attorney Marshal, FY 1896
		[Fees of Clerks]	$130,000.00	fees of clerks, FY 1897
			$16,128.57	fees of clerks, FY 1896
		Fees of Commissioners	$100,000.00	fees of commissioners, FY 1897
			$32,228.69	fees of commissioners, FY 1896
			$1,911.50	fees of commissioners, FY 1895

Heading	Appropriation	Line-item Details
[Fees of Jurors]	$22.00	fees of jurors, FY 1890
[Fees of Witnesses]	$50,000.00	fees of witnesses, FY 1897
	$55.40	fees of witnesses, FY 1891
	$96.10	fees of witnesses, FY 1890
	$22.00	fees of witnesses, FY 1889
[Support of Prisoners]	$240,000.00	support of prisoners, FY 1897
	$52,624.85	support of prisoners, FY 1896
	$11,689.65	support of prisoners, FY 1895
[Rent of Courtrooms]	$20,000.00	rent of courtrooms, FY 1897
[Pay of Bailiffs and Criers, etc.]	$40,000.00	pay of bailiffs and criers, etc, FY 1897
	$90.00	pay of bailiffs and criers, etc., FY 1893
	$75.00	pay of bailiffs and criers, etc., FY 1892
	$75.00	pay of bailiffs and criers, etc., FY 1891
	$75.00	pay of bailiffs and criers, etc., FY 1890
	$45.00	pay of bailiffs and criers, etc., FY 1889
[Miscellaneous Expenses]	$75,000.00	miscellaneous expenses, FY 1897
	$227.65	miscellaneous expenses, FY 1892
[Protecting Property in Hands of Receiver]	$504.20	expenses of protecting property in hands of receiver, FY 1894
Total	$1,297,849.07	
TOTAL APPROPRIATION	**$7,124,321.07**	

1899

Statute (Citation)	Date Passed	Headings	Appropriation	Line-item Details
Ch. 68, 1898 (30 Stat. 277, 314)	March 15, 1898	Supreme Court	$107,900.00	salaries of Chief Justice, associate justices, marshal, stenographic clerks
		Circuit Courts	$161,000.00	salaries of judges, clerks, and messenger/librarian/crier
		Court of Private Land Claims	$33,500.00	salaries of justices, clerk, stenographer, attorney, interpreter
			indefinite	deputy clerks, Court of Private Land Claims
		District Courts	$325,000.00	salaries of 65 district judges
		Retired Judges	indefinite	salaries
		United States Courts, Indian Territory	$20,000.00	salaries, United States courts, Indian Territory
		Court of Appeals, District of Columbia	$25,720.00	salaries of chief justice, associate justices, clerk, deputy clerk, messenger, expenses

Citation	Date	Account	Description	Amount
		Supreme Court, District of Columbia	salaries of chief justice, 5 associate judges	$30,000.00
		Clerk of District Court, Northern District of Illinois	salary	$3,000.00
		Commissioner, Yellowstone Park	salary	$1,000.00
		Court of Claims	salaries of judges, clerks, bailiff, messenger	$35,840.00
			expenses	$3,000.00
			reporting decisions	$1,000.00
		Total		$746,960.00
Ch. 546, 1898 (30 Stat. 597, 642)	July 1, 1898	Expenses of the United States Courts	salaries, fees, and expenses of marshals and deputies	$988,000.00
			salaries and expenses of district attorneys	$394,000.00
			fees of district attorney for the District of Columbia	$23,800.00
			salaries of regular assistant attorneys	$145,000.00
			payment of special assistant attorneys	$60,000.00
			fees of clerks	$280,000.00
			fees of commissioners	$200,000.00
			fees of jurors	$600,000.00
			fees of witnesses	$800,000.00
			support of prisoners	$650,000.00
			support for Leavenworth Penitentiary	$140,712.00
			rent of rooms for courts and judicial officers	$100,000.00
			pay of bailiffs, criers, jury commissioners, meals for jurors, expenses of judges sent outside their districts, expenses of judges in circuit courts of appeals	$150,000.00
			miscellaneous expenses	$215,000.00
			salaries and expenses for court of Indian Territory	$74,000.00
			supplies for courts and judicial officers	$35,000.00
			fees, district attorney, Southern District of New York	$500.00
		Total		$4,856,012.00
Ch. 571, 1898 (30 Stat. 652, 681)	July 7, 1898	United States Courts [District Attorneys]	salaries and expenses of district attorneys, FY 1898	$25,000.00
			salaries and expenses of district attorneys, FY 1897	$24,619.50
		[Regular Assistant District Attorneys]	salaries of regular assistant attorneys, FY 1899	$6,000.00

[Fees of District Attorney, Southern District of New York]	fees, district attorney, Southern District of New York, FY 1899	$66.05
[Rent of Courtrooms]	rent of rooms for courts and judicial officers, FY 1899	$10,000.00
	cleaning, repairing, U.S. court building, Columbus, Ga.	$51.00
[Fees of Jurors]	fees of jurors, FY 1895	$232.00
	fees of jurors, FY 1894	$153.75
	fees of jurors, FY 1892	$16.00
[Fees of Witnesses]	fees of witnesses, FY 1894	$177.20
	fees of witnesses, FY 1893	$168.50
	fees of witnesses, FY 1892	$84.70
	fees of witnesses, FY 1891	$166.40
	fees of witnesses, FY 1889	$39.80
	fees of witnesses, FY 1888	$25.40
	fees of witnesses, FY 1880	$10.90
[Fees of Clerks]	fees of clerks, FY 1896	$2,497.73
[Fees of Commissioners]	fees of commissioners, FY 1896	$1,840.45
[Support of Prisoners]	support of prisoners, FY 1896	$2,453.01
	support of prisoners, FY 1894	$286.38
	support of prisoners, FY 1891	$202.29
	support of prisoners, FY 1890	$82.28
[Bailiffs and Criers, etc.]	pay of bailiffs and criers, etc., FY 1899	$25,000.00
[Marshal, Western District of Tennessee]	for reimbursement to late marshal, for pay of extra bailiffs, FY 1894	$298.33
[Miscellaneous Expenses]	miscellaneous expenses, FY 1898	$45,000.00
	miscellaneous expenses, FY 1897	$6,178.68
	miscellaneous expenses, FY 1895	$594.08
	miscellaneous expenses, FY 1894	$241.53
	miscellaneous expenses, FY 1893	$113.74
	miscellaneous expenses, FY 1892	$65.22
	miscellaneous expenses, FY 1890	$22.00
[Deputy Clerks, Indian Territory]	FY 1898 and FY 1899	$7,200.00
Total		$158,886.92

Ch. 427, 1899 (30 Stat. 1214, 1237)

March 3, 1899

United States Courts

[Marshals]	$200,000.00	salaries, fees, and expenses of marshals, FY 1899
[District Attorneys]	$6,000.00	salaries and expenses of district attorneys, FY 1899
	$0.30	salaries and expenses of district attorneys, FY 1898
[Regular Assistant District Attorneys]	$15,000.00	salaries of regular assistant attorneys, FY 1899
[Fees of Jurors]	$100,000.00	fees of jurors, FY 1899
	$9.70	fees of jurors, FY 1898
[Fees of Witnesses]	$300,000.00	fees of witnesses, FY 1899
	$533.90	fees of witnesses, FY 1896
	$369.80	fees of witnesses, FY 1895
	$9.50	fees of witnesses, FY 1879
[Support of Prisoners]	$20,000.00	support of prisoners, FY 1899
	$35.20	support of prisoners, FY 1896
	$15.30	support of prisoners, FY 1894
[Support of Leavenworth]	$5,400.00	fuel, miscellaneous expenses, hospital supplies, subsistence, Leavenworth Penitentiary, FY 1899
[Bailiffs and Criers, etc.]	$35,000.00	pay of bailiffs and criers, etc., FY 1899
	$55.00	pay of bailiffs and criers, etc., FY 1896
	$135.00	pay of bailiffs and criers, etc., FY 1895
	$188.75	pay of bailiffs and criers, etc., FY 1894
	$10.00	pay of bailiffs and criers, etc., FY 1893
[Miscellaneous Expenses]	$25,000.00	miscellaneous expenses, FY 1899
	$207.45	miscellaneous expenses, FY 1896
	$21.32	miscellaneous expenses, FY 1894
[Special Assistant Attorneys]	$3,000.00	pay of special assistant attorneys, FY 1895
[District Attorneys]	$6,166.04	FY 1898
[U.S. Court, Indian Territory]	$18.00	salaries and expenses, U.S. court, Indian Territory, FY 1895
Total	$717,175.26	
TOTAL APPROPRIATION	$6,479,034.18	

1900

Statute (Citation)	Date Passed	Headings	Appropriation	Line-item Details
Ch. 187, 1899 (30 Stat. 846, 888)	February 24, 1899	Supreme Court	$107,900.00	salaries of Chief Justice, associate justices, marshal, stenographic clerks
		Circuit Courts	$161,000.00	salaries of 22 circuit judges, clerks, messenger/librarian/crier
		Court of Private Land Claims	$33,500.00	salaries of justices, clerk, stenographer, attorney, interpreter
			indefinite	deputy clerks, Court of Private Land Claims
			$12,000.00	to allow Attorney General to hire additional attorneys, agents, stenographers, and experts for Court of Private Land Claims
		District Courts	$325,000.00	salaries of 65 district judges
		Retired Judges	indefinite	salaries
		United States Courts, Indian Territory	$20,000.00	salaries, United States courts, Indian Territory
		Court of Appeals, District of Columbia	$25,720.00	salaries of chief justice, associate justices, clerk, deputy clerk, messenger, expenses
		Supreme Court, District of Columbia	$30,000.00	salaries of chief justice, 5 associate judges
		Clerk of District Court, Northern District of Illinois	$3,000.00	
		Commissioner Yellowstone Park	$1,000.00	
		Court of Claims	$35,840.00	salaries of judges, clerks, bailiff, messenger
			$3,000.00	expenses
			$1,000.00	reporting decisions
		Total	$758,960.00	
Ch. 424, 1899 (30 Stat. 1074, 1114)	March 3, 1899	Expenses of United States Courts	$1,000,000.00	salaries, fees, and expenses of marshals and deputies
			$400,000.00	salaries and expenses of district attorneys
			$23,800.00	fees of district attorney for the District of Columbia
			$160,000.00	salaries of regular assistant attorneys
			$60,000.00	payment of special assistant attorneys
			$250,000.00	fees of clerks
			$150,000.00	fees of commissioners
			$600,000.00	fees of jurors
			$800,000.00	fees of witnesses

Date	Citation	Agency	Description	Amount
			support of prisoners	$650,000.00
			support for Leavenworth Penitentiary	$149,912.00
			rent of rooms for courts and judicial officers	$100,000.00
			pay of bailiffs, criers, jury commissioners, meals for jurors, expenses of judges sent outside their districts, expenses of judges in circuit courts of appeals	$150,000.00
			miscellaneous expenses	$215,000.00
			salaries and expenses for court of Indian Territory	$70,000.00
			supplies for courts and judicial officers	$35,000.00
			fees, district attorney, Southern District of New York	$100.00
			movement of circuit court records in New Hampshire	$200.00
			Total	$4,814,012.00
February 9, 1900	Ch. 14, 1900 (31 Stat. 7, 23)	Support of U.S. Penitentiary, Leavenworth [Salaries of Additional Circuit Judges]	miscellaneous expenses, FY 1900	$9,000.00
			salaries of new judges appointed in 1899, FY 1899	$5,000.37
			salaries of new judges appointed in 1899, FY 1900	$18,000.00
			Total	$32,000.37
April 23, 1900	Ch. 253, 1900 (31 Stat. 138)	United States Courts	salaries, fees, and expenses of marshals, FY 1900	$165,000.00
			fees of jurors, FY 1900	$55,000.00
			fees of witnesses, FY 1900	$155,000.00
			miscellaneous expenses, FY 1900	$30,000.00
			Total	$405,000.00
June 6, 1900	Ch. 785, 1900 (31 Stat. 303, 306)	Department of Justice	salary, U.S. district judge for Territory of Hawaii	$233.52
			salary, additional judge, Southern District of New York, FY 1900	$686.83
			salary, clerk, U.S. district court, Territory of Hawaii	$140.11
			salary, reporter of the U.S. district court, Territory of Hawaii	$56.04
		United States Courts	salaries and expenses of district attorneys, FY 1898	$193.04
			salary, district attorney for Southern District of New York, FY 1900	$2,441.24
			support of prisoners, FY 1900	$50,000.00
			support of prisoners, FY 1899	$30,871.71
			pay of bailiffs and criers, etc., FY 1900	$10,000.00
			rent of rooms for courts and judicial officers, FY 1899	$3,600.00

		miscellaneous expenses, FY 1900	$15,000.00
		support for Leavenworth Penitentiary, FY 1900	$1,000.00
	Total		$114,222.49
	TOTAL APPROPRIATION		**$6,124,194.86**

1901

Statute (Citation)	Date Passed	Headings	Appropriation	Line-item Details
Ch. 192, 1900 (31 Stat. 86, 131)	April 17, 1900	Supreme Court	$107,900.00	salaries of Chief Justice, associate justices, marshal, stenographic clerks
		Circuit Courts	$179,000.00	salaries of 25 circuit judges, clerks, messenger/librarian/crier
		Court of Private Land Claims	$33,500.00	salaries of justices, clerk, stenographer, attorney, interpreter
			indefinite	deputy clerks, Court of Private Land Claims
			$8,000.00	to allow Attorney General to hire additional attorneys, agents, stenographers, and experts for Court of Private Land Claims
		District Courts	$325,000.00	salaries of 65 district judges
		Retired Judges	indefinite	salaries
		United States Courts, Indian Territory	$20,000.00	salaries, United States courts, Indian Territory
		Court of Appeals, District of Columbia	$25,720.00	salaries of chief justice, associate justices, clerk, deputy clerk, messenger, expenses
		Supreme Court, District of Columbia	$30,000.00	salaries of chief justice, 5 associate judges
		Clerk of District Court, Northern District of Illinois	$3,000.00	salary
		Commissioner, Yellowstone Park	$1,500.00	salary
		Court of Claims	$44,540.00	salaries of judges and staff
			$8,000.00	cost of auditors
			$2,000.00	miscellaneous expenses
			$1,400.00	fuel and electricity
			$1,000.00	reporting decisions
		Total	$790,560.00	
Ch. 791, 1900 (31 Stat. 588, 639)	June 6, 1900	Expenses of United States Courts	$1,000,000.00	salaries, fees, and expenses of marshals
			$400,000.00	salaries and expenses of district attorneys
			$23,800.00	fees of district attorney for the District of Columbia

			salaries of regular assistant attorneys	$160,000.00
			payment of special assistant attorneys	$60,000.00
			fees of clerks	$240,000.00
			fees of commissioners	$150,000.00
			fees of jurors	$600,000.00
			fees of witnesses	$950,000.00
			support of prisoners	$650,000.00
			support for Leavenworth Penitentiary	$163,400.00
			rent of rooms for courts and judicial officers	$100,000.00
			pay of bailiffs, criers, and jury commissioners, meals for jurors, expenses of judges sent outside their districts, expenses of judges in circuit courts of appeals	$150,000.00
			miscellaneous expenses	$225,000.00
			salaries and expenses for court of Indian Territory	$55,000.00
			supplies for courts and judicial officers	$30,000.00
			salary, additional district judge in New York and district judge in Territory of Hawaii	$10,000.00
			salary, clerk and reporter, district court, Territory of Hawaii	$4,200.00
			fees of district attorney, Southern District of New York	$100.00
		Total		$4,971,500.00
Ch. 831, 1901 (31 Stat. 1046)	March 3, 1901	United States Courts	salary, additional judge, Northern District of Ohio, FY 1901	$2,097.18
			salaries, fees, and expenses of marshals, FY 1901	$220,000.00
			salaries and expenses, district attorneys, FY 1901	$10,000.00
			pay of regular assistant attorneys, FY 1901	$10,000.00
			pay of special assistant attorneys, FY 1899	$2,000.00
			pay of special assistant attorneys, FY 1898	$2,000.00
			pay of special assistant attorneys, FY 1897	$1,000.00
			pay of special assistant attorneys, FY 1899	$1,970.65
			pay of special assistant attorneys, FY 1898	$500.00
			pay to special assistant attorneys in cases appealed from Court of Private Land Claims	$8,000.00
			fees of jurors, FY 1901	$75,000.00
			support of prisoners, FY 1901	$100,000.00
			rent of rooms for courts and judicial officers, FY 1901	$5,000.00
			rent of rooms for courts and judicial officers, FY 1900	$5,655.07

	Appropriation	Line-item Details
	$15.00	rent of rooms for courts and judicial officers, FY 1899
	$12,000.00	pay of bailiffs and criers, etc., FY 1901
	$50,000.00	miscellaneous expenses, FY 1901
Total	$505,237.90	
TOTAL APPROPRIATION	$6,267,297.90	

1902

Statute (Citation)	Date Passed	Headings	Appropriation	Line-item Details
Ch. 830, 1901 (31 Stat. 960, 1007)	March 3, 1901	Supreme Court	$107,900.00	salaries of Chief Justice, associate justices, marshal, stenographic clerks
		Circuit Courts	$179,000.00	salaries of 25 circuit judges, clerks, messenger
		District Courts	$335,000.00	salaries of 67 district judges
		United States Courts, Indian Territory	$20,000.00	salaries of judges
		District Court, Territory of Hawaii	$4,200.00	salaries of clerk and reporter
		Retired Judges	indefinite	salaries
		Court of Private Land Claims	$33,500.00	salaries of justices, clerk, stenographer, attorney, interpreter
			$5,000.00	to allow Attorney General to hire additional attorneys, agents, stenographers, and experts for Court of Private Land Claims
			indefinite	deputy clerks, Court of Private Land Claims
		Court of Appeals, District of Columbia	$25,920.00	salaries of chief justice, associate justices, clerk, deputy clerk, reporter, messenger, expenses
		Supreme Court, District of Columbia	$30,000.00	salaries of chief justice, 5 associate judges
		Clerk of District Court, Northern District of Illinois	$3,000.00	
		Commissioner, Yellowstone Park	$1,500.00	salary
			$250.00	fuel, furniture, miscellaneous expenses
		Court of Claims	$45,040.00	salaries of judges and staff
			$8,000.00	cost of auditors
			$3,400.00	miscellaneous expenses
			$1,000.00	reporting decisions
		Total	$802,710.00	

Statute (Citation)	Date Passed	Headings	Appropriation	Line-item Details
Ch. 853, 1901 (31 Stat. 1133, 1182)	March 3, 1901	Expenses of the United States Courts	$1,200,000.00	salaries, fees, and expenses of marshals
			$410,000.00	salaries and expenses of district attorneys
			$23,800.00	fees of district attorney for the District of Columbia
			$185,000.00	salaries of regular assistant attorneys
			$60,000.00	payment of special assistant attorneys
			$240,000.00	fees of clerks
			$150,000.00	fees of commissioners
			$650,000.00	fees of jurors
			$950,000.00	fees of witnesses
			$105,000.00	rent of rooms for courts and judicial officers
			$160,000.00	pay of bailiffs, criers, and jury commissioners, meals for jurors, expenses of judges sent outside their districts, expenses of judges in circuit courts of appeals
			$260,000.00	miscellaneous expenses
			$60,000.00	salaries and expenses for court of Indian Territory
			$30,000.00	supplies for courts and judicial officers
			$100.00	fees of district attorney, Southern District of New York
			$650,000.00	support of prisoners
			$166,400.00	support for Leavenworth Penitentiary
			$94,200.00	support of penitentiary in Atlanta
		Total	$5,394,500.00	
		TOTAL APPROPRIATION	**$6,197,210.00**	

1903

Statute (Citation)	Date Passed	Headings	Appropriation	Line-item Details
Ch. 594, 1902 (32 Stat. 120, 169)	April 28, 1902	Supreme Court	$107,900.00	salaries of Chief Justice, associate justices, marshal, stenographic clerks
		Circuit Courts	$179,000.00	salaries of 25 circuit judges, clerks, messenger
			$9,000.00	purchase of law books for circuit court of appeals libraries
		District Courts	$355,000.00	salaries of 71 district judges
		United States Courts, Indian Territory	$20,000.00	salaries of judges
		District Court, Territory of Hawaii	$4,200.00	salaries of clerk and reporter

	Retired Judges	indefinite	salaries
	Court of Private Land Claims	$33,500.00	salaries of justices, clerk, stenographer, attorney, interpreter
		$4,000.00	to allow Attorney General to hire additional attorneys, agents, stenographers, and experts for Court of Private Land Claims
		indefinite	deputy clerks, Court of Private Land Claims
	Court of Appeals, District of Columbia	$25,920.00	salaries of chief justice, associate justices, clerk, deputy clerk, reporter, messenger, expenses
	Supreme Court, District of Columbia	$30,000.00	salaries of chief justice, 5 associate judges
	Clerk of District Court, Northern District of Illinois	$3,000.00	salary
	Commissioner, Yellowstone Park	$1,500.00	salary
	Court of Claims	$45,540.00	salaries of judges and staff
		$8,000.00	cost of auditors
		$3,400.00	miscellaneous expenses
		$1,000.00	reporting decisions
		$400.00	fireproof safe
	Total	$831,360.00	
Ch. 1301, 1902 (32 Stat. 419, 475) June 28, 1902	Expenses of the United States Courts	$1,200,000.00	salaries, fees, and expenses of marshals
		$435,000.00	salaries and expenses of district attorneys
		$23,800.00	fees of district attorney for the District of Columbia
		$200,000.00	salaries of regular assistant attorneys
		$60,000.00	payment of special assistant attorneys
		$240,000.00	fees of clerks
		$150,000.00	fees of commissioners
		$650,000.00	fees of jurors
		$900,000.00	fees of witnesses
		$105,000.00	rent of rooms for courts and judicial officers
		$160,000.00	pay of bailiffs, criers, and jury commissioners, meals for jurors, expenses of judges sent outside their districts, expenses of judges in circuit courts of appeals
		$260,000.00	miscellaneous expenses
		$53,500.00	salaries and expenses for court of Indian Territory
		$30,000.00	supplies for courts and judicial officers
		$100.00	fees of district attorney for Southern District of New York

Statute (Citation)	Date Passed	Headings	Appropriation	Line-item Details
			$725,000.00	support of prisoners
			$166,400.00	support for Leavenworth Penitentiary
			$97,980.00	support of penitentiary in Atlanta
		Total	$5,456,780.00	
Ch. 1351, 1902 (32 Stat. 552, 579)	July 1, 1902	United States Courts	$50,000.00	salaries and expenses of marshals, FY 1902
			$25,000.00	salaries and expenses of district attorneys, FY 1902
			$100,000.00	support of prisoners, FY 1902
			$1,665.00	rent of rooms for courts and judicial officers, FY 1901
			$75.00	rent of rooms for courts and judicial officers, FY 1900
		United States Penitentiary, Leavenworth	$1,000.00	miscellaneous expenses, FY 1902
			$5,000.00	construction of sidewalks, jail, Fort Smith, Ark.
			$800.00	steam launch, penitentiary, Atlanta, Ga.
		Court of Claims	$54.00	electricity
		Total	$183,594.00	
		TOTAL APPROPRIATION	**$6,471,734.00**	

1904

Statute (Citation)	Date Passed	Headings	Appropriation	Line-item Details
Ch. 755, 1903 (32 Stat. 854, 905)	February 25, 1903	Supreme Court	$108,400.00	salaries of Chief Justice, associate justices, marshal, stenographic clerks
		Circuit Courts	$189,500.00	salaries of 26 circuit judges, clerks, messenger
		District Courts	$360,000.00	salaries of 72 district judges
		United States Courts, Indian Territory	$20,000.00	salaries of judges
		District Court, Territory of Hawaii	$4,200.00	salaries of clerk and reporter
		Retired Judges	indefinite	salaries
		Court of Appeals, District of Columbia	$26,820.00	salaries of justices and staff
		Supreme Court, District of Columbia	$30,000.00	salaries of chief justice, 5 associate judges
		Clerk of District Court, Northern District of Illinois	$3,000.00	salaries
		Commissioner, Yellowstone Park	$1,500.00	salary

	Court of Claims	law books for circuit courts of appeals	$9,000.00
		salaries of judges and staff	$45,540.00
		cost of auditors	$8,000.00
		miscellaneous expenses	$3,400.00
		reporting decisions	$1,000.00
	Total		$810,360.00
Ch. 1007, 57 Cong. (32 Stat. 1083, 1140)			
March 3, 1903	Expenses of the United States Courts	salaries, fees, and expenses of marshals	$1,300,000.00
		salaries and expenses of district attorneys	$435,000.00
		fees of district attorney for the District of Columbia	$23,800.00
		salaries of regular assistant attorneys	$200,000.00
		payment of special assistant attorneys	$85,000.00
		fees of clerks	$240,000.00
		fees of commissioners	$140,000.00
		fees of jurors	$900,000.00
		fees of witnesses	$900,000.00
		rent of rooms for courts and judicial officers	$110,000.00
		pay of bailiffs, criers, and jury commissioners, meals for jurors, expenses of judges sent outside their districts, expenses of judges in circuit courts of appeals	$160,000.00
		miscellaneous expenses	$290,000.00
		salaries and expenses for court of Indian Territory	$75,000.00
		supplies for courts and judicial officers	$30,000.00
		fees of district attorney for Southern District of New York	$1,000.00
		support of prisoners	$750,000.00
		support for Leavenworth Penitentiary	$170,400.00
		support of penitentiary in Atlanta	$123,980.00
	United States Penitentiary, Atlanta, Ga.	construction	$30,000.00
	United States Penitentiary, McNeil Island		
	Court of Private Land Claims	salaries and expenses of Court of Private Land Claims	$33,500.00
		deputy clerks, Court of Private Land Claims	indefinite
	Total		$5,997,680.00

Ch. 1006, 57 Cong. (32 Stat. 1031, 1064)	March 3, 1903	United States Court, Indian Territory	$5,000.00
		Salaries, Circuit Courts	
		additional judge, Eighth Circuit, FY 1903	$12,649.68
		additional judge, Eighth Circuit, FY 1904	$33,000.00
		Salaries, District Judges	
		additional judge, Southern District of New York, FY 1903	$29,899.07
		additional judge, District of Minnesota, FY 1904	$84,000.00
		Salaries, Supreme Court	
		increase in salaries of justices, FY 1903	$8,625.24
		increase in salaries of justices, FY 1904	$22,500.00
		Salaries, Court of Claims	
		increase in salaries of judges, FY 1903	$366.76
		increase in salaries of judges, FY 1904	$8,000.00
		Salaries, Court of Appeals, D.C.	
		increase in salaries of judges, FY 1903	$1,149.96
		increase in salaries of judges, FY 1904	$3,000.00
		Salaries, Supreme Court, D.C.	
		increase in salaries of judges, FY 1903	$2,299.92
		increase in salaries of judges, FY 1904	$6,000.00
		United States Courts	
		salaries, fees, and expenses of marshals, FY 1903	$100,000.00
		fees of clerks, FY 1903	$5,000.00
		fees of clerks, FY 1902	$5,314.16
		fees of jurors, FY 1903	$300,000.00
		pay of bailiffs, FY 1903	$15,000.00
		miscellaneous expenses, FY 1903	$40,000.00
		rent of rooms for courts and judicial officers, FY 1903	$5,000.00
		rent of rooms for courts and judicial officers, FY 1902	$9,499.50
		support of prisoners, FY 1903	$25,000.00
		penitentiary, Atlanta, FY 1903	$3,000.00
		Total	$724,304.29
Ch. 160, 58 Cong. (33 Stat. 15, 37)	February 18, 1904	Expenses of United States Courts	
		district attorneys, FY 1903	$2,690.91
		fees of clerks, FY 1903	$3,000.00
		fees of clerks FY 1903	$15,567.51
		fees of clerks, FY 1902	$3,352.15
		fees of jurors, FY 1904	$50,000.00
		rent of courtrooms, FY 1903	$2,500.00
		rent of courtrooms, FY 1903	$6,247.24
		rent of courtrooms, FY 1902	$20.00
		supplies, FY 1903	$2,622.12

Statute (Citation)	Date Passed	Headings	Appropriation	Line-item Details
			$60,000.00	miscellaneous expenses, FY 1904
			$12,500.00	miscellaneous expenses, FY 1903
			$200,000.00	penitentiary, Atlanta, FY 1904–1905
		Total	$358,499.93	
Ch. 1630, 58 Cong. (33 Stat. 394, 417)	April 27, 1904	Judicial	$1,500.00	salary, additional judge, Eastern District of Pennsylvania, FY 1904
		United States Courts	$6,000.00	salary, additional judge, Eastern District of Pennsylvania, FY 1905
			$40,000.00	marshals, FY 1904
			$7,000.00	district attorneys, FY 1904
			$131.35	district attorneys, FY 1903
			$35,000.00	fees of clerks, FY 1904
			$1,051.79	fees of clerks, FY 1902
			$1,802.12	rent of courtrooms, FY 1903
			$10,000.00	rent of courtrooms, FY 1904
			$10,000.00	pay of bailiffs, etc., FY 1904
			$221.95	supplies, FY 1903
			$4,000.00	penitentiary, Atlanta, FY 1904
		Total	$116,707.21	
		TOTAL APPROPRIATION	**$8,007,551.43**	

1905

Statute (Citation)	Date Passed	Headings	Appropriation	Line-item Details
Ch. 716, 58 Cong. (33 Stat. 85, 140)	March 18, 1904	Supreme Court	$130,900.00	Chief Justice and 8 associate justices, marshal, stenographic clerks
		Circuit Courts	$222,500.00	salaries of 27 circuit judges, clerks, messenger
		District Courts	$438,000.00	salaries of 73 district judges
		United States Courts, Indian Territory	$20,000.00	salaries of 4 judges
		District Court, Territory of Hawaii	$9,200.00	salaries of judge, clerk, and reporter of District Court of Hawaii Territory
		Retired Judges	indefinite	salaries
		Court of Appeals, District of Columbia	$30,620.00	salaries of justices and staff

Act	Entity	Amount	Purpose
	Supreme Court, District of Columbia	$36,000.00	salaries of chief justice, 5 associate judges
	Clerk of District Court, Northern District of Illinois	$3,000.00	salary
	Commissioner, Yellowstone Park	$1,500.00	salary
	Books for Libraries of Circuit Courts of Appeals	$9,500.00	purchase of law books for circuit courts of appeals libraries
	Choctaw and Chickasaw Citizenship Court	$6,000.00	travel expenses of judges, stenographer, reporter, and bailiff
	Court of Claims	$53,540.00	salaries of judges and staff
		$8,000.00	cost of auditors
		$3,400.00	miscellaneous expenses
		$1,000.00	reporting decisions
	Total	$973,160.00	
Ch. 1762, 58 Cong. (33 Stat. 452, 507) April 28, 1904	Expenses of the United States Courts	$1,350,000.00	salaries, fees, and expenses of marshals
		$440,000.00	salaries and expenses of district attorneys
		$23,800.00	fees of district attorney for the District of Columbia
		$210,000.00	salaries of regular assistant attorneys
		$85,000.00	payment of special assistant attorneys
		$240,000.00	fees of clerks
		$135,000.00	fees of commissioners
		$950,000.00	fees of jurors
		$900,000.00	fees of witnesses
		$110,000.00	rent of rooms for courts and judicial officers
		$165,000.00	pay of bailiffs, criers, and jury commissioners, meals for jurors, expenses of judges sent outside their districts, expenses of judges in circuit courts of appeals.
		$325,000.00	miscellaneous expenses
		$75,000.00	salaries and expenses for court of Indian Territory
		$30,000.00	supplies for courts and judicial officers
		$100.00	fees of district attorney for Southern District of New York
		$750,000.00	support of prisoners
		$177,400.00	support for Leavenworth Penitentiary

			support of penitentiary in Atlanta	$134,480.00
		Total		$6,100,780.00
Ch. 1484, 58 Cong. (33 Stat. 1214, 1240)	March 3, 1905	United States Courts		
		[Marshals]	salaries, fees, and expenses of marshals, FY 1905	$50,000.00
			salaries, fees, and expenses of marshals, FY 1901	$19.78
		[District Attorneys]	salaries and expenses of district attorneys, FY 1905	$10,000.00
			salaries and expenses of district attorneys, FY 1904	$24.73
			salaries and expenses of district attorneys, FY 1904	$3,007.83
			salaries and expenses of district attorneys, FY 1903	$224.76
			fees, district attorney, Southern District of New York, FY 1904	$173.74
		[Fees of Clerks]	fees of clerks, FY 1905	$40,000.00
			fees of clerks, FY 1904	$5,000.00
			fees of clerks, FY 1903	$2,968.24
		[Fees of Jurors]	fees of jurors, FY 1905	$125,000.00
			fees of jurors, FY 1904	$6,000.00
		[Fees of Witnesses]	fees of witnesses, FY 1905	$40,000.00
		[Rent of Courtrooms]	rent of rooms for courts and judicial officers, FY 1905	$15,000.00
			rent of rooms for courts and judicial officers, FY 1904	$7,132.50
			rent of rooms for courts and judicial officers, FY 1903	$1,690.00
		[Supplies]	supplies, FY 1903	$340.48
		[Pay of Bailiffs]	pay of bailiffs and criers, etc., FY 1905	$35,000.00
		[Miscellaneous Expenses]	miscellaneous expenses, FY 1905	$175,000.00
			miscellaneous expenses, FY 1904	$14,000.00
			miscellaneous expenses, FY 1904	$215.15
			miscellaneous expenses, FY 1903	$786.50
		United States Penitentiary, Leavenworth	FY 1904	$37.16
		Spanish Treaty Claims Commission	salary and expenses	$25,000.00
			purchase of law books	$200.00
			award to representative of Gasper A. Bentancourt	$10,000.00
		Total		$566,820.87
		TOTAL APPROPRIATION		$7,640,760.87

1906

Statute (Citation)	Date Passed	Headings	Appropriation	Line-item Details
Ch. 297, 58 Cong. (33 Stat. 631, 686)	February 3, 1905	Supreme Court	$130,900.00	Chief Justice and 8 associate justices, marshal, stenographic clerks
		Circuit Courts	$222,500.00	salaries of 27 circuit judges, clerks, messenger
		District Courts	$444,000.00	salaries of 74 district judges
		United States Courts, Indian Territory	$40,000.00	salaries of 8 judges
		District Court, Territory of Hawaii	$9,200.00	salaries of judge, clerk, and reporter
		Retired Judges	indefinite	salaries
		Court of Appeals, District of Columbia	$30,120.00	salaries of justices and staff
		Supreme Court, District of Columbia	$36,000.00	salaries of chief justice, 5 associate judges
		Clerk of District Court, Northern District of Illinois	$3,000.00	salary
		Commissioner, Yellowstone Park	$1,500.00	salary
		Books for Libraries of Circuit Courts of Appeals	$9,500.00	purchase of law books for circuit courts of appeals libraries
		Court of Claims	$53,540.00	salaries of judges and staff
			$8,000.00	cost of auditors
			$3,400.00	miscellaneous expenses
			$1,000.00	reporting decisions
		Total	$992,660.00	
Ch. 1483, 58 Cong. (33 Stat. 1156, 1207)	March 3, 1905	Expenses of the United States Courts	$1,400,000.00	salaries, fees, and expenses of marshals
			$440,000.00	salaries and expenses of district attorneys
			$23,800.00	fees of district attorney for the District of Columbia
			$225,000.00	salaries of regular assistant attorneys
			$85,000.00	payment of special assistant attorneys
			$240,000.00	fees of clerks
			$135,000.00	fees of commissioners

		fees of jurors	$1,000,000.00
		fees of witnesses	$900,000.00
		rent of rooms for courts and judicial officers	$80,000.00
		pay of bailiffs, criers, and jury commissioners, meals for jurors, expenses of judges sent outside their districts, expenses of judges in circuit courts of appeals	$165,000.00
		miscellaneous expenses	$360,000.00
		salaries and expenses for court of Indian Territory	$101,400.00
		supplies for courts and judicial officers	$30,000.00
		fees of district attorney for Southern District of New York	$100.00
		support of prisoners	$750,000.00
		support for Leavenworth Penitentiary	$180,100.00
		support of penitentiary in Atlanta	$136,180.00
		reform school, District of Columbia	$29,552.00
	Total		$6,281,132.00
Ch. 510, 59 Cong. (34 Stat. 27, 40)	February 27, 1906	[District Attorneys]	salaries and expenses of district attorneys, FY 1906	$35,000.00
			salaries and expenses of district attorneys, FY 1904	$12.90
			salaries and expenses of district attorneys, FY 1905	$750.00
		[District Judges]	salaries of additional judges, New Jersey and Eastern District of Washington, FY 1906	$12,000.00
			salaries of additional judges, New Jersey and Eastern District of Washington, FY 1905	$3,000.00
		[Territory of Arizona]	salary, additional justice, FY 1906	$3,000.00
			salary, additional justice, FY 1905	$825.00
		[U.S. Court, Indian Territory]	salaries of additional judges, FY 1904–1905	$2,348.94
		[Court of Appeals, District of Columbia]	salaries of stenographers, FY 1906	$1,125.00
		[Special Assistant Attorneys]	pay of special assistant attorneys, FY 1905	$5,000.00
			pay of special assistant attorneys, FY 1903	$250.00
			pay of special assistant attorneys, FY 1905	$290.65
		[Fees of Jurors]	fees of jurors, FY 1906	$100,000.00
		[Rent of Courtrooms]	rent of rooms for courts and judicial officers, FY 1906	$15,000.00
			rent of rooms for courts and judicial officers, FY 1904	$900.00
		[Pay of Bailiffs]	pay of bailiffs and criers, etc., FY 1906	$85,000.00

1907

		[Miscellaneous Expenses]	$115,000.00	miscellaneous expenses, FY 1906
		Total	$379,502.49	
		TOTAL APPROPRIATION	**$7,653,294.49**	

Statute (Citation)	Date Passed	Headings	Appropriation	Line-item Details
Ch. 3514, 59 Cong. (34 Stat. 389, 446)	June 22, 1906	Supreme Court	$130,900.00	Chief Justice and 8 associate justices, marshal, stenographic clerks
		Circuit Courts	$237,500.00	salaries of 29 circuit judges, clerks, messenger
		District Courts	$468,000.00	salaries of 78 district judges
		United States Courts, Indian Territory	$40,000.00	salaries of 8 judges
		District Court, Territory of Hawaii	$9,200.00	salaries of judge, clerk, and reporter
		Retired Judges	indefinite	salaries
		Court of Appeals, District of Columbia	$33,741.00	salaries of justices and staff; purchase of case reports
		Supreme Court, District of Columbia	$41,400.00	salaries of chief justice, 5 associate judges, stenographic clerks
		Clerk of District Court, Northern District of Illinois	$3,000.00	
		Commissioner, Yellowstone Park	$1,500.00	salary
		Books for Libraries of Circuit Courts of Appeals	$11,000.00	purchase and rebinding of law books
		Court of Claims	$53,900.00	salaries of judges and staff
			$8,000.00	cost of auditors
			$3,900.00	miscellaneous expenses
			$1,000.00	reporting decisions
		Total	$1,043,041.00	
Ch. 3914, 59 Cong. (34 Stat. 697, 753)	June 30, 1906	Expenses of the United States Courts	$1,380,000.00	salaries, fees, and expenses of marshals
			$475,000.00	salaries and expenses of district attorneys
			$23,800.00	fees of district attorney for the District of Columbia
			$250,000.00	salaries of regular assistant attorneys

Date	Citation	Category	Purpose	Amount
			payment of special assistant attorneys	$90,000.00
			fees of clerks	$275,000.00
			fees of commissioners	$125,000.00
			fees of jurors	$1,075,000.00
			fees of witnesses	$860,000.00
			rent of rooms for courts and judicial officers	$95,000.00
			pay of bailiffs, criers, and jury commissioners, meals for jurors, expenses of judges sent outside their districts, expenses of judges attending circuit courts of appeals outside their residence	$250,000.00
			miscellaneous expenses	$475,000.00
			pay and expenses of special master in case of U.S. v. George Edward Adams	$12,000.00
			salaries and expenses for court of Indian Territory	$102,400.00
			supplies for courts and judicial officers	$30,000.00
			purchase of books for district courts of Hawaii	$10,000.00
			support of prisoners	$715,000.00
			support for Leavenworth Penitentiary	$185,600.00
			support of penitentiary in Atlanta	$126,220.00
			reform school, District of Columbia	$30,980.00
		Total		$6,586,000.00
June 30, 1906	Ch. 3912, 59 Cong. (34 Stat. 634)	Judicial	salaries of deputy clerks, U.S. court, Indian Territory, FY 1907	$4,800.00
			salaries of clerks, commissioners, and constables, U.S. court, Indian Territory, FY 1906	$500.00
		United States Courts	salary, additional judge for Southern District of New York, FY 1907	$6,000.00
			salary, additional judge for Southern District of New York, FY 1906	$500.00
			support for penitentiary, Leavenworth, FY 1906	$600.00
			rent of rooms for courts and judicial officers, FY 1906	$10,000.00
			fees of clerks, FY 1906	$45,000.00
			salaries and expenses of district attorneys, FY 1905	$360.00
			pay of special assistant attorneys, FY 1906	$45,000.00
		Total		$112,760.00
March 4, 1907	Ch. 2919, 59 Cong. (34 Stat. 1371, 1390)	Judicial	additional judges in Northern District of Alabama and Southern District of Ohio, District of Nebraska, FY 1907	$6,000.00
		United States Courts	salaries, fees, and expenses of marshals, FY 1907	$30,000.00

Line-item Details	Appropriation
fees of jurors, FY 1907	$30,000.00
fees of witnesses, FY 1907	$100,000.00
pay of bailiffs and criers, etc., FY 1907	$10,000.00
miscellaneous expenses, FY 1907	$50,000.00
miscellaneous expenses, FY 1906	$3,000.00
miscellaneous expenses, FY 1903	$15.00
supplies, FY 1907	$20,000.00
rent of rooms for courts and judicial officers, FY 1907	$10,000.00
fees of clerks, FY 1907	$15,000.00
pay of special assistant attorneys, FY 1907	$35,000.00
pay of special assistant attorneys, FY 1906	$20,000.00
pay of special assistant attorneys, FY 1905	$1,035.00
Total	$330,050.00
TOTAL APPROPRIATION	**$8,071,851.00**

1908

Statute (Citation)	Date Passed	Headings	Appropriation	Line-item Details
Ch. 1635, 59 Cong. (34 Stat. 935, 991)	February 26, 1907	Supreme Court	$130,900.00	salaries of the Chief Justice and 8 associate justices, marshal, stenographic clerks
		Circuit Courts	$237,500.00	salaries of 29 circuit judges, clerks, messenger
		District Courts	$474,000.00	salaries of 79 district judges
		United States Courts, Indian Territory	$40,000.00	salaries of 8 judges
		District Court, Territory of Hawaii	$9,200.00	salaries of judge, clerk, and reporter
		Retired Judges	indefinite	salaries
		Court of Appeals, District of Columbia	$33,720.00	salaries of justices and staff
		Supreme Court, District of Columbia	$41,400.00	salaries of chief justice, 5 associate judges, stenographic clerks
		Clerk of District Court, Northern District of Illinois	$3,000.00	salary
		Commissioner, Yellowstone Park	$1,500.00	salary
		Books for Libraries of Circuit Courts of Appeals	$9,500.00	purchase and rebinding of law books

	Court of Claims	salaries of judges and staff	$55,820.00	
		cost of auditors	$8,000.00	
		miscellaneous expenses	$3,900.00	
		reporting decisions	$1,000.00	
		custodian	$500.00	
	Total		$1,049,940.00	
Ch. 2918, 59 Cong. (34 Stat. 1295, 1360)	March 4, 1907	Expenses of the United States Courts	salaries, fees, and expenses of marshals	$1,300,000.00
			salaries and expenses of district attorneys	$460,000.00
			fees of district attorney for the District of Columbia	$23,800.00
			salaries of regular assistant attorneys	$250,000.00
			payment of special assistant attorneys	$125,000.00
			payment of special assistant attorneys in naturalization cases	$100,000.00
			fees of clerks	$275,000.00
			fees of commissioners	$125,000.00
			fees of jurors	$1,020,000.00
			fees of witnesses	$850,000.00
			rent of rooms for courts and judicial officers	$85,000.00
			pay of bailiffs, criers, and jury commissioners, meals for jurors, expenses of judges sent outside their districts, expenses of judges attending circuit courts of appeals outside their residence	$250,000.00
			miscellaneous expenses	$540,000.00
			supplies for courts and judicial officers	$35,000.00
			support of prisoners	$700,000.00
			support for Leavenworth Penitentiary	$187,500.00
			support of penitentiary in Atlanta	$129,220.00
			support of reform school, District of Columbia	$56,300.00
		Total		$6,511,820.00
Ch. 2919, 59 Cong. (34 Stat. 1371, 1390)	March 4, 1907	Judicial	salaries of district judges in Eastern and Western District of Oklahoma	$12,000.00
			salaries for new judges for Northern District of Alabama, Southern District of Ohio, District of Nebraska	$18,000.00
		Total		$30,000.00

Ch. 27, 60 Cong. (35 Stat. 8, 21)	February 15, 1908	Judicial	$1,350.00	salary of district judge, Northern District of California, FY 1907

Ch. 27, 60 Cong. (35 Stat. 8, 21)	February 15, 1908	Judicial	$1,350.00	salary of district judge, Northern District of California, FY 1907
			$6,000.00	salary of district judge, Northern District of California, FY 1908
		United States Courts		
		[Marshals]	$40,000.00	salaries and expenses, marshals, FY 1908
		[District Attorneys]	$60,000.00	salaries and expenses, district attorneys, FY 1908
			$28,500.00	salaries and expenses, district attorneys, FY 1907
		[Fees of Jurors]	$200,000.00	fees of jurors, FY 1908
		[Fees of Witnesses]	$350,000.00	fees of witnesses, FY 1908
		[Pay of Bailiffs]	$5,000.00	pay of bailiffs and criers, etc., FY 1908
		[Miscellaneous Expenses]	$25,000.00	miscellaneous expenses, FY 1908
			$30.00	miscellaneous expenses, FY 1903
			$54.00	miscellaneous expenses, FY 1904
			$33.50	miscellaneous expenses, FY 1905
		[Supplies]	$3,000.00	supplies, FY 1908
			$137.16	supplies, FY 1907
		[Special Assistant Attorneys]	$20,000.00	pay of special assistant attorneys, FY 1907
			$8,034.58	pay of special assistant attorneys, FY 1906
		[Regular Assistant Attorneys]	$25,000.00	pay of regular assistant attorneys, FY 1908
			$93,000.00	pay of special assistant attorneys in naturalization cases, FY 1907–1908
		[Indian Territory]	$41,000.00	salaries, U.S. court, Indian Territory, FY 1907
		Reform School, Washington, D.C.	$5,250.00	FY 1908
		Total	$911,389.24	
Ch. 227, 60 Cong. (35 Stat. 478, 509)	May 30, 1908	United States Courts	$10,000.00	salaries of clerks and marshals, District of Oklahoma, FY 1908
			$40,000.00	fees of clerks, FY 1908
			$10,697.09	fees of clerks, FY 1907
			$447.80	fees of clerks, FY 1906
			$10,000.00	fees of witnesses, FY 1908
			$25,000.00	miscellaneous expenses, FY 1908
			$250.25	miscellaneous expenses, FY 1906
			$60.80	miscellaneous expenses, FY 1905
			$46.78	miscellaneous expenses, FY 1904
			$10,000.00	rent of rooms for courts and judicial officers, FY 1908
			$287.74	supplies, FY 1907

	Appropriation	Line-item Details
	$5,000.00	pay of bailiffs and criers, etc., FY 1908
	$500.00	support of prisoners, FY 1905
	$2,700.00	support of inmates, reform school, Washington, D.C., FY 1908
	$13.80	contingent expenses, repair of furniture, FY 1907
	$3.50	contingent expenses, court messenger
Court of Claims	$108.00	payment to Lucien B. Howry, services to the court, FY 1906
Total	$115,115.76	
TOTAL APPROPRIATION	$8,618,265.00	

1909

Statute (Citation)	Date Passed	Headings	Appropriation	Line-item Details
Ch. 186, 60 Cong. (35 Stat. 184, 242)	May 22, 1908	Supreme Court	$130,900.00	salaries of the Chief Justice and 8 associate justices, marshal, stenographic clerks
		Circuit Courts	$237,500.00	salaries of 29 circuit judges, clerks, messenger
		District Courts	$510,000.00	salaries of 85 district judges
		District Court, Territory of Hawaii	$9,200.00	salaries of judge, clerk, and reporter
		Retired Judges	indefinite	salaries
		Court of Appeals, District of Columbia	$34,440.00	salaries of justices and staff
		Supreme Court, District of Columbia	$41,400.00	salaries of chief justice, 5 associate judges, stenographic clerks
		Clerk of District Court, Northern District of Illinois	$3,000.00	salary
		Commissioner, Yellowstone Park	$1,500.00	salary
		Books for Libraries of Circuit Courts of Appeals	$9,500.00	purchase and rebinding of law books
		Court of Claims	$55,820.00	salaries of judges and staff
			$6,000.00	cost of auditors
			$3,900.00	miscellaneous expenses
			$500.00	repairs to building
			$1,000.00	reporting decisions
			$500.00	custodian
		Total	$1,045,160.00	

Citation	Date	Category	Purpose	Amount
Ch. 200, 60 Cong. (35 Stat. 317, 375)	May 27, 1908	Expenses of the United States Courts	salaries, fees, and expenses of marshals	$1,350,000.00
			salaries and expenses of district attorneys	$520,000.00
			fees of district attorney for the District of Columbia	$23,800.00
			salaries of regular assistant attorneys	$275,000.00
			payment of special assistant attorneys	$106,000.00
			payment of assistant attorneys in naturalization cases	$150,000.00
			fees of clerks	$300,000.00
			fees of commissioners	$125,000.00
			fees of jurors	$1,250,000.00
			fees of witnesses	$1,250,000.00
			rent of rooms for courts and judicial officers	$95,000.00
			pay of bailiffs, criers, and jury commissioners, meals for jurors, expenses of district judges directed to hold court outside their districts, expenses of judges attending circuit courts of appeals outside their residence	$260,000.00
			miscellaneous expenses	$560,000.00
			supplies for courts and judicial officers	$35,000.00
			purchase of a library circuit court of appeals for Ninth Circuit	$15,000.00
			support of prisoners	$625,000.00
			support for Leavenworth Penitentiary	$194,700.00
			support of penitentiary in Atlanta	$134,180.00
			support of reform school, District of Columbia	$82,900.00
		Total		$7,351,580.00
Ch. 298, 60 Cong. (35 Stat. 907, 928)	March 4, 1909	United States Courts	Salaries, District Judges	
			FY 1909 (additional judges in Western District of Pennsylvania, Western District of Washington, and Oregon)	$6,000.00
			FY 1909 (additional judge in Southern District of New York)	$2,000.00
		[District Attorneys]	salaries and expenses of district attorneys, FY 1909	$10,000.00
		[Fees of Clerks]	fees of clerks, FY 1909	$15,000.00
		[Miscellaneous Expenses]	miscellaneous expenses, FY 1909	$15,000.00
			miscellaneous expenses, FY 1906	$355.60
			miscellaneous expenses, FY 1905	$182.15
			miscellaneous expenses, FY 1904	$61.69
			miscellaneous expenses, FY 1902	$31.40

[Supplies]	supplies, FY 1907	$88.02
	supplies, FY 1906	$1.67
	supplies, FY 1904	$1.20
[Assistant Attorneys]	pay to assistant attorneys in naturalization cases, FY 1907–1908	$1,031.78
[Court of Claims]	reimbursement of special commissioner, Court of Claims	$138.98
Total		$49,892.49
TOTAL APPROPRIATION		**$8,446,632.49**

1910

Statute (Citation)	Date Passed	Headings	Line-item Details	Appropriation
Ch. 297, 60 Cong. (35 Stat. 845, 905)	March 4, 1909	Supreme Court	salaries of the Chief Justice and 8 associate justices, marshal, stenographic clerks	$130,900.00
		Circuit Courts	salaries of 29 circuit judges, clerks, messenger	$237,500.00
		District Courts	salaries of 84 district judges	$504,000.00
		District Court, Territory of Hawaii	salaries of judge, clerk, and reporter	$9,200.00
		Retired Judges	salaries	indefinite
		Court of Appeals, District of Columbia	salaries of justices and staff	$35,160.00
		Supreme Court, District of Columbia	salaries of chief justice, 5 associate judges, stenographic clerks	$41,400.00
		Clerk of District Court, Northern District of Illinois	salary	$3,000.00
		Commissioner, Yellowstone Park	salary	$1,500.00
		Books for Libraries of Circuit Courts of Appeals	purchase and rebinding of law books	$9,500.00
		Court of Claims	salaries of judges and staff	$55,820.00
			cost of auditors	$6,000.00
			miscellaneous expenses	$3,900.00
			reporting decisions	$1,000.00
			custodian	$500.00
		Total		$1,039,380.00

Ch. 299, 60 Cong. (35 Stat. 945, 1014)	March 4, 1909	Expenses of the United States Courts	$1,350,000.00	salaries, fees, and expenses of marshals
			$540,000.00	salaries and expenses of district attorneys
			$23,800.00	fees of district attorney for the District of Columbia
			$275,000.00	salaries of regular assistant attorneys
			$125,000.00	payment of special assistant attorneys
			$315,000.00	fees of clerks
			$125,000.00	fees of commissioners
			$1,250,000.00	fees of jurors
			$1,250,000.00	fees of witnesses
			$95,000.00	rent of rooms for courts and judicial officers
			$260,000.00	pay of bailiffs, criers, and jury commissioners, meals for jurors, expenses of district judges directed to hold court outside their districts, expenses of judges attending circuit courts of appeals outside their residence
			$575,000.00	miscellaneous expenses
			$35,000.00	supplies for courts and judicial officers
			$625,000.00	support of prisoners
			$197,960.00	support for Leavenworth Penitentiary
			$155,620.00	support of penitentiary in Atlanta
			$47,620.00	support of penitentiary, McNeil Island
			$48,300.00	support of National Training School for Boys (reform school), District of Columbia
		Total	$7,293,300.00	
Ch. 298, 60 Cong. (35 Stat. 907, 928)	March 4, 1909	Salaries, District Judges	$18,000.00	salaries of additional judges in Western District of Pennsylvania, Western District of Washington, District of Oregon
			$6,000.00	salary for additional judge in Southern District of New York
		Salaries, District Court, Territory of Hawaii	$7,000.00	increased salary and additional judge for Territory of Hawaii
		Salaries, Territory of Alaska	$33,500.00	salaries for Territory of Alaska
		Salaries, Territory of New Mexico	$3,000.00	additional judge for Territory of New Mexico
		Total	$67,500.00	

Ch. 7, 61 Cong. (36 Stat. 118)	August 5, 1909	Department of Justice	pay of special assistant attorneys and assistants to Attorney General, FY 1909	$27,000.00
			salary, district judge for Northern District of Alabama, FY 1907–1909	$12,733.33
			miscellaneous expenses, United States Courts, FY 1910	$10,000.00
			National Training School for Boys, District of Columbia, FY 1909	$3,000.00
		Total		$52,733.33
Ch. 62, 61 Cong. (36 Stat. 202, 214)	February 25, 1910	Court of Customs Appeals	salaries of judges and clerks	$27,440.00
		United States Courts	rent, traveling expenses, books, bailiffs and other employees	$15,000.00
			miscellaneous expenses, FY 1910	$100,000.00
			miscellaneous expenses, FY 1909	$20,000.00
			miscellaneous expenses, FY 1907	$5.00
			miscellaneous expenses, FY 1906	$204.00
			miscellaneous expenses, FY 1902	$44.00
			pay of special assistant attorneys, FY 1910	$50,000.00
			pay of special assistant attorneys, FY 1909	$15,000.00
			support of prisoners, FY 1906	$14.80
			supplies, FY 1907	$5.35
			support of Leavenworth Penitentiary, FY 1909	$2,500.00
		Total		$230,213.15
Ch. 385, 61 Cong. (36 Stat. 774, 799)	June 25, 1910	Judicial	payment to widow of Justice Brewer	$12,000.00
			additional district judges in Maryland and Ohio, FY 1910	$4,150.00
		United States Courts	salaries and expenses, marshals	$28,000.00
			salaries of district attorneys	$9,000.00
			fees of clerks, FY 1910	$20,000.00
			fees of clerks, FY 1909	$4,000.00
			miscellaneous expenses, FY 1910	$45,000.00
			miscellaneous expenses, FY 1909	$2,500.00
			supplies, FY 1907	$1.75
			pay of special assistant attorneys	$15,000.00
			pay to district attorney, South Dakota, FY 1907	$2,599.99
		National Training School for Boys	FY 1910	$3,000.00
		Total		$145,251.74
		TOTAL APPROPRIATION		**$8,828,378.22**

1911

Statute (Citation)	Date Passed	Headings	Appropriation	Line-item Details
Ch. 297, 61 Cong. (36 Stat. 468, 529)	June 17, 1910	Supreme Court	$131,900.00	salaries of the Chief Justice and 8 associate justices, marshal, stenographic clerks
		Circuit Courts	$237,500.00	salaries of 29 circuit judges, clerks, messenger
		District Courts	$528,000.00	salaries of 88 district judges
		District Court, Territory of Hawaii	$16,200.00	salaries of judges, clerk, and reporter
		Retired Judges	indefinite	salaries
		Court of Appeals, District of Columbia	$35,160.00	salaries of justices and staff
		Supreme Court, District of Columbia	$41,400.00	salaries of chief justice, 5 associate judges, stenographic clerks
		Clerk of District Court, Northern District of Illinois	$3,000.00	
		Commissioner, Yellowstone Park	$1,500.00	salary
		Books for Libraries of Circuit Courts of Appeals	$9,500.00	purchase and rebinding of law books
		Court of Customs Appeals	$54,840.00	salaries of judges, clerks, stenographers, reporters, messenger
			$40,000.00	rent and expenses
		Court of Claims	$55,820.00	salaries of judges, clerks, stenographers, bailiff, etc.
			$6,000.00	salary of auditor and additional stenographers
			$3,900.00	contingent expenses
			$1,000.00	reporting decisions
			$500.00	custodian
		Total	$1,166,220.00	
Ch. 384, 61 Cong. (36 Stat. 703, 749)	June 25, 1910	Expenses of the United States Courts	$1,450,000.00	salaries, fees, and expenses of marshals
			$545,000.00	salaries and expenses of district attorneys
			$23,800.00	fees of district attorney for the District of Columbia
			$285,000.00	payment of regular assistant attorneys
			$175,000.00	payment of special assistant attorneys
			$325,000.00	fees of clerks

Federal Judiciary Appropriations: 1792–2010

Law	Category	Amount	Purpose
		$115,000.00	fees of commissioners
		$1,125,000.00	fees of jurors
		$875,000.00	fees of witnesses
		$70,000.00	rent of rooms for courts and judicial officers
		$260,000.00	pay of bailiffs, criers, and jury commissioners, meals for jurors, expenses of district judges directed to hold court outside their districts, expenses of judges attending circuit courts of appeals outside their residence
		$440,000.00	miscellaneous expenses
		$35,000.00	supplies for courts and judicial officers
		$550,000.00	support of prisoners
		$201,480.00	support for Leavenworth Penitentiary
		$157,220.00	support of penitentiary in Atlanta
		$47,620.00	support of penitentiary, McNeil Island
		$48,800.00	support of National Training School for Boys (reform school), District of Columbia
	Total	$6,728,920.00	
June 25, 1910 Ch. 385, 61 Cong. (36 Stat. 774, 799)	Salaries, District Judges	$18,000.00	additional district judges in Maryland and Ohio, FY 1911
December 23, 1910 Ch. 7, 61 Cong. (36 Stat. 888, 890)	Salaries, Circuit Judges	$17,500.00	salaries for 5 additional circuit judges, for Commerce Court
	Commerce Court	$39,750.00	salaries, rent, and other expenses
	Salaries, District Judges	$3,000.00	salary, additional judge, Eastern District of New York, FY 1911
	Total	$60,250.00	
March 4, 1911 Ch. 240, 61 Cong. (36 Stat. 1289, 1311)	Judicial	$248.00	purchase of law books, libraries of circuit courts of appeals, FY 1908
	Expenses of United States Courts	$13,000.00	salaries and expenses, district attorneys, FY 1911
		$60.00	salaries and expenses, district attorneys, FY 1908
		$114.65	salaries and expenses, district attorneys, FY 1907
		$15,000.00	fees of clerks, FY 1911
		$75,000.00	fees of witnesses, FY 1911
		$50,000.00	miscellaneous expenses, FY 1911
		$761.62	miscellaneous expenses, FY 1908
		$197.70	miscellaneous expenses, FY 1907

			$6.00	miscellaneous expenses, FY 1904
			$0.54	supplies, FY 1906
		Total	$154,388.51	
		TOTAL APPROPRIATION	**$8,109,778.51**	

1912

Statute (Citation)	Date Passed	Headings	Appropriation	Line-item Details
Ch. 237, 61 Cong. (36 Stat. 1170, 1232)	March 4, 1911	Supreme Court	$135,500.00	salaries of Chief Justice, 8 associate justices, marshal, stenographic clerks
		Circuit Courts of Appeals	$272,000.00	salaries of 34 circuit judges, 9 clerks, and messenger
		District Courts	$546,000.00	salaries of 91 district judges
		District Court, Territory of Hawaii	$16,200.00	salaries of 2 judges, clerk, and reporter
		Retired Judges	indefinite	salaries
		Court of Appeals, District of Columbia	$36,510.00	salaries of chief justice, 2 associate justices, clerks, reporter, messenger, stenographers
		Supreme Court, District of Columbia	$41,400.00	salaries of chief justice and 5 associate judges, 6 stenographers
		Clerk of District Court, Northern District of Illinois	$3,000.00	salary
		Commissioner, Yellowstone Park	$1,500.00	salary
		Books, Libraries of Circuit Courts of Appeals	$9,500.00	purchase of law books for circuit courts of appeals libraries
		Books for Judicial Officers	$15,000.00	books for judges and judicial officers
		Court of Claims	$56,480.00	salaries of judges, clerks, stenographers, bailiff, etc.
			$6,000.00	salary of auditor and additional stenographers
			$3,900.00	contingent expenses
			$1,000.00	reporting decisions
			$500.00	custodian
		Court of Customs Appeals	$54,840.00	salaries of judges, clerks, stenographers, reporters, messenger
			$23,000.00	rent and expenses
		Commerce Court	$94,500.00	salaries (except judges) and expenses
		Total	$1,316,830.00	

Ch. 285, 61 Cong. (36 Stat. 1363, 1425)	March 4, 1911	Expenses of the United States Courts	
		salaries, fees, and expenses of marshals	$1,400,000.00
		additional salary, Supreme Court justices	$9,000.00
		salaries and expenses of district attorneys	$550,000.00
		fees of district attorney for the District of Columbia	$28,940.00
		payment of regular assistant attorneys	$325,000.00
		payment of special assistant attorneys	$200,000.00
		fees of clerks	$325,000.00
		fees of commissioners	$115,000.00
		fees of jurors	$1,125,000.00
		fees of witnesses	$1,000,000.00
		rent of rooms for courts and judicial officers	$70,000.00
		pay of bailiffs and criers, travel expenses of circuit and district judges, meals and lodging of jurors in U.S. cases, compensation of jury commissioners	$250,000.00
		miscellaneous expenses	$450,000.00
		supplies for courts and judicial officers	$35,000.00
		to procure a marble bust for Supreme Court of Justice Fuller	$1,500.00
		to procure an oil portrait for Supreme Court of Justice Fuller	$1,500.00
		support of prisoners	$510,000.00
		support for Leavenworth Penitentiary	$198,580.00
		support of penitentiary in Atlanta	$158,080.00
		support of penitentiary, McNeil Island	$47,900.00
		support of National Training School for Boys (reform school), District of Columbia	$44,996.00
	Total		$6,845,496.00
	Judicial	salary of district judge for state of New Mexico	$2,133.33
Ch. 408, 62 Cong. (37 Stat. 595, 611)	August 26, 1912	United States Courts	
		payment to the widow of John Marshall Harlan	$12,500.00
		miscellaneous expenses, FY 1908	$58.75
		miscellaneous expenses, FY 1907	$260.00
		salaries and expenses of marshals	$80,000.00
		salaries and expenses of district attorneys, FY 1912	$35,000.00
		salaries and expenses of district attorneys, FY 1911	$1,200.00
		pay of special assistant attorneys, FY 1912	$50,000.00

Statute (Citation)	Date Passed		Line-item Details	Appropriation
			pay of special assistant attorneys, FY 1911	$4,500.00
			fees of clerks, FY 1911	$13,250.00
			fees of clerks, FY 1910	$2,227.78
			supplies, FY 1907	$26.75
			pay of bailiffs and criers, etc., FY 1912	$9,000.00
			support of prisoners, FY 1909	$23.35
			support of prisoners, FY 1908	$29.20
		[Penal Institutions]	miscellaneous expenses, penitentiary, Atlanta, FY 1912	$2,087.13
			subsistence, penitentiary, Atlanta, FY 1912	$2,904.62
			miscellaneous expenses, FY 1912	$2,087.13
			support of penitentiary, McNeil Island, FY 1912	$1,184.17
		Total		$218,472.21
Pub Res., No. 32, 62 Cong. (37 Stat. 634)	May 30, 1912	United States Courts	fees of witnesses	$90,000.00
			miscellaneous expenses	$50,000.00
		Total		$140,000.00
		TOTAL APPROPRIATION		**$8,520,798.21**

1913

Statute (Citation)	Date Passed	Headings	Appropriation	Line-item Details
Ch. 350, 62 Cong. (37 Stat. 360, 411)	August 23, 1912	Supreme Court	$153,500.00	salaries of the Chief Justice and 8 associate justices of the Supreme Court, marshal, stenographic clerks
		Circuit Courts of Appeals	$272,500.00	salaries of 34 circuit judges, 9 clerks, and messenger
		District Courts	$558,000.00	salaries of 93 district judges
		District Court, Territory of Hawaii	$16,200.00	salaries of 2 judges, clerk, and reporter
		Retired justices and Judges	indefinite	salaries
		Court of Appeals, District of Columbia	$36,510.00	salaries of chief justice, 2 associate justices, clerks, reporter, messenger, stenographers
		Supreme Court, District of Columbia	$41,400.00	salaries of chief justice and 5 associate judges, 6 stenographers
		Commissioner, Yellowstone Park	$1,500.00	salary
		Court of Customs Appeals	$54,840.00	salaries of presiding judge and 4 associate judges, marshals, clerks, stenographers, messenger

	Commerce Court	rent and expenses	$15,330.00
		salaries (except judges) and expenses	$42,022.22
	Court of Claims	salaries of judges, clerks, stenographers, bailiff, etc.	$56,480.00
		auditors and additional stenographers	$6,000
		contingent expenses	$3,900
		reporting decisions	$1,000
		custodian	$500
	Books for Judicial Officers	books for judges and judicial officers	$16,000.00
	Total		$1,264,282.22
Ch. 355, 62 Cong. (37 Stat. 417, 465)	August 24, 1912		
	United States Courts	salaries, fees, and expenses of marshals	$1,400,000.00
		salaries and expenses of district attorneys	$550,000.00
		fees of district attorney for the District of Columbia	$28,940.00
		payment of regular assistant attorneys	$325,000.00
		payment of special assistant attorneys	$200,000.00
		fees of clerks	$300,000.00
		fees of commissioners	$115,000.00
		fees of jurors	$1,125,000.00
		fees of witnesses	$1,000,000.00
		rent of rooms for courts and judicial officers	$50,000.00
		pay of bailiffs and criers, expenses of circuit and district judges, meals and lodging of jurors in U.S. cases, compensation of jury commissioners	$275,000.00
		miscellaneous expenses	$490,000.00
		supplies for courts and judicial officers	$35,000.00
		support of prisoners	$500,000.00
		support for Leavenworth Penitentiary	$190,080.00
		support of penitentiary in Atlanta	$154,580.00
		support of penitentiary, McNeil Island	$46,100.00
		support of National Training School for Boys, District of Columbia	$49,296.00
	Total		$6,833,996.00

Ch. 149, 62 Cong. (37 Stat. 912, 926)   March 4, 1913

Judicial		
Commerce Court	expenses, March 5 to June 20, 1913	$19,977.78
United States Courts		
[Marshals]	salaries and expenses of marshals, FY 1913	$125,000.00
[District Attorneys]	salaries and expenses of district attorneys, FY 1913	$50,000.00
[Fees of Commissioners]	fees of commissioners, FY 1913	$3,000.00
	fees of commissioners, FY 1912	$500.00
[Fees of Witnesses]	fees of witnesses, FY 1913	$300,000.00
[Pay of Bailiffs]	pay of bailiffs and criers, etc., FY 1913	$25,000.00
[Miscellaneous Expenses]	miscellaneous expenses, FY 1913	$88,000.00
	miscellaneous expenses, FY 1911	$1,221.86
	miscellaneous expenses, FY 1910	$446.09
	miscellaneous expenses, FY 1909	$19.60
[Support of Prisoners]	support of prisoners, FY 1913	$35,000.00
	support of prisoners, FY 1912	$9,500.00
	support of prisoners, FY 1910	$300.00
	support of prisoners, FY 1909	$61.25
	support of prisoners, FY 1906	$6.80
[Supplies]	supplies, FY 1913	$2,709.00
	supplies, FY 1907	$7.10
[Special Assistant Attorneys]	pay of special assistant attorneys, FY 1912	$3,953.78
	pay of special assistant attorneys, FY 1910	$2,500.00
[Penal Institutions]	subsistence, FY 1913	$6,000.00
	subsistence, FY 1912	$1,725.41
	miscellaneous expenditures, FY 1912	$483.10
	hospital supplies	$500.00
	subsistence, penitentiary, Atlanta	$8,700.00
	miscellaneous expenses, penitentiary, Atlanta	$15,000.00
	hospital supplies, penitentiary, Atlanta, FY 1913	$600.00
	hospital supplies, penitentiary, Atlanta, FY 1912	$73.09
	subsistence, penitentiary, McNeil Island	$1,000.00
	miscellaneous expenditures, penitentiary, McNeil Island	$1,000.00
	miscellaneous expenditures, penitentiary, McNeil Island, FY 1912	$307.01
Total		$702,591.87
TOTAL APPROPRIATION		**$8,800,870.09**

1914

Statute (Citation)	Date Passed	Headings	Line-item Details	Appropriation
Ch. 142, 62 Cong. (37 Stat. 739, 789)	March 4, 1913	Supreme Court	Salaries of the Chief Justice and 8 associate justices of the Supreme Court, marshal, stenographic clerks	$153,500.00
		Circuit Courts of Appeals	salaries of 34 circuit judges, 9 clerks, and messenger	$272,500.00
		District Courts	salaries of 93 district judges	$558,000.00
		District Court, Territory of Hawaii	salaries of 2 judges, clerk, and reporter	$16,200.00
		Retired Judges	salaries	indefinite
		Court of Appeals, District of Columbia	salaries of chief justice, 2 associate justices, clerks, reporter, messenger, stenographers	$36,710.00
		Supreme Court, District of Columbia	salaries of chief justice and 5 associate judges, 6 stenographers	$41,400.00
		Commissioner, Yellowstone Park	salary	$1,500.00
		Books for Judicial Officers	books for judges and judicial officers	$16,000.00
		Court of Claims	salaries	$56,680.00
			auditors	$7,000.00
			miscellaneous	$3,900.00
			reporting of decisions	$1,000.00
			custodian	$500.00
		Court of Customs Appeals	salaries of presiding judge and 4 associate judges, marshals, clerks, stenographers, messenger	$54,840.00
			rent and expenses	$14,650.00
		Total		$1,234,380.00
Ch. 3, 63 Cong. (38 Stat. 4, 54)	June 23, 1913	Expenses of United States Courts	salaries, fees, and expenses of marshals	$1,480,000.00
			salaries and expenses of district attorneys	$600,000.00
			fees of district attorney for the District of Columbia	$28,940.00
			salaries of regular assistant attorneys	$325,000.00
			payment of special assistant attorneys	$200,000.00
			fees of clerks	$300,000.00
			fees of commissioners	$115,000.00
			fees of jurors	$1,125,000.00
			fees of witnesses	$1,000,000.00

		rent of rooms for courts and judicial officers	$50,000.00
		pay of bailiffs and criers, expenses of circuit and district judges, meals and lodging of jurors in U.S. cases, compensation of jury commissioners	$275,000.00
		miscellaneous expenses	$490,000.00
		supplies for courts and judicial officers	$35,000.00
		support of prisoners	$500,000.00
		support for Leavenworth Penitentiary	$207,980.00
		support of penitentiary, Atlanta	$175,780.00
		support of penitentiary, McNeil Island	$51,100.00
		support of National Training School for Boys (reform school), District of Columbia	$45,776.00
		Total	$7,004,576.00
Ch. 32, 63 Cong. (38 Stat. 208, 219)	October 2, 1913	Commerce Court	
		United States Courts	
		salaries and expenses, first half of FY 1914	$23,500.00
		marshals	$4,500.00
		special assistant attorneys	$20,000.00
		district attorney for D.C., FY 1911	$57.05
		support of prisoners, FY 1910	$1,250.00
		miscellaneous expenses, FY 1909	$548.85
		miscellaneous expenses, FY 1910	$294.25
		miscellaneous expenses, FY 1911	$64.20
		penitentiary, Leavenworth	$13,495.00
		Total	$63,709.35
Ch. 52, 63 Cong. (38 Stat. 312, 323)	April 6, 1914	United States Courts	
		salaries and expenses of marshals	$60,000.00
		fees of witnesses	$200,000.00
		miscellaneous expenses, FY 1914	$60,000.00
		miscellaneous expenses, FY 1911	$542.76
		miscellaneous expenses, FY 1910	$475.00
		miscellaneous expenses, FY 1909	$198.70
		miscellaneous expenses, FY 1907	$62.50
		miscellaneous expenses, FY 1904	$13.70
		supplies, FY 1908	$3.13
		support of prisoners, FY 1911	$11.00
		rent of rooms for courts and judicial officers, FY 1914	$3,668.75

1915

Statute (Citation)	Date Passed	Headings	Appropriation	Line-item Details
		[Penal Institutions]	$10,000.00	furniture for court rooms of New York
			$15,074.94	penitentiary, Leavenworth
			$16,848.61	penitentiary, Atlanta
			$2,000.00	penitentiary, McNeil Island
		Total	$368,899.09	
		TOTAL APPROPRIATION	**$8,671,564.44**	
Ch. 141, 63 Cong. (38 Stat. 454, 506)	July 9, 1914	Supreme Court	$153,500.00	salaries of the Chief Justice and 8 associate justices of the Supreme Court, marshal, stenographic clerks
		Circuit Courts of Appeals	$272,500.00	salaries of 34 circuit judges, 9 clerks and messenger
		District Courts	$558,000.00	salaries of 93 district judges
		District Court, Territory of Hawaii	$16,200.00	salaries of 2 judges, clerk, and reporter
		Court of Appeals, District of Columbia	$36,710.00	salaries of chief justice, 2 associate justices, clerks, reporter, messenger, stenographers
		Supreme Court, District of Columbia	$41,400.00	salaries of chief justice and 5 associate judges, 6 stenographers
		Commissioner, Yellowstone Park	$1,500.00	salary
		Books for Judges and Judicial Officers	$16,000.00	
		Court of Customs Appeals	$54,840.00	salaries of presiding judge and 4 associate judges, marshals, clerks, stenographers, messenger
			$13,650.00	rent and expenses
		Court of Claims	$56,680.00	salaries
			$7,000.00	auditors
			$3,900.00	miscellaneous expenses
			$1,000.00	reporting of decisions
			$500.00	custodian
		Total	$1,233,380.00	
Ch. 223, 63 Cong. (38 Stat. 609, 653)	August 1, 1914	Expenses of the United States Courts	$1,530,000.00	salaries, fees, and expenses of marshals
			$615,000.00	salaries and expenses of district attorneys

Appropriation	Line-item Details
$28,940.00	fees of district attorney for the District of Columbia
$350,000.00	salaries of regular assistant attorneys
$220,000.00	payment of special assistant attorneys
$250,000.00	fees of clerks
$120,000.00	fees of commissioners
$1,125,000.00	fees of jurors
$1,100,000.00	fees of witnesses
$64,000.00	rent of rooms for courts and judicial officers
$275,000.00	pay of bailiffs and criers, expenses of circuit and district judges, meals and lodging of jurors in U.S. cases, compensation of jury commissioners
$550,000.00	miscellaneous expenses
$35,000.00	supplies for courts and judicial officers
$500,000.00	support of prisoners
$222,780.00	support for Leavenworth Penitentiary
$175,680.00	support of penitentiary, Atlanta
$49,100.00	support of penitentiary, McNeil Island
$50,826.00	support of National Training School for Boys (reform school), District of Columbia
$7,261,326.00	Total
$8,494,706.00	TOTAL APPROPRIATION

1916

Statute (Citation)	Date Passed	Headings	Line-item Details	Appropriation
Ch. 75, 63 Cong. (38 Stat. 822, 867)	March 3, 1915	Judicial	payment to widow of Justice Horace H. Lurton	$14,500.00
		United States Courts	salaries, fees, and expenses of marshals	$1,530,000.00
			salaries and expenses of district attorneys	$615,000.00
			fees of district attorney for the District of Columbia	$28,940.00
			salaries of regular assistant attorneys	$350,000.00
			payment of special assistant attorneys	$200,000.00
			fees of clerks	$240,000.00
			fees of commissioners	$120,000.00
			fees of jurors	$1,125,000.00
			fees of witnesses	$1,100,000.00

Date / Citation	Court / Category	Description	Amount
		rent of rooms for courts and judicial officers	$64,000.00
		pay of bailiffs and criers, expenses of circuit and district judges, meals and lodging of jurors in U.S. cases, compensation of jury commissioners	$275,000.00
		miscellaneous expenses	$550,000.00
		supplies for courts and judicial officers	$35,000.00
		support of prisoners	$500,000.00
		support for Leavenworth Penitentiary	$232,580.00
		support of penitentiary, Atlanta	$175,200.00
		support of penitentiary, McNeil Island	$49,100.00
		support of National Training School for Boys (reform school), District of Columbia	$49,276.00
	Total		$7,253,596.00
March 4, 1915 Ch. 141, 63 Cong. (38 Stat. 997, 1047)	Supreme Court	salaries of Chief Justice and 8 associate justices of the Supreme Court, marshal, stenographic clerks	$153,500.00
	Circuit Courts of Appeals	salaries of 34 circuit judges, 9 clerks, and messenger	$272,500.00
	District Courts	salaries of 94 district judges	$564,000.00
	District Court, Territory of Hawaii	salaries of 2 judges, clerk, and reporter	$16,200.00
	Court of Appeals, District of Columbia	salaries of chief justice, 2 associate justices, clerks, reporter, messenger, stenographers	$36,710.00
	Supreme Court, District of Columbia	salaries of chief justice and 5 associate judges, 6 stenographers	$41,400.00
	Commissioner, Yellowstone Park	salary	$1,500.00
	Books	books for judges and judicial officers	$16,000.00
	Court of Customs Appeals	salaries of presiding judge and 4 associate judges, marshals, clerks, stenographers, messenger	$54,840.00
		rent and expenses	$13,350.00
	Court of Claims	salaries	$56,680.00
		auditors	$7,000.00
		miscellaneous expenses	$3,900.00
		reporting of decisions	$1,000.00
		custodian	$500.00
	Total		$1,170,000.00

Statute (Citation)	Date	Headings		
Ch. 55, 64 Cong. (39 Stat. 41, 43)	March 31, 1916	United States Courts	salaries and expenses of marshals, FY 1916	$50,000.00
			salaries and expenses of marshals, FY 1915	$27,633.91
			salaries and expenses of district attorneys, FY 1916	$5,000.00
			salaries and expenses of district attorneys, FY 1913	$0.33
			fees of commissioners, FY 1916	$30,000.00
			fees of jurors, FY 1916	$25,000.00
			fees of witnesses, FY 1916	$100,000.00
			pay of bailiffs and criers, etc., FY 1915	$444.82
			miscellaneous expenses, FY 1913	$92.23
			miscellaneous expenses, FY 1912	$218.17
			miscellaneous expenses, FY 1910	$82.80
			support of prisoners, FY 1916	$200,000.00
			support of prisoners, FY 1915	$101,893.05
		[Penal Institutions]	National Training School for Boys, FY 1914	$13.42
			support for penitentiary, Leavenworth, FY 1916	$57,800.00
			support for penitentiary, Leavenworth, FY 1915	$3,520.93
			support of penitentiary, Atlanta, FY 1916	$41,000.00
			support of penitentiary, Atlanta, FY 1915	$17,630.36
		Total		$660,330.02
		TOTAL APPROPRIATION		**$9,083,926.02**

1917

Statute (Citation)	Date Passed	Headings	Appropriation	Line-item Details
Ch. 117, 64 Cong. (39 Stat. 66, 118)	May 10, 1916	Supreme Court	$153,500.00	salaries of Chief Justice and 8 associate justices of the Supreme Court, marshal, stenographic clerks
		Circuit Courts of Appeals	$265,000.00	salaries of 33 circuit judges, 9 clerks, and messenger
		District Courts	$570,000.00	salaries of 95 district judges
		District Court, Territory of Hawaii	$16,200.00	salaries of 2 judges, clerk, and reporter
		Court of Appeals, District of Columbia	$36,710.00	salaries of chief justice, 2 associate justices, clerks, reporter, messenger, stenographers
		Supreme Court, District of Columbia	$41,900.00	salaries of chief justice and 5 associate judges, 6 stenographers
		Commissioner, Yellowstone Park	$1,500.00	salary

Commissioner of Glacier National Park		$1,500.00
Books	books for judges and judicial officers	$16,000.00
Court of Customs Appeals	salaries of presiding judge and 4 associate judges, marshals, clerks, stenographers, messenger	$54,840.00
	rent and expenses	$12,870.00
Court of Claims	salaries	$56,680.00
	auditors	$7,000.00
	miscellaneous expenses	$3,900.00
	reporting of decisions	$1,000.00
	custodian	$500.00
Total		**$1,170,020.00**

Ch. 209, 64 Cong. (39 Stat. 262, 313)	July 1, 1916		
	United States Courts	salaries, fees, and expenses of marshals	$1,580,000.00
		salaries and expenses of district attorneys	$620,000.00
		fees of district attorney for the District of Columbia	$28,940.00
		salaries of regular assistant attorneys	$350,000.00
		payment of special assistant attorneys	$175,000.00
		fees of clerks	$215,000.00
		fees of commissioners	$150,000.00
		fees of jurors	$1,150,000.00
		fees of witnesses	$1,200,000.00
		rent of rooms for courts and judicial officers	$58,000.00
		pay of bailiffs and criers, expenses of circuit and district judges, meals and lodging of jurors in U.S. cases, compensation of jury commissioners	$250,000.00
		miscellaneous expenses	$475,000.00
		supplies for courts and judicial officers	$35,000.00
		support of prisoners	$625,000.00
		support for Leavenworth Penitentiary	$268,080.00
		support of penitentiary in Atlanta	$227,600.00
		support of penitentiary, McNeil Island	$48,200.00
		support of National Training School for Boys (reform school), District of Columbia	$44,776.00
	Total		**$7,500,596.00**

Statute (Citation)	Date Passed	Headings	Appropriation	Line-item Details
Ch. 464, 64 Cong. (39 Stat. 801, 818)	September 8, 1916	Judicial	$14,500.00	payment to widow of Justice Joseph Lamar
			$533.33	salary, additional district judge of New Jersey, FY 1916
			$6,000.00	salary, additional district judge of New Jersey, FY 1917
			$1,366.67	commissioner, Mt. Ranier National Park, FY 1917
			$1,250.00	commissioner, Crater Lake National Park, FY 1917
		United States Courts	$25,000.00	salaries and expenses of marshals, FY 1916
			$35,000.00	support of prisoners, FY 1916
			$5,000.00	creation of commission on prisons
			$191.67	salaries and expenses of district attorneys, FY 1914
		[Penal Institutions]	$3,066.12	penitentiary, Atlanta
			$8,232.59	penitentiary, Leavenworth
			$282.50	penitentiary, McNeil Island
		Total	$100,422.88	
Ch. 3, 65 Cong. (40 Stat. 2, 21)	April 17, 1917	United States Courts	$1,500.00	salary, additional district judge, Texas
			$1,652.78	salary, additional district judge, Puerto Rico
			$991.67	clerk, district court, Puerto Rico
			$255,000.00	salaries and expenses of marshals
			$50,000.00	miscellaneous expenses
			$7,500.00	supplies
			$50,000.00	support of prisoners
		[Penal Institutions]	$46,500.00	penitentiary, Leavenworth
			$30,000.00	penitentiary, Atlanta
			$10,500.00	penitentiary, McNeil Island
		Total	$453,644.45	
		TOTAL APPROPRIATION	$8,054,663.33	

1918

Statute (Citation)	Date Passed	Headings	Appropriation	Line-item Details
Ch. 163, 64 Cong. (39 Stat. 1070, 1119)	March 3, 1917	Supreme Court	$153,500.00	salaries of Chief Justice and 8 associate justices, marshal, 9 stenographic clerks
		Circuit Courts of Appeals	$265,500.00	salaries of 33 circuit judges, 9 clerks, and messenger
		District Courts	$576,000.00	salaries of 96 district judges

	District Court, Territory of Hawaii	salaries of 2 judges, clerk, and reporter	$16,200.00	
	Court of Appeals, District of Columbia	salaries of chief justice, 2 associate justices, clerks, reporter, messenger, stenographers	$36,710.00	
	Supreme Court, District of Columbia	salaries of chief justice and 5 associate judges, 6 stenographers	$41,900.00	
	National Park Commissioners	salaries	$6,000.00	
	Books	books for judges and judicial officers	$16,000.00	
	Court of Customs Appeals	salaries of presiding judge and 4 associate judges, marshals, clerks, stenographers, messenger	$54,840.00	
		rent and expenses	$12,660.00	
	Court of Claims	salaries	$59,080.00	
		auditors	$9,000.00	
		miscellaneous expenses	$3,900.00	
		reporting of decisions	$1,000.00	
		custodian	$500.00	
	Total		$1,179,310.00	
Ch. 27, 65 Cong. (40 Stat. 105, 156)	June 12, 1917	United States Courts	salary, additional judge, Texas	$6,000.00
			salary, additional judge, Puerto Rico	$5,000.00
			salary, clerk, Puerto Rico	$3,000.00
			salaries, fees, and expenses of marshals	$1,580,000.00
			salaries and expenses of district attorneys	$620,000.00
			fees of district attorney for the District of Columbia	$33,500.00
			salaries of regular assistant attorneys	$350,000.00
			payment of special assistant attorneys	$150,000.00
			fees of clerks	$215,000.00
			fees of commissioners	$150,000.00
			fees of jurors	$1,150,000.00
			fees of witnesses	$1,200,000.00
			rent of rooms for courts and judicial officers	$58,000.00
			pay of bailiffs and criers, expenses of circuit and district judges, meals and lodging of jurors in U.S. cases, compensation of jury commissioners	$250,000.00
			miscellaneous expenses	$450,000.00
			supplies for courts and judicial officers	$37,500.00
			support of prisoners	$725,000.00

		support for Leavenworth Penitentiary	$344,980.00
		support of penitentiary, Atlanta	$250,460.00
		support of penitentiary, McNeil Island	$52,100.00
		support of National Training School for Boys (reform school), District of Columbia	$45,856.00
		Total	$7,676,396.00
Ch. 28, 65 Cong. (40 Stat. 459, 493)	March 28, 1918	United States Courts	
		salaries and expenses of district attorneys	$12,266.30
		fees of commissioners	$90,000.00
		supplies	$7,500.00
		[Penal Institutions]	
		support of penitentiary, Leavenworth	$18,110.47
		support of penitentiary, Atlanta	$25,000.00
		support of penitentiary, McNeil Island	$14,000.00
		support of National Training School for Boys	$1,500.00
		Total	$168,376.77
		TOTAL APPROPRIATION	$9,024,082.77

1919

Statute (Citation)	Date Passed	Headings	Line-item Details	Appropriation
Ch. 113, 65 Cong. (40 Stat. 634, 682)	July 1, 1918	United States Courts	salaries, fees, and expenses of marshals	$1,730,000.00
			salaries and expenses of district attorneys	$660,000.00
			fees of district attorney for the District of Columbia	$33,300.00
			salaries of regular assistant attorneys	$385,000.00
			payment of special assistant attorneys	$175,000.00
			fees of clerks	$235,000.00
			fees of commissioners	$175,000.00
			fees of jurors	$1,150,000.00
			fees of witnesses	$1,200,000.00
			rent of rooms for courts and judicial officers	$58,000.00
			pay of bailiffs and criers, expenses of circuit and district judges, meals and lodging of jurors in U.S. cases, compensation of jury commissioners	$250,000.00
			miscellaneous expenses	$450,000.00
			supplies for courts and judicial officers	$45,000.00

			Amount	Description
			$700,000.00	support of prisoners
			$434,315.00	support for Leavenworth Penitentiary
			$324,040.00	support of penitentiary, Atlanta
			$64,750.00	support of penitentiary, McNeil Island
			$54,416.00	support of National Training School for Boys (reform school), District of Columbia
		Total	$17,317,780.54	
Ch. 130, 65 Cong. (40 Stat. 757, 812)	July 3, 1918	Supreme Court	$153,500.00	salaries of Chief Justice and 8 associate justices, marshal, 9 stenographic clerks
		Circuit Courts of Appeals	$265,500.00	salaries of 33 circuit judges, 9 clerks, and messenger
		District Courts	$582,000.00	salaries of 97 district judges
		District Court, Territory of Hawaii	$16,200.00	salaries of 2 judges, clerk, and reporter
		District Court for Puerto Rico	$8,000.00	salaries of judge and clerk
		Court of Appeals, District of Columbia	$36,710.00	salaries of chief justice, 2 associate justices, clerks, reporter, messenger, stenographers
		Supreme Court, District of Columbia	$43,100.00	salaries of chief justice and 5 associate judges, 6 stenographers
		National Park Commissioners	$6,000.00	salaries
		Books	$16,000.00	books for judges and judicial officers
		Court of Customs Appeals	$54,840.00	salaries of presiding judge and 4 associate judges, marshals, clerks, stenographers, messenger
			$12,660.00	rent and expenses
		Court of Claims	$59,080.00	salaries
			$9,000.00	auditors
			$3,900.00	miscellaneous expenses
			$1,000.00	reporting of decisions
			$500.00	custodian
		Total	$1,194,510.00	
		TOTAL APPROPRIATION	$18,512,290.54	

1920

Statute (Citation)	Date Passed	Headings	Appropriation	Line-item Details
Ch. 86, 65 Cong. (40 Stat. 1213, 1264)	March 4, 1919	Supreme Court	$153,500.00	salaries of Chief Justice and 8 associate justices, marshal, 9 stenographic clerks
		Circuit Courts of Appeals	$331,500.00	salaries of 33 circuit judges, March 1, 1919, to June 30, 1920, 9 clerks, messenger
		District Courts	$776,000.00	salaries of 97 district judges, March 1, 1919, to June 30, 1920
		District Court, Territory of Hawaii	$20,200.00	salaries of 2 judges, clerk, and reporter, March 1, 1919, to June 30, 1920
		District Court for Puerto Rico	$11,333.34	salaries of judge and clerk, March 1, 1919, to June 30, 1920
		Court of Appeals, District of Columbia	$42,043.34	salaries of chief justice, 2 associate justices, clerks, reporter, messenger, stenographers, March 1, 1919, to June 30, 1920
		Supreme Court, District of Columbia	$54,433.34	salaries of chief justice, 5 associate justices, 6 stenographers, March 1, 1919, to June 30, 1920
		National Park Commissioners	$6,000.00	salaries
		Court of Claims	$69,080.00	salaries of judges, clerks, stenographers, bailiff, etc.
			$9,000.00	auditors and additional stenographers
			$5,000.00	miscellaneous expenses
			$1,000.00	reporting of decisions
			$500.00	custodian
		Court of Customs Appeals	$64,840.00	salaries of presiding judge and 4 associate judges, marshals, clerks, stenographers, messenger, March 1, 1919, to June 30, 1920
			$12,660.00	rent and expenses
		Books	$16,000.00	books for judges and judicial officers
		Total	$1,573,090.02	
Ch. 24, 66 Cong. (41 Stat. 163, 209)	July 19, 1919	Supreme Court	$32,400.00	salaries of 9 law clerks
		United States Courts	$7,500.00	salary, additional district judge, Northern District of Texas
			$1,730,000.00	salaries, fees, and expenses of marshals
			$708,300.00	salaries and expenses of district attorneys
			$400,000.00	salaries of regular assistant attorneys
			$300,000.00	payment of special assistant attorneys
			$800,000.00	salaries of clerks
			$18,000.00	fees of clerks
			$225,000.00	fees of commissioners

		fees of jurors	$1,150,000.00
		fees of witnesses	$1,200,000.00
		rent of rooms for courts and judicial officers	$55,000.00
		pay of bailiffs and criers, expenses of circuit and district judges, meals and lodging of jurors in U.S. cases, compensation of jury commissioners	$250,000.00
		miscellaneous expenses	$450,000.00
		supplies for courts and judicial officers	$70,000.00
		support of prisoners	$975,000.00
		support for Leavenworth Penitentiary	$553,225.00
		support of penitentiary in Atlanta	$441,700.00
		support of penitentiary, McNeil Island	$80,850.00
		support of National Training School for Boys (reform school), District of Columbia	$60,136.00
		Total	$9,507,111.00
Ch. 6, 66 Cong. (41 Stat. 35, 51)	July 11, 1919	United States Courts	
		salary, additional judge, Northern District of Texas	$2,229.17
		salaries, fees, and expenses of marshals	$200,000.00
		salaries and expenses of district attorneys	$45,000.00
		fees of clerks	$50,000.00
		fees of commissioners	$120,000.00
		fees of jurors	$50,000.00
		fees of jurors, FY 1918	$2,602.25
		fees of witnesses	$50,000.00
		increased cost of envelopes	$4,000.00
		miscellaneous expenses	$35,000.00
		support for Leavenworth Penitentiary	$150,760.28
		support of penitentiary, Atlanta	$108,500.00
		support of penitentiary, McNeil Island	$24,000.00
		support of prisoners	$500,000.00
		support of National Training School for Boys (reform school), District of Columbia	$7,300.00
		Total	$1,349,391.70

Ch. 93, 66 Cong. (41 Stat. 327)	November 4, 1919	United States Courts	salaries and expenses of marshals, FY 1920	$200,000.00
			salaries and expenses of marshals, FY 1919	$45,000.00
			salaries and expenses of district attorneys, FY 1919	$35,000.00
			salaries of clerks, FY 1920	$150,000.00
			special assistant attorneys, FY 1920	$300,000.00
			FY 1919	$25,000.00
			miscellaneous expenses, FY 1919	$15,000.00
		United States Penitentiaries	salaries, Leavenworth Penitentiary	$10,875.00
			salaries, Atlanta Penitentiary	$8,325.00
			miscellaneous expenses, Atlanta Penitentiary	$2,947.60
			salaries, McNeil Island Penitentiary	$1,600.00
			clothing, transportation, travel expenses, etc., McNeil Island Penitentiary	$634.99
		Total		$794,382.59
Ch. 253, 66 Cong. (41 Stat. 1015, 1032)	June 5, 1920	United States Courts	salaries and expenses of marshals	$120,000.00
			salaries and expenses of district attorneys	$125,000.00
			coal and electricity for district attorney's office in D.C., FY 1919	$73.27
			regular assistant attorneys	$3,500.00
			special assistant attorneys	$3,600.00
			fees of jurors	$100,000.00
			fees of witnesses	$60,000.00
			pay of bailiffs and criers, etc.	$30,000.00
			miscellaneous expenses	$100,000.00
			supplies	$5,000.00
			support of penitentiary, Leavenworth, FY 1919	$23,909.12
			support of penitentiary, Leavenworth, FY 1920	$105,000.00
			national park commissioners, FY 1920	$250.00
			national park commissioners, FY 1921	$3,000.00
		Total		$679,332.39
		TOTAL APPROPRIATION		**$13,108,925.11**

1921

Statute (Citation)	Date Passed	Headings	Line-item Details	Appropriation
Ch. 214, 66 Cong. (41 Stat. 631, 686)	May 29, 1920	Supreme Court	salaries of Chief Justice and 8 associate justices, marshal, 9 law clerks, 9 stenographic clerks	$185,900.00
		Circuit Courts of Appeals	salaries of 33 circuit judges, 9 clerks, and messenger	$324,000.00
		District Courts	salaries of 98 district judges	$735,000.00
		District Court, Territory of Hawaii	salaries of 2 judges, clerk, and reporter	$19,200.00
		District Court for Puerto Rico	salaries of judge and clerk	$10,500.00
		Court of Appeals, District of Columbia	salaries of chief justice, 2 associate justices, clerk, custodian, reporter, crier, messengers, stenographers	$42,410.00
		Supreme Court, District of Columbia	salaries of chief justice, 5 associate judges, 6 stenographers	$52,100.00
		National Park Commissioners	salaries	$6,000.00
		Books	books for judges and judicial officers	$16,000.00
		Court of Customs Appeals	salaries of presiding judge and 4 associate judges, marshal, clerks, reporter, messenger	$62,340.00
			rent and expenses	$12,660.00
		Court of Claims	salaries of judges, clerks, stenographers, bailiff, etc.	$66,580.00
			auditors and additional stenographers	$9,000.00
			miscellaneous expenses	$5,000.00
			reporting of decisions	$1,000.00
			custodian	$500.00
		Total		$1,466,110.00
Ch. 235, 1920 (41 Stat. 874, 923)	June 5, 1920	United States Courts	salaries, fees, and expenses of marshals	$2,061,000.00
			salaries and expenses of district attorneys	$730,000.00
			salaries of regular assistant attorneys	$500,000.00
			payment of special assistant attorneys	$450,000.00
			salaries of clerks	$990,000.00
			fees of clerks	$6,000.00
			fees of commissioners	$200,000.00
			fees of jurors	$1,150,000.00
			fees of witnesses	$1,200,000.00

Date	Citation	Category	Line item	Amount
			rent of rooms for courts and judicial officers	$55,000.00
			pay of bailiffs and criers, expenses of circuit and district judges, meals and lodging of jurors in U.S. cases, compensation of jury commissioners	$250,000.00
			miscellaneous expenses	$500,000.00
			supplies for courts and judicial officers	$75,000.00
			support of prisoners	$870,000.00
			support for Leavenworth Penitentiary	$671,300.00
			support of penitentiary, Atlanta	$503,020.00
			support of penitentiary, McNeil Island	$114,700.00
			support of National Training School for Boys (reform school), District of Columbia	$67,536.00
			Total	$10,393,556.00
March 1, 1921	Ch. 89, 66 Cong. (41 Stat. 1156)	Judicial — United States Courts	expenses, Court of Claims	$1,800.00
			salaries and expenses of marshals	$140,000.00
			salaries and expenses of district attorneys	$130,000.00
			pay of special assistant attorneys, FY 1921	$400,000.00
			pay of special assistant attorneys, FY 1920	$75,650.00
			pay of special assistant attorneys, FY 1919	$925.00
			salaries of clerks, FY 1920	$5,203.27
			salaries of clerks, FY 1921	$56,000.00
			fees of commissioners	$100,000.00
			miscellaneous expenses	$50,000.00
			supplies	$15,000.00
		[Penal Institutions]	support of penitentiary, Leavenworth, FY 1920	$28,691.69
			support of penitentiary, Leavenworth, FY 1921	$21,000.00
			support of penitentiary, Atlanta, FY 1920	$17,657.69
			support of penitentiary, Atlanta, FY 1921	$5,000.00
			support of penitentiary, McNeil Island, FY 1920	$8,856.31
			Total	$1,055,783.96
June 16, 1921	Ch. 23, 1921 (42 Stat. 29, 40)	Judicial — United States Courts	pay to the widow of Chief Justice Edward White	$15,000.00
			special assistant attorneys, FY 1919	$300.00
			special assistant attorneys, FY 1921	$150,000.00
			clerks	$5,000.00

commissioners	$75,000.00	
jurors	$100,000.00	
supplies	$15,000.00	
support of prisoners	$50,000.00	
miscellaneous expenses, FY 1920	$1,059.88	
miscellaneous expenses, FY 1921	$40,000.00	
Atlanta Penitentiary	$5,000.00	
Atlanta Penitentiary	$463.11	
Books for Judicial Officers	books, FY 1918	$10.00
	books, FY 1920	$258.35
Total	$457,091.34	
TOTAL APPROPRIATION	**$13,372,541.30**	

1922

Statute (Citation)	Date Passed	Headings	Appropriation	Line-item Details
Ch. 124, 66 Cong. (41 Stat. 1252, 1306)	March 3, 1921	Supreme Court	$185,900.00	salaries of Chief Justice and 8 associate justices, marshal, 9 law clerks, 9 stenographic clerks
		Circuit Courts of Appeals	$324,000.00	salaries of 33 circuit judges, 9 clerks, messenger
		District Courts	$742,500.00	salaries of 99 district judges
		District Court, Territory of Hawaii	$16,200.00	salaries of 2 judges, clerk, and reporter
		District Court for Puerto Rico	$7,500.00	salary of district judge
		Court of Appeals, District of Columbia	$42,410.00	salaries of chief justice, 2 associate justices, clerk, custodian, reporter, crier, messengers, stenographers
		Supreme Court, District of Columbia	$52,100.00	salaries of chief justice, 5 associate judges, 6 stenographers
		National Park Commissioners	$9,000.00	salaries
		Books	$16,000.00	books for judges and judicial officers
		Court of Customs Appeals	$62,340.00	salaries of presiding judge and 4 associate judges, marshal, clerks, reporter, messenger
			$12,660.00	rent and expenses
		Court of Claims	$66,580.00	salaries of judges, clerks, stenographers, bailiff, etc.
			$12,000.00	auditors and additional stenographers
			$5,000.00	miscellaneous expenses

			reporting of decisions	$1,000.00
			custodian	$500.00
		Total		$1,470,610.00
Ch. 161, 66 Cong. (41 Stat. 1367, 1412)	March 4, 1921	United States Courts	salaries, fees, and expenses of marshals	$2,160,000.00
			salaries and expenses of district attorneys	$800,000.00
			salaries of regular assistant attorneys	$550,000.00
			payment of special assistant attorneys	$600,000.00
			salaries of clerks	$1,050,000.00
			fees of commissioners	$225,000.00
			fees of jurors	$1,150,000.00
			fees of witnesses	$1,200,000.00
			rent of rooms for courts and judicial officers	$52,000.00
			pay of bailiffs and criers, expenses of circuit and district judges, meals and lodging of jurors in U.S. cases, compensation of jury commissioners	$240,000.00
			miscellaneous expenses	$550,000.00
			supplies for courts and judicial officers	$75,000.00
			support of prisoners	$800,000.00
			support for Leavenworth Penitentiary	$646,600.00
			support of penitentiary, Atlanta	$505,520.00
			support of penitentiary, McNeil Island	$114,700.00
			support of National Training School for Boys (reform school), District of Columbia	$64,036.00
		Total		$10,782,856.00
Ch. 89, 67 Cong. (42 Stat. 192, 194)	August 24, 1921	United States Courts	salaries and expenses of marshals	$72,000.00
			salaries and expenses of district attorneys	$29,000.00
			salaries of clerks, FY 1921	$66,000.00
			fees of jurors, FY 1921	$31,000.00
			support of prisoners	$138,000.00
			miscellaneous expenses, FY 1918	$7.04
			miscellaneous expenses, FY 1919	$524.57
			miscellaneous expenses, FY 1920	$1,618.04
			miscellaneous expenses, FY 1921	$42,000.00

Citation	Date	Category	Line item	Amount
			Atlanta Penitentiary	$21,449.10
			Leavenworth Penitentiary	$121,500.00
			McNeil Island Penitentiary	$8,200.00
			Total	$531,298.75
Ch. 1, 67 Cong. (42 Stat. 327, 332)	December 15, 1921	District Courts	salaries of district judges of North Dakota and Southern District of West Virginia	$11,812.50
		District Court, Territory of Hawaii	salary, reporter, July 9, 1921, to June 30, 1922	$1,760.00
		Supreme Court, Territory of Hawaii	salaries of justices, June 9 to June 30, 1922	$4,400.01
		Books for Judicial Officers	FY 1917	$115.00
			FY 1918	$33.93
			FY 1919	$20.50
		Court of Claims Building	building maintenance and repair	$7,500.00
		[Expenses of United States Courts]	salaries and expenses of marshals	$140,000.00
			salaries and expenses of district attorneys	$100,000.00
			salaries of clerks, FY 1920	$392.27
			salaries of clerks, FY 1922	$125,000.00
			fees of commissioners, FY 1920	$74.70
			fees of commissioners, FY 1922	$150,000.00
			fees of jurors, FY 1921	$9,155.32
			miscellaneous expenses, FY 1916	$35.00
			miscellaneous expenses, FY 1919	$659.85
			miscellaneous expenses, FY 1920	$1,978.52
			supplies	$25,000.00
			support of prisoners, FY 1921	$27,147.58
			support of prisoners, FY 1922	$300,000.00
			Total	$905,085.18
Ch. 104, 67 Cong. (42 Stat. 437, 448)	March 20, 1922	Court of Claims	miscellaneous expenses	$1,800.00
		... Expenses of United States Courts	special assistant attorneys	$250,000.00
			clerks, FY 1920	$827.28
			commissioners, FY 1920	$4,577.45

		Appropriation	Line-item Details
		$150,000.00	jurors
		$115,000.00	miscellaneous expenses
		$1,718.86	supplies, FY 1921
Penal Institutions		$25,000.00	Atlanta Penitentiary
		$6,500.00	McNeil Island Penitentiary
		$16,907.98	support of prisoners
Total		$572,331.57	
TOTAL APPROPRIATION		**$14,262,181.50**	

1923

Statute (Citation)	Date Passed	Headings	Appropriation	Line-item Details
Ch. 204, 67 Cong. (42 Stat. 599, 614)	June 1, 1922	United States Supreme Court	$185,900.00	salaries of Chief Justice and 8 associate justices, marshal, 9 law clerks, 9 stenographic clerks
			$17,000.00	printing and binding
		Circuit Court of Appeals	$280,500.00	salaries of 33 circuit judges
		District Courts	$757,500.00	salaries of district judges
			$16,200.00	salaries of judges and reporter, Territory of Hawaii
			$7,500.00	salary of district judge of Puerto Rico
		Retired Judges	$140,000.00	salaries for judges retired under sec. 260 of Judicial Code
		National Park Commissioners	$9,000.00	commissioners
		Court of Customs Appeals	$62,340.00	salaries
			$10,965.00	rent and miscellaneous expenses
		Court of Claims	$68,080.00	salaries of judges and all other officers and employees
			$12,000.00	auditors and stenographers
			$6,600.00	miscellaneous expenses
			$1,000.00	reports of decisions
			$500.00	custodian
			$25,470.00	printing and binding
		Territorial Courts	$80,000.00	Alaska, salaries of judges, attorneys, marshals, clerks
			$21,500.00	Hawaii, salaries of chief justice and associate justices
			$42,000.00	Hawaii, salaries of judges of circuit courts
		. . . Expenses of United States Courts	$2,275,000.00	salaries, fees, and expenses of marshals
			$900,000.00	salaries and expenses of district attorneys

Headings	Appropriation	Line-item Details
	$550,000.00	salaries of regular assistant attorneys
	$850,000.00	payment of special assistant attorneys
	$1,300,000.00	fees of clerks
	$375,000.00	fees of commissioners
	$1,250,000.00	fees of jurors
	$1,100,000.00	fees of witnesses
	$50,000.00	rent of rooms for courts and judicial officers
	$240,000.00	pay of bailiffs and criers, expenses of circuit and district judges, meals and lodging of jurors in U.S. cases, compensation of jury commissioners
	$600,000.00	miscellaneous expenses
	$90,000.00	supplies for courts and judicial officers
	$25,000.00	purchase and binding of books
	$4,205.00	purchase of copies of case reports
Penal Institutions	$757,800.00	Leavenworth Penitentiary
	$578,500.00	Atlanta Penitentiary
	$149,300.00	McNeil Island Penitentiary
	$60,736.00	National Training School for Boys
	$1,050,000.00	support of prisoners
	$12,000.00	inspection of prisons
Total	$13,961,596.00	

Statute (Citation)	Date Passed	Headings	Appropriation	Line-item Details
Ch. 258, 67 Cong. (42 Stat. 767, 774)	July 1, 1922	United States Supreme Court	$7,666.66	salary and expenses, reporter of decisions, FY 1922
			$11,500.00	salary and expenses, reporter of decisions, FY 1923
			$21,000.00	printing and binding reports, FY 1923
		Total	$40,166.66	
		TOTAL APPROPRIATION	$14,001,762.66	

1924

Statute (Citation)	Date Passed	Headings	Appropriation	Line-item Details
Ch. 21, 67 Cong. (42 Stat. 1068, 1081)	January 3, 1923	United States Supreme Court	$185,900.00	salaries of Chief Justice and 8 associate justices, marshal, 9 law clerks, 9 stenographic clerks
			$46,000.00	printing and binding, including official reports
			$11,500.00	salary and expenses, reporter

Circuit Court of Appeals	$280,500.00	salaries of 33 circuit judges
District Courts	$937,500.00	salaries of 125 district judges
	$16,200.00	salaries of judges and reporter, Territory of Hawaii
	$7,500.00	salary of district judge of Puerto Rico
Retired Judges	$140,000.00	salaries for judges retired under sec. 260 of Judicial Code
National Park Commissioners	$9,000.00	commissioners
Court of Customs Appeals	$62,340.00	salaries of judges and all other officers and employees
	$10,460.00	rent and expenses
Court of Claims	$68,080.00	salaries of judges and all other officers and employees
	$35,000.00	printing and binding
	$12,000.00	auditors and stenographers
	$6,600.00	miscellaneous expenses
	$1,000.00	reports of decisions
	$500.00	custodian of building
Territorial Courts	$80,000.00	Alaska, salaries of judges, attorneys, marshals, clerks
	$21,500.00	Hawaii, salaries of chief justice and associate justices
	$48,000.00	Hawaii, salaries of judges of circuit courts
. . . Expenses of United States Courts	$2,300,000.00	salaries, fees, and expenses of marshals
	$925,000.00	salaries and expenses of district attorneys
	$600,000.00	salaries of regular assistant attorneys
	$850,000.00	payment of special assistant attorneys
	$1,400,000.00	salaries of clerks
	$375,000.00	fees of commissioners
	$1,250,000.00	fees of jurors
	$1,100,000.00	fees of witnesses
	$62,500.00	rent of rooms for courts and judicial officers
	$275,000.00	pay of bailiffs and criers, expenses of circuit and district judges, meals and lodging of jurors in U.S. cases, compensation of jury commissioners
	$650,000.00	miscellaneous expenses
	$70,000.00	supplies for courts and judicial officers
	$35,000.00	purchase and binding of books
	$3,620.00	purchase of copies of Federal Reporter
Penal Institutions	$663,000.00	Leavenworth Penitentiary
	$599,000.00	Atlanta Penitentiary

	McNeil Island Penitentiary	$156,000.00
	National Training School for Boys	$60,436.00
Total		$13,354,136.00

Ch. 81, 68 Cong. (43 Stat. 33, 44)   April 2, 1924

Judicial	retired judges, FY 1923	$3,923.16
	salaries, fees, and expenses of marshals, FY 1921	$408.44
	district attorneys, FY 1923	$18,754.28
	fees of commissioners, FY 1919	$155.85
	fees of commissioners, FY 1920	$740.25
	fees of commissioners, FY 1921	$1,909.70
	fees of commissioners, FY 1922	$21,553.02
	miscellaneous expenses, FY 1920	$219.24
	miscellaneous expenses, FY 1923	$31,998.49
Penal Institutions	support of prisoners, FY 1916	$40.00
	support of prisoners, FY 1919	$276.00
	support of prisoners, FY 1923	$60,053.93
	Leavenworth Penitentiary	$450,000.00
	McNeil Island Penitentiary	$64,500.00
Total		$654,532.36

Ch. 191, 68 Cong. (43 Stat. 170, 171)   May 26, 1924

United States Courts	salaries, fees, and expenses of marshals	$530,000.00
	district attorneys	$210,000.00
	salaries of clerks	$35,000.00
	fees of commissioners	$125,000.00
	fees of jurors	$250,000.00
	fees of witnesses	$200,000.00
	miscellaneous expenses	$35,000.00
Penal Institutions	support of prisoners, FY 1924	$602,000.00
Total		$1,987,000.00
TOTAL APPROPRIATION		**$15,995,668.36**

1925

Statute (Citation)	Date Passed	Headings	Appropriation	Line-item Details
Ch. 204, 68 Cong. (43 Stat. 205, 218)	May 28, 1924	United States Supreme Court	$188,060.00	salaries of Chief Justice and 8 associate justices, marshal, 9 law clerks, 9 stenographic clerks
			$50,000.00	printing and binding
			$11,500.00	reporter of decisions, salary and expenses
		Salaries of Judges	$1,380,500.00	circuit, district, and retired judges
			$1,200.00	reporter, Territory of Hawaii
		National Park Commissioners	$9,000.00	commissioners
		Court of Customs Appeals	$62,340.00	salaries of judges and all other officers and employees
			$13,960.00	rent and expenses
		Court of Claims	$68,080.00	salaries of judges and all other officers and employees
			$500.00	custodian
			$35,000.00	printing and binding
			$14,000.00	auditors and stenographers
			$6,600.00	miscellaneous expenses
			$1,000.00	reports of decisions
		Territorial Courts	$80,000.00	Alaska, salaries of judges, attorneys, marshals, clerks
			$21,500.00	Hawaii, salaries of chief justice and associate justices
			$48,000.00	Hawaii, salaries of judges of circuit courts
		. . . Expenses of United States Courts	$2,931,000.00	salaries, fees, and expenses of marshals
			$1,199,780.00	salaries and expenses of district attorneys
			$652,800.00	salaries of regular assistant attorneys
			$840,000.00	payment of special assistant attorneys
			$1,504,405.00	salaries of clerks
			$500,000.00	fees of commissioners
			$1,600,000.00	fees of jurors
			$1,430,000.00	fees of witnesses
			$80,000.00	rent of rooms for courts and judicial officers
			$290,000.00	pay of bailiffs and criers, expenses of circuit and district judges, meals and lodging of jurors in U.S. cases, compensation of jury commissioners
			$739,000.00	miscellaneous expenses

Penal Institutions	$73,000.00	supplies for courts and judicial officers
	$38,860.00	purchase and binding of books
	$659,120.00	Leavenworth Penitentiary
	$683,620.00	Atlanta Penitentiary
	$172,860.00	McNeil Island Penitentiary
	$60,436.00	National Training School for Boys
	$1,795,000.00	support of prisoners
	$15,890.00	inspection of prisons
Total	$17,118,951.00	
Ch. 4, 68 Cong. (43 Stat. 672, 686) December 5, 1924		
United States Supreme Court	$4,000.00	printing and binding
Court of Customs Appeals	$3,000.00	rent
Court of Claims	$8,000.00	printing and binding, FY 1924
	$2,225.00	building maintenance
. . . Expenses of United States Courts	$10.00	salaries, fees, and expenses of marshals, FY 1918
	$10.21	salaries, fees, and expenses of marshals, FY 1920
	$910.04	salaries, fees, and expenses of marshals, FY 1921
	$31.00	district attorneys
	$120,000.00	special assistant attorneys
	$6,591.13	fees of commissioners
	$310.00	miscellaneous expenses, FY 1920
	$150.00	miscellaneous expenses, FY 1922
	$10,100.24	miscellaneous expenses, FY 1923
	$9,000.00	supplies
	$18.00	books, FY 1921
	$1,000.00	books, FY 1924
Penal Institutions	$49,115.00	Leavenworth Penitentiary
	$3,204.25	Atlanta Penitentiary, FY 1923
	$20,000.00	Atlanta Penitentiary, FY 1924
	$2,000.00	McNeil Island Penitentiary
	$4,383.75	support of prisoners, FY 1919
	$3,672.25	support of prisoners, FY 1920
	$6,400.50	support of prisoners, FY 1921

Citation	Date	Category	Description	Amount
			support of prisoners, FY 1922	$6,275.62
			support of prisoners, FY 1923	$37,107.80
		Total		$297,514.79
Ch. 85, 68 Cong. (43 Stat. 753, 756)	January 20, 1925	United States Courts	supplies, reappropriated from FY 1924	$9,000.00
Ch. 556, 68 Cong. (43 Stat. 1313, 1332)	March 4, 1925	Court of Customs Appeals	books, FY 1925	$1,000.00
		Court of Claims	printing and binding, reappropriated from FY 1924	$8,000.00
			commissioners, salaries and expenses, FY 1925 and FY 1926	$69,000.00
		. . . Expenses of United States Courts	salaries, fees, and expenses of marshals, FY 1924	$81,654.39
			salaries, fees, and expenses of marshals, FY 1925	$149,000.00
			fees of jurors, FY 1924	$60,221.47
			fees of jurors, FY 1925	$100,000.00
			fees of witnesses, FY 1924	$34,602.43
			fees of witnesses, FY 1925	$63,000.00
			pay of bailiffs and criers, FY 1924	$19,437.48
			pay of bailiffs and criers, FY 1925	$66,000.00
			miscellaneous expenses, FY 1923	$1,479.82
			books, FY 1924–1925	$100,000.00
		Penal Institutions	Leavenworth Penitentiary, FY 1925	$21,000.00
			Atlanta Penitentiary, FY 1925	$50,000.00
			Atlanta Penitentiary, FY 1924	$10,975.12
			McNeil Island Penitentiary, FY 1925	$1,500.00
			National Training School for Boys, FY 1925	$7,000.00
			support for prisoners, FY 1923	$29,098.79
			support for prisoners, FY 1924	$89,343.72
			support for prisoners, FY 1925	$370,000.00
			Federal Institution for Women, FY 1925–1926	$909,100.00
		Total		$2,241,413.22
		TOTAL APPROPRIATION		**$19,666,879.01**

1926

Statute (Citation)	Date Passed	Headings	Appropriation	Line-item Details
Ch. 364, 68 Cong. (43 Stat. 1014, 1028)	February 27, 1925	United States Supreme Court	$188,060.00	salaries of Chief Justice and 8 associate justices, marshal, 9 law clerks, 9 stenographic clerks
			$50,000.00	printing and binding
			$11,500.00	reporter of decisions, salary and expenses
		Salaries of Judges	$1,353,000.00	district, circuit, and retired judges
		National Park Commissioners	$11,160.00	salaries of commissioners
		Court of Customs Appeals	$70,000.00	salaries of judges and all other officers and employees
			$13,100.00	rent and expenses
		Court of Claims	$83,432.00	salaries of judges and all other officers and employees
			$45,000.00	printing and binding
			$12,000.00	auditors and stenographers
			$6,600.00	miscellaneous expenses
			$5,660.00	building maintenance
		Territorial Courts	$81,200.00	Alaska, salaries of judges, attorneys, marshals, clerks
			$21,500.00	Hawaii, salaries of chief justice and associate justices
			$48,000.00	circuit judges
		. . . Expenses of United States Courts	$3,500,000.00	salaries, fees, and expenses of marshals
			$1,334,000.00	salaries and expenses of district attorneys
			$919,000.00	salaries of regular assistant attorneys
			$650,000.00	payment of special assistant attorneys
			$1,758,000.00	clerks, salaries
			$500,000.00	fees of commissioners
			$1,850,000.00	fees of jurors
			$1,670,000.00	fees of witnesses
			$80,000.00	rent of rooms for courts and judicial officers
			$348,000.00	pay of bailiffs and criers, expenses of circuit and district judges, meals and lodging of jurors in U.S. cases, compensation of jury commissioners
			$925,000.00	miscellaneous expenses
			$73,000.00	supplies for courts and judicial officers
			$65,000.00	purchase and binding of books

Statute (Citation)	Date Passed	Headings	Appropriation	Line-item Details
		Penal Institutions	$730,000.00	Leavenworth Penitentiary
			$764,000.00	Atlanta Penitentiary
			$201,500.00	McNeil Island Penitentiary
			$85,710.00	National Training School for Boys
			$2,035,000.00	support of prisoners
			$20,000.00	inspection of prisons
		Total	$19,508,422.00	
Ch. 44, 69 Cong. (44 Stat. 161, 175)	March 3, 1926	Supreme Court	$500.00	reappropriated for bracket or pedestal for bust of Chief Justice White
		Court of Claims	$9,000.00	building repairs
		United States Courts	$81,150.00	regular assistant attorneys, FY 1926
			$46,000.00	special assistant attorneys, FY 1926
			$65,000.00	salaries, fees, and expenses of marshals, FY 1925
		Penal Institutions	$115,000.00	support of prisoners, FY 1925
			$37,500.00	Industrial Reformatory, Chillicothe, Ohio
			$12,000.00	National Training School for Boys, FY 1926
		Total	$366,150.00	
		TOTAL APPROPRIATION	**$19,874,572.00**	

1927

Statute (Citation)	Date Passed	Headings	Appropriation	Line-item Details
Ch. 195, 69 Cong. (44 Stat. 330, 344)	April 29, 1926	United States Supreme Court	$237,046.00	salaries of Chief Justice and 8 associate justices, marshal, 9 law clerks, 9 stenographic clerks
			$50,000.00	printing and binding
		Miscellaneous Expenses, Supreme Court	$18,874.00	miscellaneous expenses
			$11,500.00	reporter of decisions, salary and expenses
		Salaries of Judges	$1,350,000.00	circuit, district, and retired judges
		National Park Commissioners	$11,160.00	commissioners, salaries
		Court of Customs Appeals	$69,890.00	salaries of presiding judge and 4 associate judges and other officers and employees
			$14,000.00	rent and expenses
		Court of Claims	$96,212.00	salaries of judges and all other officers and employees
			$40,000.00	printing and binding

	Amount	Description
	$6,600.00	miscellaneous expenses
	$69,000.00	commissioners and stenographers
Territorial Courts	$81,200.00	Alaska, salaries of judges, attorneys, marshals, clerks
	$21,500.00	Hawaii, salaries of chief justice and associate justices
	$48,000.00	circuit judges
. . . Expenses of United States Courts	$3,400,000.00	salaries, fees, and expenses of marshals
	$1,334,000.00	salaries and expenses of district attorneys
	$1,000,000.00	salaries of regular assistant attorneys
	$400,000.00	payment of special assistant attorneys
	$1,750,000.00	clerks, salaries
	$500,000.00	fees of commissioners
	$1,575,000.00	fees of jurors
	$1,400,000.00	fees of witnesses
	$80,000.00	rent of rooms for courts and judicial officers
	$330,000.00	pay of bailiffs and criers, expenses of circuit and district judges, meals and lodging of jurors in U.S. cases, compensation of jury commissioners
	$755,000.00	miscellaneous expenses
	$70,000.00	supplies for courts and judicial officers
	$65,000.00	purchase and binding of books
Penal and Correctional Institutions	$971,493.00	Leavenworth Penitentiary
	$1,066,072.00	Atlanta Penitentiary
	$419,047.00	McNeil Island Penitentiary
	$190,100.00	Industrial Institution for Women
	$350,000.00	Industrial Reformatory, Ohio
	$142,793.00	National Training School for Boys
	$50,000.00	probation system
	$1,974,000.00	support of prisoners
	$10,000.00	inspection of prisons
Total	$19,640,067.00	
. . . Expenses of United States Courts	$3,000.00	special assistant attorneys, FY 1922
	$90,000.00	fees of commissioners, FY 1926
	$63.21	fees of jurors, FY 1924

Ch. 771, 69 Cong. (44 Stat. 841, 858)   July 3, 1926

Line-item	Appropriation
bailiff and criers, FY 1925	$50,000.00
supplies, FY 1926	$24,000.00
books, FY 1927	$20,000.00
Penal Institutions	
Leavenworth Penitentiary, FY 1925 and 1926	$88,867.12
Atlanta Penitentiary, FY 1926	$75,000.00
McNeil Island Penitentiary, FY 1926	$26,000.00
National Training School for Boys	$5,000.00
support of prisoners, FY 1922	$3,526.40
support of prisoners, FY 1924	$26,330.46
support of prisoners, FY 1926	$600,000.00
inspection of prisons, FY 1926	$2,000.00
jail, Nome, Alaska	$5,000.00
Federal Institution for Women	$1,509,300.00
GAO Approved Claims, FY 1925	$67,534.25
Total	$2,595,621.44
TOTAL APPROPRIATION	$22,235,688.44

1928

Statute (Citation)	Date Passed	Headings	Appropriation	Line-item Details
Ch. 189, 69 Cong (44 Stat. 1178, 1194)	February 24, 1927	United States Supreme Court	$290,046.00	salaries of justices and all other officers and employees
			$25,000.00	printing and binding
			$18,874.00	miscellaneous expenses
			$8,000.00	reporter of decisions, salary and expenses
		Salaries of Judges	$1,813,500.00	circuit, district, and retired judges
		National Park Commissioners	$11,160.00	commissioners, salaries
		Court of Customs Appeals	$91,280.00	salaries of judges and all other officers and employees
			$14,800.00	rent and expenses
		Court of Claims	$122,962.00	salaries of judges and all other officers and employees
			$40,000.00	printing and binding
			$6,600.00	miscellaneous expenses
		Salaries and Expenses, Commissioners, Court of Claims	$43,387.50	under 43 Stat. 964

Territorial Courts	Alaska, salaries of judges, attorneys, marshals, clerks	$91,200.00
	Hawaii, salaries of chief justice and associate justices	$21,500.00
	Hawaii, salaries of judges of circuit courts	$48,000.00
... Expenses of United States Courts	salaries, fees, and expenses of marshals	$3,650,000.00
	salaries and expenses of district attorneys	$1,400,000.00
	salaries of regular assistant attorneys	$1,100,000.00
	payment of special assistant attorneys	$400,000.00
	clerks, salaries	$1,775,000.00
	fees of commissioners	$600,000.00
	mileage and per diem of jurors	$1,900,000.00
	mileage and per diems of witnesses	$1,850,000.00
	rent of rooms for courts and judicial officers	$80,000.00
	pay of bailiffs and criers, expenses of circuit and district judges, meals and lodging of jurors in U.S. cases, compensation of jury commissioners	$425,000.00
	miscellaneous expenses	$800,000.00
	supplies for courts and judicial officers	$70,000.00
	purchase and binding of books	$65,000.00
	Leavenworth Penitentiary	$849,240.00
Penal and Correctional Institutions	construction, Leavenworth Penitentiary	$17,500.00
	Atlanta Penitentiary	$850,000.00
	McNeil Island Penitentiary	$260,000.00
	construction, McNeil Island Penitentiary	$143,000.00
	Industrial Institution for Women	$230,000.00
	Industrial Reformatory, Ohio	$360,000.00
	National Training School for Boys	$165,000.00
	construction, National Training School for Boys	$75,000.00
	probation system	$30,000.00
	support of prisoners	$2,300,000.00
	inspection of prisons	$12,000.00
Total		$22,053,049.50

Ch. 5, 70 Cong. (45 Stat. 2, 20)	December 22, 1927	Salaries of Judges	$17,452.75	pay increases, Supreme Court, FY 1927
			$198,457.00	pay increases, circuit, district, and retired judges, FY 1927
			$10,000.00	pay increases, court of customs appeals, FY 1927
			$11,441.29	pay increases, court of claims, FY 1927
			$4,503.88	Alaska, FY 1927
			$51,000.00	district judges, FY 1928
		. . . Expenses of United States Courts	$3,841.56	salaries, fees, and expenses of marshals, FY 1924
			$5,000.00	special assistant attorneys, FY 1923
			$25,000.00	salaries of clerks, FY 1928
			$585.70	fees of commissioners, FY 1922
			$13,098.70	fees of commissioners, FY 1925
			$25,000.00	fees of commissioners, FY 1927
			$33.20	costs taxed against the U.S., FY 1926
			$672.00	cost of transcript for defendant in case against U.S., FY 1928
			$18,000.00	compensation and expenses of commissioner in State of Oklahoma v. State of Texas
			$20,162.78	pay of bailiffs and criers, FY 1927
			$10.00	books, FY 1924
			$55,399.00	books, FY 1928
		Penal and Correctional Institutions	$5,000.00	Leavenworth Penitentiary, FY 1927
			$250,000.00	Atlanta Penitentiary, FY 1928 and 1929
			$12,900.00	McNeil Island Penitentiary, FY 1928
			$62,250.00	McNeil Island Penitentiary, FY 1928 and 1929
			$1,805.37	National Training School for Boys, FY 1927
			$6,141.18	support for prisoners, FY 1924
			$7,576.26	support for prisoners, FY 1925
			$420,965.07	support of prisoners, FY 1927
		Total	$1,226,295.74	
		TOTAL APPROPRIATION	$23,279,345.24	

1929

Statute (Citation)	Date Passed	Headings	Appropriation	Line-item Details
Ch. 57, 70 Cong. (45 Stat. 64, 79)	February 15, 1928	United States Supreme Court	$290,046.00	salaries of justices and all other officers and employees
			$25,000.00	printing and binding
		Miscellaneous Expenses, Supreme Court	$20,374.00	miscellaneous expenses
			$8,000.00	salary of the reporter
		Salaries of Judges	$1,864,500.00	circuit, district, and retired judges
		National Park Commissioners	$11,160.00	commissioners, salaries
		Court of Customs Appeals	$91,280.00	salaries of presiding judge and 4 associate judges
			$14,800.00	rent and expenses
		Court of Claims	$124,085.00	salaries of judges and all other officers and employees
			$36,000.00	printing and binding
			$6,600.00	miscellaneous expenses
			$90,112.50	commissioners and stenographers
			$5,825.00	building repairs
		Territorial Courts	$91,200.00	Alaska, salaries of judges, attorneys, marshals, clerks
			$21,500.00	Hawaii, salaries of chief justice and associate justices
			$48,000.00	Hawaii, salaries of judges of circuit courts
		. . . Expenses of United States Courts	$3,672,500.00	salaries, fees, and expenses of marshals
			$1,440,000.00	salaries and expenses of district attorneys
			$1,130,000.00	salaries of regular assistant attorneys
			$380,000.00	payment of special assistant attorneys
			$1,820,000.00	clerks, salaries
			$550,000.00	fees of commissioners
			$1,875,000.00	mileage and per diem of jurors
			$1,725,000.00	mileage and per diems of witnesses
			$76,000.00	rent of rooms for courts and judicial officers
			$445,000.00	pay of bailiffs and criers, expenses of circuit and district judges, meals and lodging of jurors in U.S. cases, compensation of jury commissioners
			$838,000.00	miscellaneous expenses

		supplies for courts and judicial officers	$71,000.00	
		purchase and binding of books	$65,000.00	
		Leavenworth Penitentiary	$880,000.00	
	Penal and Correctional Institutions	Atlanta Penitentiary	$852,500.00	
		McNeil Island Penitentiary	$332,500.00	
		construction, McNeil Island Penitentiary	$177,100.00	
		Industrial Institution for Women	$270,000.00	
		Industrial Reformatory, Ohio	$372,500.00	
		National Training School for Boys	$192,710.00	
		construction, National Training School for Boys	$60,000.00	
		probation system	$25,000.00	
		support of prisoners	$2,350,000.00	
		inspection of prisons	$13,000.00	
	Total		$22,361,292.50	
Ch. 853, 70 Cong. (45 Stat. 883, 905)	May 29, 1928	United States Supreme Court	transfer from "miscellaneous expenses, Supreme Court, FY 1929"	$(3,730.00)
			transfer to "salaries, Supreme Court, FY 1929"	$3,730.00
		National Park Commissioners	commissioners salaries, FY 1929	$4,030.00
		Court of Claims	printing and binding, FY 1928	$10,000.00
		...Expenses of United States Courts	salaries, fees, and expenses of marshals, FY 1924	$1,861.35
			marshals, purchase of 2 vans, FY 1928	$5,000.00
			fees of commissioners, FY 1925	$1,627.75
			pay of bailiffs and criers, FY 1926	$1,958.24
			pay of bailiffs and criers, FY 1928	$30,000.00
			miscellaneous expenses, FY 1929	$100,000.00
			supplies, FY 1928, transfer from "printing and binding, Department of Justice and courts"	$11,100.00
			books, FY 1924	$12.50
		Penal and Correctional Institutions	Leavenworth Penitentiary, FY 1929	$130,000.00
			transfer from "Industrial Reformatory, Ohio, FY 1928"	$(25,000.00)
			transfer from to "Penitentiary, Atlanta, FY 1928"	$25,000.00
			McNeil Island Penitentiary, FY 1929	$65,000.00

Industrial Reformatory, Ohio	$400,000.00
National Training School for Boys	$9,973.00
support of prisoners, FY 1924	$377.10
support of prisoners, FY 1925	$14,838.80
support of prisoners, FY 1928	$200,000.00
Total	$985,778.74
TOTAL APPROPRIATION	**$23,347,071.24**

1930

Statute (Citation)	Date Passed	Headings	Appropriation	Line-item Details
Ch. 102, 70 Cong. (45 Stat. 1094, 1109)	January 25, 1929	United States Supreme Court	$293,776.00	salaries of justices and all other officers and employees
			$25,000.00	printing and binding
		Miscellaneous Expenses, Supreme Court	$16,644.00	miscellaneous expenses
			$8,000.00	salary of the reporter
		Salaries of Judges	$1,930,000.00	circuit, district, and retired judges
		National Park Commissioners	$16,000.00	commissioners, salaries
		Court of Customs Appeals	$95,460.00	salaries of judges and all other officers and employees
			$14,800.00	rent and expenses
		Court of Claims	$129,829.00	salaries of judges and all other officers and employees
			$38,000.00	printing and binding
			$6,600.00	miscellaneous expenses
		Salaries and Expenses, Commissioners, Court of Claims	$79,180.00	commissioners and stenographers
		Territorial Courts	$93,600.00	Alaska, salaries of judges, attorneys, marshals, clerks
			$30,500.00	Hawaii, salaries of chief justice and associate justices
			$58,000.00	Hawaii, salaries of judges of circuit courts
		...Expenses of United States Courts	$3,780,000.00	salaries, fees, and expenses of marshals
			$1,526,000.00	salaries and expenses of district attorneys
			$1,223,400.00	salaries of regular assistant attorneys
			$359,600.00	payment of special assistant attorneys
			$1,943,400.00	clerks, salaries
			$550,000.00	fees of commissioners

Category	Description	Date / Act	Amount
	fees of jurors and witnesses		$3,550,000.00
	rent of rooms for courts and judicial officers		$78,000.00
	pay of bailiffs and criers, expenses of circuit and district judges, meals and lodging of jurors in U.S. cases, compensation of jury commissioners		$455,000.00
	miscellaneous expenses		$890,360.00
	supplies for courts and judicial officers		$85,000.00
	purchase and binding of books		$65,000.00
	Leavenworth Penitentiary		$1,036,910.00
Penal and Correctional Institutions	bridge repairs, Leavenworth Penitentiary		$50,000.00
	Atlanta Penitentiary		$923,319.00
	McNeil Island Penitentiary		$381,872.00
	construction, McNeil Island Penitentiary		$65,000.00
	Industrial Institution for Women		$286,210.00
	Industrial Reformatory, Ohio		$331,320.00
	construction, Industrial Reformatory, Ohio		$150,000.00
	National Training School for Boys		$208,000.00
	probation system		$25,000.00
	support of prisoners		$2,450,000.00
	inspection of prisons		$13,000.00
Total			$23,261,780.00
Salaries of Judges	FY 1927	March 4, 1929 — Ch. 706, 70 Cong. (45 Stat. 1607, 1610)	$57.29
Territorial Courts	judges' salaries, Hawaii, FY 1928		$1,583.36
	judges' salaries, Hawaii, FY 1929		$19,000.00
Expenses of United States Courts	fees of commissioners, FY 1922		$3,400.20
	pay of bailiffs, FY 1926		$798.07
	transfer from fees of witnesses, FY 1928		$(44,000.00)
	transfer to fees of jurors, FY 1928		$44,000.00
Penal Institutions	support of prisoners, FY 1924		$208.48
	support of prisoners, FY 1928		$172,000.00
Total			$197,047.40

Law	Date	Category	Description	Amount
Ch. 707, 70 Cong. (45 Stat. 1623, 1645)	March 4, 1929	Salaries of Judges	circuit, district, and retired, FY 1929	$48,000.00
		Court of Claims	building maintenance, FY 1929–1930	$28,450.00
		. . . Expenses of United States Courts	special assistant attorneys, FY 1929–1930	$121,600.00
			regular assistant attorneys, FY 1929	$12,145.00
			salaries of clerks, FY 1928	$2,813.74
			salaries of clerks, FY 1929	$12,700.00
			fees of commissioners, FY 1922	$69.30
			fees of commissioners, FY 1929	$50,000.00
			books, FY 1929	$58,730.00
			miscellaneous expenses, FY 1929–1930	$28,800.00
			repair, courthouse in Nome, Alaska, FY 1929	$4,000.00
		Penal and Correctional Institutions	Leavenworth Penitentiary	$52,000.00
			repairs and construction, Leavenworth Penitentiary, FY 1929–1930	$52,400.00
			Atlanta Penitentiary, construction, FY 1929	$40,000.00
			McNeil Island Penitentiary	$27,000.00
			support of prisoners, FY 1929	$1,284,875.00
			support of prisoners, FY 1924	$9.50
		Total		$1,823,592.54
Ch. 92, 71 Cong. (46 Stat. 90, 107)	March 26, 1930	Salaries of Judges	FY 1929	$3,082.84
		National Park Commissioners	commissioner salary, FY 1930	$500.00
		Court of Customs and Patent Appeals	FY 1929	$15,000.00
		. . . Expenses of United States Courts	salaries, fees, and expenses of marshals, FY 1930	$100,000.00
			district attorneys, FY 1930	$109,990.00
			regular assistant attorneys, FY 1930	$57,500.00
			special assistant attorneys, FY 1924	$115.64
			salaries of clerks, FY 1929	$6,640.00
			salaries of clerks, FY 1930	$75,400.00
			fees of jurors, FY 1925	$30.00
			fees of jurors, FY 1929	$15,800.00
			fees of commissioners, FY 1922	$528.30

$3,284.72	fees of commissioners, FY 1925
$1,109.47	rent, FY 1929
$22,000.00	rent, FY 1930
$600.00	pay of bailiffs, etc., FY 1929
$54,606.64	books, FY 1930
$979.95	Leavenworth Penitentiary, FY 1927

Penal and Correctional Institutions

$357,693.00	Leavenworth Penitentiary, FY 1930
$85,456.00	Leavenworth Penitentiary, machinery and equipment, FY 1930–1931
$10,000.00	Leavenworth Penitentiary, construction
$148,000.00	Atlanta Penitentiary, FY 1930
$25,615.00	Atlanta Penitentiary, machinery and equipment, FY 1930–1931
$86,198.00	McNeil Island Penitentiary, FY 1930
$237,000.00	McNeil Island Penitentiary, machinery and equipment, FY 1930–1931
$84,539.00	Industrial Institution for Women, FY 1930
$120,000.00	support of prisoners, FY 1929
$5,900.00	inspection of prisons, FY 1930

Total	$1,627,568.56
TOTAL APPROPRIATION	**$26,909,988.50**

1931

Statute (Citation)	Date Passed	Headings	Appropriation	Line-item Details
Ch. 184, 71 Cong. (46 Stat. 173, 188)	April 18, 1930	United States Supreme Court	$293,776.00	salaries of justices and all other officers and employees
		Miscellaneous Expenses, Supreme Court	$25,000.00	printing and binding
			$16,644.00	miscellaneous expenses
		Salaries of Judges	$8,000.00	salary of the reporter
			$2,099,000.00	circuit, district, and retired judges
		National Park Commissioners	$18,000.00	commissioners, salaries
		Court of Customs and Patent Appeals	$104,820.00	salaries of judges and all other officers and employees
			$6,500.00	rent and expenses
		Court of Claims	$129,829.00	salaries of judges and all other officers and employees
			$38,000.00	printing and binding

	miscellaneous expenses	$7,950.00
Salaries and Expenses, Commissioners, Court of Claims	commissioners and stenographers	$41,790.00
Territorial Courts	building repairs	$1,763.00
	Alaska, salaries of judges, attorneys, marshals, clerks	$93,600.00
	Hawaii, salaries of chief justice and associate justices	$30,500.00
	Hawaii, salaries of judges of circuit courts	$58,000.00
. . . Expenses of United States Courts	salaries, fees, and expenses of marshals	$3,880,000.00
	salaries and expenses of district attorneys	$1,678,550.00
	salaries of regular assistant attorneys	$1,479,700.00
	payment of special assistant attorneys	$450,000.00
	clerks, salaries	$2,105,056.00
	fees of commissioners	$600,000.00
	fees of jurors and witnesses	$3,650,000.00
	rent of rooms for courts and judicial officers	$118,000.00
	pay of bailiffs and criers, expenses of circuit and district judges, meals and lodging of jurors in U.S. cases, compensation of jury commissioners	$485,000.00
	miscellaneous expenses	$950,000.00
	supplies for courts and judicial officers	$86,000.00
	purchase and binding of books	$72,000.00
Penal and Correctional Institutions	Leavenworth Penitentiary	$1,623,357.00
	repairs, Leavenworth Penitentiary	$22,300.00
	Atlanta Penitentiary	$1,037,437.00
	construction, Atlanta Penitentiary	$79,000.00
	McNeil Island Penitentiary	$431,268.00
	construction, McNeil Island Penitentiary	$139,000.00
	Industrial Institution for Women	$377,125.00
	Industrial Reformatory, Ohio	$568,690.00
	construction, Industrial Reformatory, Ohio	$450,000.00
	National Training School for Boys	$215,080.00
	probation system	$25,000.00
	support of prisoners	$3,000,000.00
Total		$26,495,735.00

Ch. 846, 71 Cong. (46 Stat. 860, 880)	July 3, 1930	Salaries of Judges	circuit, district, retired, FY 1930	$135,000.00
			payment to widow of Justice Sanford	$20,000.00
		National Park Commissioners	commissioners, FY 1931	$2,000.00
		Court of Customs and Patent Appeals	salaries, FY 1931	$2,000.00
			printing and binding	$3,500.00
			printing, transferred from treasury and justice departments	$3,100.00
		. . . Expenses of United States Courts	salaries of clerks, FY 1928	$1,340.30
			fees of commissioners, FY 1925	$126.15
			fees of commissioners, FY 1930	$50,000.00
			pay of bailiffs, etc., FY 1930	$40,000.00
			miscellaneous expenses, FY 1928	$284.22
			miscellaneous expenses, FY 1930	$112,000.00
			supplies, FY 1930	$20,000.00
			hospitals, FY 1930	$65,000.00
		Penal and Correctional Institutions	Leavenworth Penitentiary, FY 1930	$129,940.08
			Leavenworth Penitentiary, FY 1930	$293,623.00
			Atlanta Penitentiary, FY 1930–1931	$92,133.00
			construction of new penitentiary	$1,700,000.00
			Industrial Reformatory, Chillicothe, Ohio, FY 1930	$30,177.00
			Chillicothe, FY 1931	$24,300.00
			consolidated prisons working capital fund, FY 1931	$500,000.00
			building federal jails	$1,000,000.00
			building prison camps, FY 1931	$750,000.00
			support of prisoners, FY 1924	$3,324.50
			inspection of prisons, FY 1930	$3,000.00
			probation system, FY 1931	$175,000.00
			Total	$5,155,848.25
Ch. 111, 71 Cong. (46 Stat. 1064, 1071)	February 6, 1931	Judicial	commissioners, salaries and expenses, Court of Claims, FY 1931	$37,930.00
			TOTAL APPROPRIATION	$31,689,513.25

1932

Statute (Citation)	Date Passed	Headings	Appropriation	Line-item Details
Ch. 280, 71 Cong. (46 Stat. 1309, 1323)	February 23, 1931	United States Supreme Court	$293,776.00	salaries of justices and all other officers and employees
			$25,000.00	printing and binding
			$16,644.00	miscellaneous expenses
		Miscellaneous Expenses, Supreme Court	$8,000.00	salary of the reporter
		Salaries of Judges	$2,184,000.00	circuit, district, retired judges
		National Park Commissioners	$20,000.00	commissioners, salaries
		Court of Customs and Patent Appeals	$106,820.00	salaries of judges and all other officers and employees
			$6,600.00	printing and binding
			$6,000.00	expenses
		Customs Court	$246,260.00	salaries of judges and all other officers and employees
			$19,350.00	expenses
			$3,300.00	printing and binding
		Court of Claims	$130,123.00	salaries of judges and all other officers and employees
			$38,000.00	printing and binding
			$7,500.00	miscellaneous expenses
			$84,870.00	commissioners and stenographers
			$12,565.00	building repairs
		Territorial Courts	$30,500.00	Hawaii, salaries of Supreme Court
			$58,000.00	Hawaii, salaries of judges of circuit courts
		... Expenses of United States Courts	$4,350,460.00	salaries, fees, and expenses of marshals
			$3,295,620.00	salaries and expenses of district attorneys and regular assistants
			$450,000.00	payment of special assistant attorneys
			$2,175,920.00	clerks, salaries
			$600,000.00	fees of commissioners
			$4,150,000.00	fees of jurors and witnesses
			$115,000.00	rent of rooms for courts and judicial officers
			$500,000.00	pay of bailiffs and criers, expenses of circuit and district judges, meals and lodging of jurors in U.S. cases, compensation of jury commissioners

Citation	Date	Category	Item	Amount
			miscellaneous expenses	$1,270,980.00
			supplies for courts and judicial officers	$90,000.00
			purchase and binding of books	$75,000.00
		Penal Institutions	Leavenworth Penitentiary	$1,942,440.00
			Atlanta Penitentiary	$1,198,212.00
			construction, Atlanta Penitentiary	$100,000.00
			McNeil Island Penitentiary	$516,060.00
			construction, McNeil Island Penitentiary	$214,135.00
			Northeastern Penitentiary	$287,000.00
			Industrial Institution for Women	$352,400.00
			Industrial Reformatory, Ohio	$790,448.00
			construction, Industrial Reformatory, Ohio	$1,000,000.00
			construction of U.S. Reformatory, Oklahoma	$500,000.00
			federal jails	$871,220.00
			construction of federal jails	$500,000.00
			prison camps	$837,640.00
			National Training School for Boys	$258,260.00
			construction and repair, Training School	$200,000.00
			probation system	$230,400.00
			support of prisoners	$3,996,040.00
			Total	$34,164,543.00
Ch. 522, 71 Cong. (46 Stat. 1552, 1572)	March 4, 1931	Court of Customs and Patent Appeals	printing and binding, FY 1931	$2,900.00
		Customs Court	miscellaneous salaries and expenses, FY 1931	$15,000.00
		… Expenses of United States Courts	salaries, fees, and expenses of marshals, FY 1931	$255,665.00
			district attorneys, FY 1931	$60,550.00
			salaries of clerks, FY 1931	$19,308.00
			fees of commissioners, FY 1925	$20.31
			fees of jurors, FY 1925	$42.00
			fees of jurors and witnesses, FY 1931	$550,000.00
			miscellaneous expenses, FY 1930	$53,360.00
			miscellaneous expenses, FY 1931	$371,250.00
			supplies, FY 1931	$20,000.00
			fees of commissioner, North Carolina	$87.45

Penal Institutions	Leavenworth Penitentiary, FY 1931	$150,000.00
	construction and repair of buildings, Leavenworth Penitentiary, FY 1931–1932	$183,900.00
	Atlanta Penitentiary, FY 1931	$113,945.00
	construction and repair of buildings, Atlanta Penitentiary, FY 1931–1932	$100,000.00
	water system, boilers, etc., Atlanta Penitentiary, FY 1929	$3,200.00
	McNeil Island Penitentiary, FY 1931	$34,971.00
	construction and repair of buildings, McNeil Island Penitentiary, FY 1931–1932	$33,252.00
	construction, Northeastern Penitentiary, FY 1931–1932	$1,900,000.00
	Industrial Institution for Women, FY 1931–1932	$7,090.00
	Industrial Reformatory, Ohio, FY 1931	$77,000.00
	Hospital for Defective Delinquents, FY 1931–1932	$1,250,000.00
	construction and repair of buildings, prison camps, FY 1931–1932	$150,000.00
	National Training School for Boys, FY 1931	$27,000.00
	support of prisoners, 1929	$23,828.55
	support of prisoners, 1931	$1,000,000.00
Total		$6,402,369.31
February 2, 1932 / Ch. 12, 72 Cong. (47 Stat. 15, 23)	. . . Expenses of United States Courts	
	salaries, fees, and expenses of marshals, FY 1931	$27,000.00
	fees of commissioners, FY 1930	$5,195.35
	fees of jurors and witnesses, FY 1932	$150,000.00
	pay of bailiffs, etc., FY 1931	$14,000.00
	pay of bailiffs, etc., FY 1932	$30,000.00
	miscellaneous expenses, FY 1930	$4,834.81
	support of prisoners, FY 1929	$16,826.05
Total		$247,856.21
TOTAL APPROPRIATION		**$40,814,768.52**

1933

Statute (Citation)	Date Passed	Headings	Appropriation	Line-item Details
Ch. 361, 72 Cong. (47 Stat. 475, 490)	July 1, 1932	Supreme Court	$280,500.00	salaries of justices and all other officers and employees
			$21,000.00	printing and binding
		Miscellaneous Expenses, Supreme Court	$15,000.00	miscellaneous expenses
			$8,000.00	salary of the reporter
		Salaries of Judges	$2,174,000.00	circuit, district, and retired judges
		Court of Customs and Patent Appeals	$100,000.00	salaries of judges and all other officers and employees
			$5,000.00	printing and binding
			$4,500.00	expenses
		Customs Court	$230,000.00	salaries of judges and all other officers and employees
			$15,000.00	expenses
			$3,000.00	printing and binding
		Court of Claims	$117,500.00	salaries of judges and all other officers and employees
			$35,000.00	printing and binding
			$6,000.00	miscellaneous expenses
			$75,000.00	commissioners and stenographers
			$4,000.00	building repairs
		Territorial Courts	$30,500.00	salaries, Supreme Court, Hawaii
			$58,000.00	Hawaii, salaries of judges of circuit courts
		. . . Expenses of United States Courts	$4,100,000.00	salaries, fees, and expenses of marshals
			$3,050,000.00	salaries and expenses of district attorneys and regular assistants
			$360,000.00	payment of special assistant attorneys
			$1,925,000.00	clerks, salaries
			$550,000.00	fees of commissioners
			$3,750,000.00	fees of jurors and witnesses
			$90,000.00	rent of rooms for courts and judicial officers
			$400,000.00	pay of bailiffs and criers, expenses of circuit and district judges, meals and lodging of jurors in U.S. cases, compensation of jury commissioners
			$900,000.00	miscellaneous expenses

Penal Institutions		supplies for courts and judicial officers	$75,000.00
		purchase and binding of books	$75,000.00
		medical and hospital services	$312,000.00
		Leavenworth Penitentiary	$1,645,000.00
		construction, Leavenworth Penitentiary	$8,000.00
		Atlanta Penitentiary	$1,045,000.00
		construction, Atlanta Penitentiary	$8,500.00
		McNeil Island Penitentiary	$428,500.00
		construction, McNeil Island Penitentiary	$32,000.00
		Northeastern Penitentiary	$440,000.00
		Industrial Institution for Women	$300,000.00
		Industrial Reformatory, Ohio	$634,000.00
		construction, Industrial Reformatory, Ohio	$521,000.00
		Southwestern Reformatory	$284,000.00
		construction, Southwestern Reformatory	$520,000.00
		Hospital for Defective Delinquents	$270,000.00
		construction, Hospital for Defective Delinquents	$468,000.00
		federal jails	$815,000.00
		construction of federal jails	$500.00
		prison camps	$800,000.00
		National Training School for Boys	$248,000.00
		construction and repair, Training School	$76,000.00
		probation system	$415,000.00
		support of prisoners	$2,855,000.00
		Total	$30,582,500.00
Ch. 364, 72 Cong. (47 Stat. 525, 536)	July 1, 1932	... Expenses of United States Courts	fees of commissioners, FY 1930	$6,014.95
			fees of commissioners, FY 1925	$124.19
			fees of commissioners, FY 1922	$176.55
			miscellaneous expenses, FY 1930	$2,405.88
		Penal and Correctional Institutions	support of prisoners, FY 1929	$971.35
			Total	$9,692.92

Statute (Citation)	Date Passed	Headings	Line-item Details	Appropriation
Ch. 26, 72 Cong. (47 Stat. 780, 782)	January 30, 1933	. . . Expenses of United States Courts	fees of commissioners, FY 1925	$138.50
			fees of commissioners, FY 1930	$1,007.15
			fees of commissioners, FY 1931	$3,275.80
			fees of commissioners, FY 1932	$43,812.67
			fees of jurors and witnesses, FY 1931	$11,356.85
			pay of bailiffs, etc., FY 1931	$1,261.07
			miscellaneous expenses, FY 1930	$244.55
		Penal and Correctional Institutions	construction, Hospital for Defective Delinquents, FY 1933	$177,983.00
			transfer from federal jails, FY 1932	$(185,000.00)
			transfer to support of prisoners, FY 1932	$185,000.00
		Total		$239,079.59
		TOTAL APPROPRIATION		**$30,831,272.51**

1934

Statute (Citation)	Date Passed	Headings	Line-item Details	Appropriation
Ch. 144, 72 Cong. (47 Stat. 1371, 1382)	March 1, 1933	United States Supreme Court	salaries of justices and all other officers and employees	$279,173.00
			printing and binding	$21,000.00
			miscellaneous expenses	$15,000.00
		Salaries and Expenses of Judges	circuit, district, and retired judges	$2,217,417.00
			expenses of judges	$111,000.00
		Court of Customs and Patent Appeals	salaries of judges and all other officers and employees	$84,300.00
			general expenses	$4,500.00
			printing and binding	$6,000.00
		Customs Court	salaries of judges and all other officers and employees	$209,300.00
			expenses	$15,700.00
			printing and binding	$2,000.00
		Court of Claims	salaries of judges and all other officers and employees	$102,000.00
			commissioners and stenographers	$52,000.00
			printing and binding	$30,000.00
			miscellaneous expenses	$6,000.00
			building maintenance and repairs	$4,500.00

Territorial Courts

	salaries of justices and circuit judges, Hawaii	$81,167.00
... Expenses of United States Courts	salaries, fees, and expenses of marshals	$3,935,500.00
	salaries and expenses of district attorneys and regular assistants	$3,049,020.00
	payment of special assistant attorneys	$336,717.00
	clerks, salaries	$1,856,580.00
	fees of commissioners	$550,000.00
	fees of jurors and witnesses	$3,135,000.00
	rent of rooms for courts and judicial officers	$73,500.00
	salaries and expenses of bailiffs, etc.	$253,000.00
	miscellaneous expenses	$884,000.00
	supplies for courts and judicial officers	$85,000.00
	purchase and binding of books	$75,000.00
	medical and hospital services	$426,000.00

Penal and Correctional Institutions

	Leavenworth Penitentiary	$1,468,000.00
	construction, Leavenworth Penitentiary	$5,400.00
	Atlanta Penitentiary	$920,000.00
	McNeil Island Penitentiary	$406,400.00
	construction, McNeil Island Penitentiary	$36,000.00
	transfer from "federal jails, construction" to "construction, McNeil Island Penitentiary"	$(36,000.00)
	Northeastern Penitentiary	$493,000.00
	Industrial Institution for Women	$285,700.00
	Industrial Reformatory, Ohio	$543,000.00
	transfer from "federal jails" to "construction, Industrial Reformatory, Ohio"	$(40,000.00)
	construction, Industrial Reformatory, Ohio	$40,000.00
	Southwestern Reformatory	$263,000.00
	Hospital for Defective Delinquents	$311,500.00
	transfer from "federal jails" to "construction, Hospital for Delinquents"	$(145,000.00)
	construction, Hospital for Delinquents	$145,000.00
	federal jails	$600,000.00
	prison camps	$346,000.00
	federal correctional camp, Eustis, Va.	$236,000.00

Date / Citation	Category	Purpose	Amount
		Federal Reformatory Camp, Petersburg, Va.	$232,000.00
		National Training School for Boys	$218,000.00
		probation system	$434,543.00
		support of prisoners	$3,088,000.00
		transfer from unexpended balance of federal jails, construction, FY 1932	$(175,000.00)
		salaries and expense of clerks, salaries and expenses of district attorneys, enforcement of antitrust laws, FY 1934	$175,000.00
	Total		$27,750,917.00
March 4, 1933 Ch. 282, 72 Cong. (47 Stat. 1602, 1610)	United States Courts	fees of commissioners, FY 1930	$3.45
		fees of commissioners, FY 1931	$1,236.90
		fees of commissioners, FY 1932	$23,901.37
		miscellaneous expenses, FY 1930	$1,823.49
		supplies, FY 1931	$176.52
		supplies, FY 1932	$3.93
		support of prisoners, FY 1929	$51.03
		support of prisoners, FY 1931	$49.80
	Total		$27,246.49
May 29, 1933 Ch. 42, 73 Cong. (48 Stat. 97, 98)	Contingent Expenses United States Courts	transfer from "salaries, fees, and expenses of marshals, FY 1933" to Department of Justice	$(3,500.00)
		transfer from "salaries, fees, and expenses of marshals, FY 1933" to conciliation commissioners, FY 1934	$(25,000.00)
		compensation and expenses of conciliation commissioners, FY 1934	$25,000.00
	Total		$(3,500.00)
June 16, 1933 Ch. 100, 73 Cong. (48 Stat. 274, 277)	... Expenses of United States Courts	fees of commissioners, FY 1925	$7.80
		fees of commissioners, FY 1930	$11.05
		fees of commissioners, FY 1931	$3,896.70
		fees of commissioners, FY 1932	$12,374.92
		miscellaneous expenses, FY 1930	$24.61

1935

				supplies, FY 1931
			$1.40	supplies, FY 1932
			$545.00	
		Total	$16,861.48	
		TOTAL APPROPRIATION	$27,791,524.97	

Statute (Citation)	Date Passed	Headings	Appropriation	Line-item Details
Ch. 104, 73 Cong. (48 Stat. 529, 539)	April 7, 1934	United States Supreme Court	$282,000.00	salaries of justices and all other officers and employees
			$21,000.00	printing and binding
			$15,000.00	miscellaneous expenses
		Salaries of Judges	$2,220,000.00	circuit, district, and retired judges
		Expenses of Judges	$95,000.00	expenses of judges
		Court of Customs and Patent Appeals	$90,040.00	salaries of judges and all other officers and employees
			$4,000.00	general expenses
			$5,000.00	printing and binding
		Customs Court	$205,560.00	salaries of judges and all other officers and employees
			$15,700.00	expenses
			$2,000.00	printing and binding
		Court of Claims	$109,940.00	salaries of judges and all other officers and employees
			$51,130.00	commissioners and stenographers
			$25,000.00	printing and binding
			$6,000.00	general expenses
			$14,000.00	building maintenance and repairs
		Territorial Courts	$79,650.00	salaries of justices and circuit judges, Hawaii
		District Court, Panama Canal Zone	$41,205.00	salaries of judges, officials, and employees, Panama Canal Zone
		United States Court for China	$42,440.00	salaries of judges, officials, and employees
		. . . Expenses of United States Courts	$2,971,730.00	salaries, fees, and expenses of marshals
			$2,344,580.00	salaries and expenses of district attorneys and regular assistants
			$600,000.00	payment of special assistant attorneys
			$1,797,000.00	clerks, salaries
			$400,000.00	fees of commissioners

	fees of jurors and witnesses	$2,230,000.00
	rent of rooms for courts and judicial officers	$55,000.00
	salaries and expenses of bailiffs	$235,000.00
	miscellaneous expenses	$827,460.00
	supplies for courts and judicial officers	$80,000.00
	purchase and binding of books	$75,000.00
	medical and hospital services	$418,478.00
Penal Institutions	Leavenworth Penitentiary	$1,146,000.00
	Atlanta Penitentiary	$626,000.00
	McNeil Island Penitentiary	$338,000.00
	construction, McNeil Island Penitentiary	$60,800.00
	Northeastern Penitentiary	$491,000.00
	Alcatraz	$231,475.00
	transfer from unexpended balance of Northeastern Penitentiary, FY 1934 to Alcatraz	$(15,000.00)
	Alcatraz	$15,000.00
	Industrial Institution for Women	$226,000.00
	Industrial Reformatory, Ohio	$453,000.00
	Southwestern Reformatory	$191,500.00
	Hospital for Defective Delinquents	$254,000.00
	federal jails	$435,000.00
	prison camps	$231,500.00
	federal correctional camp, Eustis, Va.	$175,000.00
	Federal Reformatory Camp, Petersburg, Va.	$158,000.00
	National Training School for Boys	$185,000.00
	probation system	$454,160.00
	support of prisoners	$1,400,000.00
Total		$22,415,348.00
Ch. 648, 73 Cong. (48 Stat. 1021, 1036)	June 19, 1934	Supreme Court	care of building by marshal	$40,830.00
	care of building by Architect of Capital	$30,348.00
... Expenses of United States Courts	salaries, fees, and expenses of marshals, FY 1931	$6,537.81
	salaries, fees, and expenses of marshals, FY 1935	$100,000.00
	salaries of clerks, FY 1935	$75,000.00

	$5.00	fees of commissioners, FY 1922
	$10.00	fees of commissioners, FY 1925
	$4,105.75	fees of commissioners, FY 1930
	$7,065.37	fees of commissioners, FY 1931
	$14,258.52	fees of commissioners, FY 1932
	$25,684.33	fees of commissioners, FY 1933
	$1,116.58	fees of jurors and witnesses, FY 1931
	$465.99	miscellaneous expenses, FY 1930
	$136.55	supplies, FY 1931
	$180.63	supplies, FY 1932
	$15,000.00	supplies, FY 1935
	$24.26	books, FY 1931
	$12,500.00	special master, No. Pacific Railway case
	$978.58	support of prisoners, FY 1924
	$218.44	support of prisoners, FY 1929
	$75,000.00	support of prisoners, FY 1935
Total	$409,465.81	
Ch. 36, 74 Cong. (49 Stat. 49, 52) March 21, 1935		. . . Expenses of United States Courts
	$230.53	salaries, fees, and expenses of marshals, FY 1924
	$372.07	salaries, fees, and expenses of marshals, FY 1931
	$188.33	district attorneys, FY 1933
	$471.60	fees of commissioners, FY 1931
	$15,395.89	fees of commissioners, FY 1932
	$28,582.02	fees of commissioners, FY 1933
	$135,000.00	fees of conciliation commissioners, FY 1935–1936
	$0.68	supplies, FY 1931
Penal and Correctional Institutions	$65,410.00	Leavenworth Penitentiary, buildings, FY 1935–1936
	$126,080.00	Leavenworth Penitentiary, maintenance, FY 1935
	$83,180.00	Atlanta Penitentiary, maintenance, FY 1935
	$38,715.00	McNeil Island Penitentiary, maintenance, FY 1935
	$59,180.00	Northeastern Penitentiary, maintenance, FY 1935

			Industrial Reformatory, FY 1935	$21,705.00
			Southwestern Reformatory, FY 1935	$130,500.00
			Total	$705,011.12
			TOTAL APPROPRIATION	**$23,529,824.93**

1936

Statute (Citation)	Date Passed	Headings	Appropriation	Line-item Details
Ch. 39, 74 Cong. (49 Stat. 67, 79)	March 22, 1935	Supreme Court	$416,000.00	salaries of justices and all other officers and employees
			$20,000.00	printing and binding
			$25,000.00	miscellaneous expenses
			$49,080.00	care of building and grounds
		Salaries of Judges	$2,195,000.00	circuit, district, and retired judges
		Judge's Expenses	$85,000.00	expenses of judges
		Court of Customs and Patent Appeals	$100,040.00	salaries of judges and all other officers and employees
			$13,500.00	general expenses
			$6,250.00	printing and binding
		Customs Court	$228,280.00	salaries of judges and all other officers and employees
			$15,000.00	expenses
			$1,000.00	printing and binding
		Court of Claims	$122,160.00	salaries of judges and all other officers and employees
			$25,000.00	printing and binding
			$6,000.00	general expenses
			$63,840.00	commissioners and stenographers
			$15,000.00	building maintenance and repairs
		Territorial Courts	$88,500.00	salaries of justices and circuit judges, Hawaii
		Panama Canal Zone	$45,785.00	salaries of judges, officials, and employees, Panama Canal Zone
		United States Court for China	$40,000.00	salaries of judges, officials, and employees
		. . . Expenses of United States Courts	$3,270,000.00	salaries, fees, and expenses of marshals
			$2,913,000.00	salaries and expenses of district attorneys and regular assistants
			$700,000.00	payment of special assistant attorneys
			$2,070,000.00	clerks, salaries
			$350,000.00	fees of commissioners

		conciliation commissioners	$30,000.00
		fees of jurors and witnesses	$2,100,000.00
		salaries and expenses of bailiffs	$247,000.00
		miscellaneous expenses	$1,069,000.00
		medical and hospital services	$487,500.00
	Penal and Correctional Institutions	construction and maintenance	$80,000.00
		Leavenworth Penitentiary	$1,240,670.00
		Atlanta Penitentiary	$767,660.00
		McNeil Island Penitentiary	$444,000.00
		Northeastern Penitentiary	$633,840.00
		Alcatraz	$363,000.00
		Industrial Institution for Women	$258,520.00
		Industrial Reformatory, Ohio	$531,000.00
		Southwestern Reformatory	$390,000.00
		Hospital for Defective Delinquents	$305,510.00
		federal jails	$528,940.00
		prison camps	$234,460.00
		Federal Reformatory Camp, Petersburg, Va.	$246,430.00
		National Training School for Boys	$203,000.00
		probation system	$631,035.00
		support of prisoners	$1,950,000.00
		Total	$25,605,000.00
Ch. 508, 74 Cong. (49 Stat. 571, 586)	August 12, 1935	Supreme Court	expenses of promulgating rules of civil procedure, FY 1935–1936	$25,000.00
		. . . Expenses of United States Courts	salaries, fees, and expenses of marshals, FY 1931	$72.33
			district attorneys, FY 1933	$245.68
			special assistant attorneys, FY 1936	$176,767.00
			fees of commissioners, FY 1930	$1.65
			fees of commissioners, FY 1931	$8.00
			fees of commissioners, FY 1933	$2,702.32
			fees of conciliation commissioners, FY 1935–1936	$209,000.00
			fees of jurors and witnesses, FY 1935	$140,000.00
			rent, FY 1935	$17,000.00

Statute (Citation)	Date Passed	Headings	Appropriation	Line-item Details
			$863.61	supplies, FY 1934
		Penal and Correctional Institutions	$22,000.00	Leavenworth Penitentiary, FY 1936
			$55,000.00	McNeil Island Penitentiary, FY 1936
			$48,000.00	Alcatraz, FY 1936
			$4,500.00	Chillicothe, Ohio, FY 1936
			$24,500.00	Hospital for Defective Delinquents, FY 1936
			$390,000.00	support of prisoners, FY 1935
		Total	$1,115,660.59	
Ch. 241, 74 Cong. (49 Stat. 1236)	April 20, 1936	[Expenses of United States Courts]	$900,000.00	fees of jurors and witnesses, FY 1936
		TOTAL APPROPRIATION	$27,620,660.59	

1937

Statute (Citation)	Date Passed	Headings	Appropriation	Line-item Details
Ch. 405, 74 Cong. (49 Stat. 1309, 1324)	May 15, 1936	Supreme Court	$416,000.00	salaries of justices and all other officers and employees
			$21,000.00	printing and binding
			$29,000.00	miscellaneous expenses
			$55,000.00	care of building and grounds
		Salaries of Judges	$2,295,000.00	circuit, district, and retired judges
		Judge's Expenses	$85,000.00	expenses of judges
		Court of Customs and Patent Appeals	$101,120.00	salaries of judges and all other officers and employees
			$3,000.00	general expenses
			$6,000.00	printing and binding
		Customs Court	$228,280.00	salaries of judges and all other officers and employees
			$15,000.00	expenses
			$1,000.00	printing and binding
		Court of Claims	$122,160.00	salaries of judges and all other officers and employees
			$25,500.00	printing and binding
			$6,500.00	general expenses
			$63,840.00	commissioners and stenographers
			$16,000.00	building maintenance and repairs

Territorial Courts	salaries of justices and circuit judges, Hawaii	$88,500.00
District Court, Panama Canal Zone	salaries of judges, officials, and employees, Panama Canal Zone	$45,785.00
United States Court for China	salaries of judges, officials, and employees	$49,375.00
Marshals and Other Expenses of United States Courts	salaries, fees, and expenses of marshals	$3,300,000.00
	salaries and expenses of district attorneys and regular assistants	$3,083,510.00
	payment of special assistant attorneys	$600,000.00
	clerks, salaries	$2,125,000.00
	fees of commissioners	$350,000.00
	conciliation commissioners	$200,000.00
	fees of jurors and witnesses	$3,000,000.00
	salaries and expenses of bailiffs	$247,000.00
	miscellaneous expenses	$1,040,000.00
Penal and Correctional Institutions	medical and hospital services	$500,000.00
	building and maintenance of jails	$2,550,000.00
	Leavenworth Penitentiary	$1,566,530.00
	Atlanta Penitentiary	$894,140.00
	McNeil Island Penitentiary	$504,180.00
	construction and maintenance of prisons	$300,000.00
	Northeastern Penitentiary	$686,350.00
	Alcatraz	$300,000.00
	Institution for Women	$272,175.00
	Chillicothe Reformatory	$718,460.00
	Southwestern Reformatory	$486,830.00
	Hospital for Defective Delinquents	$358,010.00
	federal jails	$715,000.00
	prison camps	$364,950.00
	Petersburg, Va., reformatory camp	$270,290.00
	National Training School for Boys	$225,000.00
	probation system	$727,540.00
	support of prisoners	$2,100,000.00
Total		$31,158,025.00

June 22, 1936	Ch. 689, 74 Cong. (49 Stat. 1597, 1625)	Supreme Court	$17,500.00	expenses, rules of civil procedure, FY 1937
		Salaries of Judges	$65,000.00	FY 1936
		Expenses of Judges	$7,500.00	for judges in Alaska, Puerto Rico, and Hawaii, FY 1936
		U.S. Court for China	$7,025.00	FY 1936
			$4,700.00	FY 1937
		. . . Expenses of United States Courts	$31,951.21	salaries, fees, and expenses of marshals, FY 1935
			$270,000.00	salaries, fees, and expenses of marshals, FY 1936
			$6,439.09	district attorneys, FY 1935
			$60,000.00	district attorneys, FY 1936
			$12,735.32	salaries of clerks, FY 1935
			$73,000.00	salaries of clerks, FY 1936
			$0.60	fees of commissioners, FY 1930
			$56.60	fees of commissioners, FY 1931
			$714.72	fees of commissioners, FY 1932
			$886.23	fees of commissioners, FY 1933
			$63,097.34	fees of jurors and witnesses, FY 1935
			$20,000.00	salaries and expenses of bailiffs, FY 1936
			$360.00	miscellaneous expenses, FY 1930
			$36,500.00	miscellaneous expenses, FY 1936
			$153.60	supplies, FY 1934
		Penal and Correctional Institutions	$21,300.00	National Training School for Boys, FY 1936
			$97.50	support of prisoners, FY 1929
		Total	$699,017.21	
February 9, 1937	Ch. 9, 75 Cong. (50 Stat. 8, 13)	Supreme Court	$25,000.00	miscellaneous expenses, FY 1937–1938
May 28, 1937	Ch. 277, 75 Cong. (50 Stat. 213, 224)	Salaries of Judges	$45,000.00	circuit, district, retired judges
		. . . Expenses of United States Courts	$170.64	salaries, fees, and expenses of marshals, FY 1931
			$33,000.00	salaries, fees, and expenses of marshals, FY 1937
			$4,000.00	special assistant attorneys, FY 1934
			$2,948.57	special assistant attorneys, FY 1935

salaries of clerks, FY 1937	$20,000.00
fees of commissioners, FY 1925	$688.10
fees of commissioners, FY 1930	$24.45
fees of commissioners, FY 1933	$52.23
fees of conciliation commissioners, FY 1935–1936	$40,000.00
salaries and expenses of bailiffs, FY 1937	$20,000.00
miscellaneous expenses, FY 1937	$75,000.00
rent, FY 1935	$245.81
supplies, FY 1934	$1.75
Penal and Correctional Institutions — McNeil Island Penitentiary	$53,000.00
support of prisoners, FY 1929	$61.45
support of prisoners, FY 1932	$201.30
National Training School for Boys, FY 1937	$11,500.00
Total	$305,894.30
TOTAL APPROPRIATION	$32,187,936.51

1938

Statute (Citation)	Date Passed	Headings	Appropriation	Line-item Details
Ch. 359, 75 Cong. (50 Stat. 261, 276)	June 16, 1937	Supreme Court	$422,700.00	salaries of justices and all other officers and employees
			$21,000.00	printing and binding
			$26,000.00	miscellaneous expenses
			$60,000.00	care of building and grounds
		Salaries of Judges	$2,410,000.00	circuit, district, and retired judges
		Court of Customs and Patent Appeals	$101,120.00	salaries of judges and all other officers and employees
			$3,000.00	general expenses
			$6,250.00	printing and binding
		Customs Court	$229,900.00	salaries of judges and all other officers and employees
			$14,500.00	expenses
			$1,000.00	printing and binding
		Court of Claims	$122,160.00	salaries of judges and all other officers and employees
			$25,500.00	printing and binding
			$6,500.00	general expenses

	commissioners and stenographers	$65,500.00
	building maintenance and repairs	$6,000.00
Territorial Courts	salaries of justices and circuit judges, Hawaii	$88,500.00
District Court, Panama Canal Zone	salaries of judges, officials, and employees	$47,000.00
United States Court for China	salaries of judges, officials, and employees	$54,000.00
Marshals and Other Expenses of United States Courts	salaries, fees, and expenses of marshals	$3,560,000.00
	salaries and expenses of district attorneys and regular assistants	$2,918,500.00
	payment of special assistant attorneys	$927,000.00
	clerks, salaries	$2,170,000.00
	fees of commissioners	$320,000.00
	conciliation commissioners	$105,000.00
	fees of jurors and witnesses	$3,040,000.00
	salaries and expenses of bailiffs	$262,000.00
	miscellaneous expenses	$1,086,000.00
Penal and Correctional Institutions	medical and hospital services	$563,040.00
	Leavenworth Penitentiary	$953,370.00
	Leavenworth Penitentiary annex	$601,540.00
	Atlanta Penitentiary	$932,610.00
	McNeil Island Penitentiary	$513,980.00
	construction and maintenance, McNeil Island Penitentiary	$800,000.00
	Northeastern Penitentiary	$734,390.00
	Alcatraz	$305,600.00
	Institution for Women	$273,900.00
	Chillicothe Reformatory	$761,360.00
	Southwestern Reformatory	$514,040.00
	Hospital for Defective Delinquents	$341,000.00
	federal jails	$1,023,465.00
	prison camps	$376,440.00
	Petersburg, Va., reformatory camp	$274,000.00
	public works construction	$1,380,000.00
	National Training School for Boys	$238,000.00
	construction and repairs, National Training School for Boys	$21,540.00

Statute (Citation)	Date Passed	Headings	Appropriation	Line-item Details
			$584,500.00	probation system
			$2,000,000.00	support of prisoners
		Total	$31,291,905.00	
Ch. 757, 75 Cong. (50 Stat. 755, 766)	August 25, 1937	Supreme Court	$1,200.00	salaries, FY 1938
			$79,000.00	additional salaries and expenses, U.S. v. No. Pacific Railway, FY 1936–1938
		. . . Expenses of United States Courts	$37.65	salaries, fees, and expenses of marshals, FY 1931
			$550.25	fees of commissioners, FY 1925
		Penal Institutions	$50,000.00	Institution for Women
			$174.50	support of prisoners, FY 1929
			$477.61	support of prisoners, FY 1932
		Total	$131,440.01	
Ch. 42, 75 Cong. (52 Stat. 85, 89)	March 5, 1938	Customs Court	$75.60	printing and binding, FY 1937
		Territorial Courts	$2,355.00	Hawaii, salaries of chief justice and associate justices, FY 1938
		United States Courts	$46,500.00	salaries, fees, and expenses of marshals, FY 1937
			$18.84	fees of commissioners, FY 1933
			$11,000.00	salaries and expenses of bailiffs, FY 1937
		Total	$59,949.44	
		TOTAL APPROPRIATION	**$31,483,294.45**	

1939

Statute (Citation)	Date Passed	Headings	Appropriation	Line-item Details
Ch. 180, 75 Cong. (52 Stat. 248, 265)	April 27, 1938	Supreme Court	$430,660.00	salaries of justices and all other officers and employees
			$23,500.00	printing and binding
			$25,000.00	miscellaneous expenses
			$61,500.00	care of building and grounds
		District of Columbia	$16,260.00	courthouse, District Court of D.C.
			$11,000.00	U.S. Court of Appeals building

Court of Customs and Patent Appeals	salaries of judges and all other officers and employees	$101,120.00
	expenses	$2,800.00
	printing and binding	$6,250.00
Customs Court	salaries of judges and all other officers and employees	$232,800.00
	expenses	$13,500.00
	printing and binding	$1,000.00
Court of Claims	salaries of judges and all other officers and employees	$122,160.00
	printing and binding	$25,500.00
	general expenses	$10,500.00
	commissioners and stenographers	$65,500.00
	building maintenance and repairs	$5,000.00
Territorial Courts	salaries of justices and circuit judges, Hawaii	$96,000.00
District Court, Panama Canal Zone	salaries of judges, officials, and employees	$46,085.00
United States Court for China	salaries of judges, officials, and employees	$51,000.00
Salaries of Judges	circuit, district, and retired judges	$2,593,000.00
. . . Expenses of United States Courts	salaries, fees, and expenses of marshals	$3,634,440.00
	salaries and expenses of district attorneys and regular assistants	$3,010,000.00
	payment of special assistant attorneys	$613,600.00
	clerks, salaries	$2,191,140.00
	fees of commissioners	$300,000.00
	fees of jurors and witnesses	$3,408,000.00
	salaries and expenses of bailiffs	$271,660.00
	miscellaneous salaries	$737,650.00
	miscellaneous expenses	$551,290.00
Total		$18,657,915.00
Judicial	judge's salaries, FY 1938	$60,000.00
. . . Expenses of United States Courts	fees of commissioners, FY 1933	$1.50
	salaries and expenses of bailiffs, FY 1938	$44,000.00
	miscellaneous expenses, FY 1936	$1,288.06
	miscellaneous expenses, FY 1938	$169,840.00

Ch. 681, 75 Cong, (52 Stat. 1114, 1137)   June 25, 1938

		Penal and Correctional Institutions	$129,840.00	additional salaries and wages, FY 1939
			$9,830.00	National Training School for Boys, FY 1938
		Total	$414,799.56	
Ch. 107, 76 Cong. (53 Stat. 626, 636)	May 2, 1939	Territorial Courts	$7,500.00	salaries of judges, Hawaii, FY 1939
		Salaries of Judges	$100,000.00	FY 1939
		. . . Expenses of United States Courts	$46,500.00	fees of jurors and witnesses, FY 1938
			$37,000.00	salaries and expenses of bailiffs, FY 1939
			$30,000.00	miscellaneous salaries, FY 1939
			$150,000.00	miscellaneous expenses, FY 1939
		Total	$371,000.00	
		TOTAL APPROPRIATION	$19,443,714.56	

1940

Statute (Citation)	Date Passed	Headings	Appropriation	Line-item Details
Ch. 248, 76 Cong. (53 Stat. 885, 903)	June 29, 1939	Supreme Court	$445,000.00	salaries of justices and all other officers and employees
			$23,000.00	printing and binding
			$25,000.00	miscellaneous expenses
			$62,500.00	care of building and grounds
			$10,000.00	books
		Courts for the District of Columbia	$47,000.00	courthouse, District Court of D.C.
			$4,500.00	U.S. Court of Appeals building
		Court of Customs and Patent Appeals	$105,780.00	salaries of judges and all other officers and employees
			$3,000.00	expenses
			$7,000.00	printing and binding
		Customs Court	$234,600.00	salaries of judges and all other officers and employees
			$14,000.00	expenses
			$1,000.00	printing and binding

Headings	Line-item Details	Appropriation
Court of Claims	salaries of judges and all other officers and employees	$122,160.00
	expenses	$11,560.00
	printing and binding	$25,500.00
	salaries of commissioners and stenographers	$75,500.00
	building maintenance and repairs	$8,000.00
Territorial Courts	salaries of justices and circuit judges, Hawaii	$103,500.00
District Court, Panama Canal Zone	salaries of judges, officials, and employees	$49,400.00
United States Court for China	salaries of judges, officials, and employees	$47,600.00
Salaries of Judges		$2,950,000.00
[Expenses of United States Courts]	salaries and expenses of clerks	$2,330,000.00
	fees of commissioners	$300,000.00
	fees of jurors and witnesses	$3,480,000.00
	salaries and expenses of bailiffs	$320,000.00
	miscellaneous salaries	$890,000.00
	miscellaneous expenses	$610,000.00
TOTAL APPROPRIATION		**$12,305,600.00**

1941

Statute (Citation)	Date Passed	Headings	Line-item Details	Appropriation
Ch. 189, 76 Cong. (54 Stat. 181, 207)	May 14, 1940	United States Supreme Court	salaries of justices and all other officers and employees	$449,500.00
			printing and binding	$23,500.00
			miscellaneous expenses	$25,000.00
			care of building and grounds	$65,000.00
		U.S. Courts for the District of Columbia	courthouse, District Court of D.C.	$20,000.00
			U.S. Court of Appeals building	$6,000.00
		Court of Customs and Patent Appeals	salaries of judges and all other officers and employees	$105,780.00
			expenses	$3,000.00
			printing and binding	$6,720.00
		Customs Court	salaries of judges and all other officers and employees	$234,500.00
			expenses	$15,000.00

Headings	Line-item Details	Appropriation
Court of Claims	printing and binding	$1,000.00
	salaries of judges and all other officers and employees	$131,000.00
	expenses	$10,800.00
	printing and binding	$25,200.00
	salaries of commissioners and stenographers	$75,500.00
	building maintenance and repairs	$4,500.00
Territorial Courts	salaries of justices and circuit judges, Hawaii	$103,500.00
District Court, Panama Canal Zone	salaries of judges, officials, and employees	$28,000.00
U.S. Court for China	salaries of judges, officials, and employees	$28,000.00
Miscellaneous Items of Expense	salaries, circuit, district, and retired judges	$3,030,000.00
	salaries and expenses of clerks	$2,330,000.00
	fees of commissioners	$290,000.00
	fees of jurors	$1,970,000.00
	miscellaneous salaries	$885,000.00
	probation system	$810,000.00
	miscellaneous expenses	$317,000.00
	traveling expenses	$473,000.00
	printing and binding	$83,000.00
Administrative Office of the U.S. Courts	salaries	$187,500.00
	expenses	$55,000.00
TOTAL APPROPRIATION		**$11,792,000.00**

1942

Statute (Citation)	Date Passed	Headings	Appropriation	Line-item Details
Ch. 258, 77 Cong. (55 Stat. 265, 298)	June 28, 1941	United States Supreme Court	$458,000.00	salaries of justices and all other officers and employees
			$23,500.00	printing and binding
			$27,000.00	miscellaneous expenses
			$25,000.00	preparation of rules of criminal procedure, FY 1941–1942
			$69,627.00	care of building and grounds
		U.S. Courts for the District of Columbia	$14,000.00	courthouse, District Court of D.C.
			$5,000.00	U.S. Court of Appeals building

Court of Customs and Patent Appeals	salaries of judges and all other officers and employees	$106,080.00
	expenses	$3,000.00
	printing and binding	$6,720.00
Customs Court	salaries of judges and all other officers and employees	$234,500.00
	expenses	$19,000.00
	printing and binding	$800.00
Court of Claims	salaries of judges and all other officers and employees	$131,410.00
	expenses	$8,300.00
	printing and binding	$25,500.00
	salaries of commissioners and stenographers	$75,500.00
	building maintenance and repairs	$12,000.00
Territorial Courts	salaries of justices and circuit judges, Hawaii	$103,500.00
District Court, Panama Canal Zone	salaries of judges, officials, and employees	$26,000.00
U.S. Court for China	salaries of judges, officials, and employees	$28,000.00
Miscellaneous Items of Expense	salaries, circuit, district, and retired judges	$3,115,000.00
	salaries and expenses of clerks	$2,418,000.00
	probation system	$860,000.00
	fees of commissioners	$350,000.00
	fees of jurors	$2,040,000.00
	miscellaneous salaries	$866,200.00
	miscellaneous expenses	$398,000.00
	traveling expenses	$538,000.00
	printing and binding	$82,000.00
Administrative Office of the U.S. Courts	salaries	$220,000.00
	expenses	$37,000.00
Total		$12,326,637.00
United States Courts	fees of commissioners, FY 1937	$6.75
	fees of commissioners, FY 1939	$781.93
Total		$788.68

Ch. 32, 77 Cong. (55 Stat. 62, 63)   April 1, 1941

Statute (Citation)	Date Passed	Headings	Appropriation	Line-item Details
Ch. 273, 77 Cong. (55 Stat. 541, 542)	July 3, 1941	United States Supreme Court	$5,400.00	salaries, FY 1942
		TOTAL APPROPRIATION	**$12,332,825.68**	

1943

Statute (Citation)	Date Passed	Headings	Appropriation	Line-item Details
Ch. 472, 77 Cong. (56 Stat. 468, 501)	July 2, 1942	United States Supreme Court	$472,400.00	salaries of justices and all other officers and employees
			$27,700.00	printing and binding
			$27,000.00	miscellaneous expenses
			$68,000.00	care of building and grounds
		U.S. Courts for the District of Columbia	$12,300.00	courthouse, District Court of D.C.
			$2,500.00	U.S. Court of Appeals building
		Court of Customs and Patent Appeals	$107,500.00	salaries of judges and all other officers and employees
			$3,000.00	expenses
			$6,700.00	printing and binding
		Customs Court	$236,500.00	salaries of judges and all other officers and employees
			$17,000.00	expenses
			$1,000.00	printing and binding
		Court of Claims	$207,000.00	salaries of judges and all other officers and employees
			$18,500.00	expenses
			$26,500.00	printing and binding
			$4,550.00	building maintenance and repairs
		Territorial Courts	$103,500.00	salaries of justices and circuit judges, Hawaii
		District Court, Panama Canal Zone	$27,300.00	salaries of judges, officials, and employees
		U.S. Court for China	$26,000.00	salaries of judges, officials, and employees
		Miscellaneous Items of Expense	$3,170,000.00	salaries, circuit, district, and retired judges
			$2,462,900.00	salaries and expenses of clerks
			$988,000.00	probation system
			$350,000.00	fees of commissioners
			$1,940,000.00	fees of jurors
			$893,100.00	miscellaneous salaries

Statute (Citation)	Date Passed	Headings	Line-item Details	Appropriation
			miscellaneous expenses	$307,200.00
			traveling expenses	$567,000.00
			printing and binding	$89,000.00
		Administrative Office of the U.S. Courts	salaries	$242,500.00
			expenses	$39,000.00
		Total		$12,443,650.00
Ch. 476, 78 Cong. (56 Stat. 593, 597)	July 2, 1942	Fees of Commissioners, U.S. Courts	FY 1939	$52.21
		Fees and Expenses, Conciliation Commissioners	FY 1935	$138.75
		Probation System, U.S. Courts	FY 1937	$200.69
			FY 1939	$6.24
		Total		$397.89
Ch. 17, 78 Cong. (57 Stat. 21, 22)	March 18, 1943	Miscellaneous Expenses, U.S. Courts	fees of commissioners, FY 1942	$15,000.00
		TOTAL APPROPRIATION		**$12,459,047.89**

1944

Statute (Citation)	Date Passed	Headings	Line-item Details	Appropriation
Ch. 173, 78 Cong. (57 Stat. 220, 239)	June 28, 1943	United States Supreme Court	salaries of justices and all other officers and employees	$484,200.00
			preparation of rules of criminal procedure	$30,000.00
			printing and binding	$26,000.00
			miscellaneous expenses	$27,000.00
			care of building and grounds	$68,000.00
		U.S. Courts for the District of Columbia	courthouse, District Court of D.C.	$11,300.00
			U.S. Court of Appeals building	$2,500.00
		Court of Customs and Patent Appeals	salaries of judges and all other officers and employees	$107,060.00
			expenses	$3,000.00
			printing and binding	$6,700.00

Statute (Citation)	Date Passed	Headings	Line-item Details	Appropriation
		Customs Court	salaries of judges and all other officers and employees	$236,500.00
			expenses	$13,500.00
			printing and binding	$1,000.00
		Court of Claims	salaries of judges and all other officers and employees	$208,000.00
			expenses	$18,000.00
			printing and binding	$26,500.00
			building maintenance and repairs	$2,550.00
		Territorial Courts	salaries of justices and circuit judges, Hawaii	$103,500.00
		Miscellaneous Items of Expense	salaries, circuit, district, and retired judges	$3,222,500.00
			salaries and expenses of clerks	$2,570,280.00
			probation system	$956,800.00
			fees of commissioners	$350,000.00
			fees of jurors	$1,680,000.00
			miscellaneous salaries	$1,087,800.00
			miscellaneous expenses	$391,000.00
			traveling expenses	$540,000.00
			printing and binding	$89,000.00
		Administrative Office of the U.S. Courts	salaries	$243,800.00
			expenses	$24,000.00
		Total		$12,530,490.00
Ch. 152, 78 Cong. (58 Stat. 150, 151)	April 1, 1944	Supreme Court of the United States	preparation of rules of criminal proceedings, FY 1944–1945	$21,000.00
			preparation of rules of civil procedure, FY 1944	$4,414.00
		Total		$25,414.00
		TOTAL APPROPRIATION		$12,555,904.00

1945

Statute (Citation)	Date Passed	Headings	Line-item Details	Appropriation
Ch. 277, 78 Cong. (58 Stat. 334, 354)	June 26, 1944	United States Supreme Court	salaries of justices and all other officers and employees	$536,509.00
			printing and binding	$49,750.00
			miscellaneous expenses	$27,000.00
			care of building and grounds	$80,000.00

U.S. Courts for the District of Columbia	$12,300.00	courthouse, District Court of D.C.
	$3,370.00	U.S. Court of Appeals building
Court of Customs and Patent Appeals	$114,860.00	salaries of judges and all other officers and employees
	$3,000.00	expenses
	$6,700.00	printing and binding
Customs Court	$250,000.00	salaries of judges and all other officers and employees
	$12,500.00	expenses
	$1,000.00	printing and binding
Court of Claims	$220,000.00	salaries of judges and all other officers and employees
	$15,000.00	expenses
	$25,000.00	printing and binding
	$2,550.00	building maintenance and repairs
Territorial Courts	$96,500.00	salaries of justices and circuit judges, Hawaii
Miscellaneous Items of Expense	$3,222,500.00	salaries, circuit, district, and retired judges
	$2,985,000.00	salaries and expenses of clerks
	$1,137,400.00	probation system
	$400,000.00	fees of commissioners
	$1,600,000.00	fees of jurors
	$1,327,885.00	miscellaneous salaries
	$366,000.00	miscellaneous expenses
	$563,500.00	traveling expenses
	$89,000.00	printing and binding
Administrative Office of the U.S. Courts	$283,700.00	salaries
	$24,000.00	expenses
Total	$13,455,024.00	
Miscellaneous Items of Expense	$133,000.00	fees of commissioners, FY 1944
	$30,000.00	miscellaneous expenses, FY 1945
Total	$163,000.00	

Ch. 304, 78 Cong. (58 Stat. 597, 599)   June 28, 1944

Federal Judiciary Appropriations: 1792–2010

Statute (Citation)	Date Passed	Headings	Line-item Details	Appropriation
Ch. 660, 78 Cong. (58 Stat. 853, 854)	December 22, 1944	Supreme Court of the United States	preparation of rules of civil procedure, FY 1945–1946	$19,700.00
		Miscellaneous Items of Expense	fees of commissioners, FY 1943	$5,500.00
		Total		$25,200.00
Ch. 95, 79 Cong. (59 Stat. 77, 92)	April 25, 1945	U.S. Courts for the District of Columbia	building repairs and improvements, FY 1945	$1,400.00
		TOTAL APPROPRIATION		**$13,644,624.00**

1946

Statute (Citation)	Date Passed	Headings	Line-item Details	Appropriation
Ch. 129, 79 Cong. (59 Stat. 169, 196)	May 21, 1945	United States Supreme Court	salaries of justices and all other officers and employees	$499,100.00
			printing and binding	$37,000.00
			miscellaneous expenses	$34,900.00
			care of building and grounds	$74,800.00
		U.S. Courts for the District of Columbia	courthouse, District Court of D.C.	$10,300.00
			U.S. Court of Appeals building	$2,500.00
		Court of Customs and Patent Appeals	salaries of judges and all other officers and employees	$111,600.00
			expenses	$3,300.00
			printing and binding	$6,700.00
		Customs Court	salaries of judges and all other officers and employees	$233,200.00
			expenses	$13,000.00
			printing and binding	$1,000.00
		Court of Claims	salaries of judges and all other officers and employees	$300,000.00
			expenses	$45,000.00
			printing and binding	$33,000.00
			building maintenance and repairs	$6,500.00
		Territorial Courts	salaries of justices and circuit judges, Hawaii	$96,500.00
		Miscellaneous Items of Expense	salaries, circuit, district, and retired judges	$3,200,000.00
			salaries and expenses of clerks	$2,635,000.00
			probation system	$1,173,000.00
			salaries of criers	$200,000.00

Statute	Date	Office / Court	Item	Amount
Ch. 589, 79 Cong. (59 Stat. 632, 634)	December 28, 1945	Administrative Office of the U.S. Courts	fees of commissioners	$450,000.00
			fees of jurors	$1,600,000.00
			miscellaneous salaries	$1,400,000.00
			miscellaneous expenses	$540,000.00
			traveling expenses	$620,000.00
			printing and binding	$89,000.00
			salaries of court reporters	$700,000.00
			salaries	$249,000.00
			expenses	$26,000.00
		Total		$14,390,400.00
		Court of Customs and Patent Appeals		
		Miscellaneous Items of Expense	printing and binding, FY 1944	$1,234.06
			salaries of criers, FY 1946	$20,000.00
			fee of commissioners, FY 1945	$34,000.00
		Total		$55,234.06
Ch. 114, 79 Cong. (60 Stat. 82)	March 28, 1946	Court of Claims	printing and binding, FY 1946	$12,000.00
Ch. 263, 79 Cong. (60 Stat. 183, 199)	May 18, 1946	United States Supreme Court	rules of criminal proceedings, FY 1946–1947	$7,500.00
		U.S. Courts for the District of Columbia	courthouse, district court, FY 1946	$5,400.00
			U.S. Circuit Court of Appeals Building, FY 1946	$11,000.00
		Total		$23,900.00
Ch. 425, 79 Cong. (60 Stat. 262, 268)	June 21, 1946	Miscellaneous Items of Expense	probation system, FY 1946	$20,000.00
			miscellaneous salaries, FY 1946	$10,000.00
			salaries of court reporters, FY 1946	$58,500.00
		Total		$88,500.00
		TOTAL APPROPRIATION		**$14,570,034.06**

1947

Statute (Citation)	Date Passed	Headings	Appropriation	Line-item Details
Ch. 541, 79 Cong. (60 Stat. 446, 475)	July 5, 1946	United States Supreme Court	$598,590.00	salaries of justices and all other officers and employees
			$37,000.00	printing and binding
			$28,600.00	miscellaneous expenses
			$102,600.00	care of building and grounds
		U.S. Courts for the District of Columbia	$12,500.00	courthouse, District Court of D.C.
			$11,000.00	U.S. court of appeals building
		Court of Customs and Patent Appeals	$136,000.00	salaries and expenses
		Customs Court	$295,700.00	salaries and expenses
		Court of Claims	$450,000.00	salaries and expenses
			$9,000.00	building repair and improvements
		Territorial Courts	$96,500.00	salaries of justices and circuit judges, Hawaii
		Miscellaneous Items of Expense	$3,200,000.00	salaries, circuit, district, and retired judges
			$3,368,000.00	salaries and expenses of clerks
			$1,472,000.00	probation system
			$320,000.00	salaries of criers
			$475,000.00	fees of commissioners
			$1,400,000.00	fees of jurors
			$1,750,000.00	miscellaneous salaries
			$500,000.00	miscellaneous expenses
			$590,000.00	traveling expenses
			$80,000.00	printing and binding
			$800,000.00	salaries of court reporters
		Administrative Office of the U.S. Courts	$295,000.00	salaries
			$30,000.00	expenses
		Total	$16,057,490.00	
Ch. 591, 79 Cong. (60 Stat. 600, 624)	July 23, 1946	United States Supreme Court	$15,116.00	salaries, FY 1947

Statute (Citation)	Date Passed	Headings	Line-item Details	Appropriation
Ch. 49, 80 Cong. (61 Stat. 58, 59)	May 1, 1947	Court of Claims	building repairs and improvements	$12,500.00
		Territorial Courts	Hawaii	$1,188.00
		Miscellaneous Items of Expense	salaries of court reporters	$15,000.00
		Total		$28,688.00
Ch. 82, 80 Cong. (61 Stat. 106)	May 26, 1947	United States Supreme Court	printing and binding, FY 1947	$5,600.00
		Administrative Office	salaries, FY 1947	$7,500.00
		Total		$13,100.00
Ch. 156, 80 Cong. (61 Stat. 183, 184)	June 27, 1947	Court of Customs and Patent Appeals	printing and binding, FY 1946	$1,074.07
		Miscellaneous Items of Expense	printing and binding, FY 1946	$7,050.00
			jurors, FY 1947	$30,000.00
			printing and binding, FY 1947	$23,700.00
		Total		$61,824.07
		TOTAL APPROPRIATION		**$16,176,218.07**

1948

Statute (Citation)	Date Passed	Headings	Line-item Details	Appropriation
Ch. 211, 80 Cong. (61 Stat. 279, 302)	July 9, 1947	United States Supreme Court	salaries of justices and all other officers and employees	$762,500.00
			printing and binding	$25,000.00
			miscellaneous expenses	$40,000.00
			care of building and grounds	$122,800.00
			rules of civil procedure	$5,420.00
		U.S. Courts for the District of Columbia	courthouse, District Court of D.C.	$11,200.00
			U.S. court of appeals building	$3,800.00
		Court of Customs and Patent Appeals	salaries and expenses	$168,000.00
		Customs Court	salaries and expenses	$356,400.00
		Court of Claims	salaries and expenses	$450,000.00
			building repair and improvements	$11,000.00
		Territorial Courts	salaries of justices and circuit judges, Hawaii	$96,500.00

	Miscellaneous Items of Expense	$4,515,000.00	salaries, circuit, district, and retired judges
		$3,631,295.00	salaries and expenses of clerks
		$1,650,000.00	probation system
		$320,000.00	salaries of criers
		$475,000.00	fees of commissioners
		$1,400,000.00	fees of jurors
		$1,800,000.00	miscellaneous salaries
		$500,000.00	miscellaneous expenses
		$590,000.00	traveling expenses
		$69,000.00	printing and binding
		$80,250.00	printing and binding opinions and reports of Supreme Court
		$865,000.00	salaries of court reporters
		$350,000.00	salaries of referees
		$350,000.00	expenses of referees
	Administrative Office of the U.S. Courts	$400,000.00	salaries and expenses
	Total	$19,048,165.00	
Ch. 361, 80 Cong. (61 Stat. 610, 612) — July 30, 1947	U.S. Courts for the District of Columbia	$370,000.00	plans for new courthouse
Ch. 91, 80 Cong. (62 Stat. 59, 61) — March 3, 1948	Court of Claims	$(25,000.00)	transfer from "salaries and expenses" to repairs and improvements, Court of Claims building
		$25,000.00	repairs and improvements, Court of Claims building
	Miscellaneous Items of Expense	$75,000.00	salaries, circuit, district, and retired judges
	Total	$75,000.00	
Ch. 658, 80 Cong. (62 Stat. 1027, 1030) — June 25, 1948	Miscellaneous Items of Expense	$23,000.00	printing and binding opinions and reports of Supreme Court, FY 1948
	TOTAL APPROPRIATION	**$19,516,165.00**	

1949

Statute (Citation)	Date Passed	Headings	Appropriation	Line-item Details
Ch. 400, 80 Cong. (62 Stat. 305, 329)	June 3, 1948	United States Supreme Court	$786,600.00	salaries of justices and all other officers and employees
			$8,500.00	printing and binding
			$45,100.00	miscellaneous expenses
			$175,700.00	care of building and grounds
		U.S. Courts, District of Columbia	$5,300.00	courthouse, District Court of D.C.
			$2,500.00	U.S. court of appeals building
		Court of Customs and Patent Appeals	$177,400.00	salaries and expenses
		Customs Court	$356,400.00	salaries and expenses
		Court of Claims	$432,000.00	salaries and expenses
			$7,100.00	building repair and improvements
		Territorial Courts	$106,500.00	salaries of justices and circuit judges, Hawaii
		Miscellaneous Items of Expense	$4,575,000.00	salaries, circuit, district, and retired judges
			$3,758,000.00	salaries and expenses of clerks
			$1,700,000.00	probation system
			$468,000.00	salaries of criers
			$475,000.00	fees of commissioners
			$1,430,000.00	fees of jurors
			$1,844,000.00	miscellaneous salaries
			$600,000.00	miscellaneous expenses
			$607,000.00	traveling expenses
			$85,800.00	printing and binding
			$91,200.00	printing and binding opinions and reports of Supreme Court
			$865,000.00	salaries of court reporters
			$170,000.00	salaries of referees
			$150,000.00	expenses of referees
		Administrative Office of the U.S. Courts	$430,000.00	salaries and expenses
		Total	$19,352,100.00	
Ch. 138, 81 Cong. (63 Stat. 76, 78)	May 24, 1949	Miscellaneous Items of Expense	$300,000.00	fees of jurors

Federal Judiciary Appropriations: 1792–2010

Statute (Citation)	Date Passed	Headings	Line-item Details	Appropriation
Ch. 236, 81 Cong. (63 Stat. 231, 253)	June 23, 1949	United States Supreme Court	salaries	$35,000.00
			care of building and grounds	$15,000.00
		Court of Customs and Patent Appeals	salaries and expenses	$5,000.00
		Customs Court	salaries and expenses	$15,000.00
		Court of Claims	salaries and expenses	$8,200.00
		Miscellaneous Items of Expense	salaries, circuit, district, and retired judges	$25,000.00
			clerks salaries	$312,600.00
			probation system	$158,000.00
			miscellaneous salaries	$49,000.00
			transfer from miscellaneous expenses to miscellaneous salaries	$(72,000.00)
			Administrative Office of the U.S. Courts	$15,600.00
			Total	$566,400.00
			TOTAL APPROPRIATION	**$20,218,500.00**

1950

Statute (Citation)	Date Passed	Headings	Line-item Details	Appropriation
Ch. 354, 81 Cong. (63 Stat. 447, 470)	July 20, 1949	Supreme Court of the United States	salaries of justices and all other officers and employees	$867,000.00
			miscellaneous expenses	$52,100.00
			care of building and grounds	$148,400.00
		Court of Customs and Patent Appeals	salaries and expenses	$187,900.00
		Customs Court	salaries and expenses	$400,600.00
		Court of Claims	salaries and expenses	$510,000.00
			building repair and improvements	$24,100.00
		Other Courts and Services	Hawaii, salaries of justices and circuit judges	$106,500.00
			salaries of judges	$4,675,000.00
			salaries of clerks of court	$4,221,300.00
			probation system	$1,965,000.00
			salaries of criers	$470,000.00
			fees of commissioners	$475,000.00
			fees of jurors	$1,850,000.00

Date	Citation	Category	Item	Amount
			miscellaneous salaries	$2,067,000.00
			miscellaneous expenses	$611,000.00
			traveling expenses	$614,000.00
			printing and binding Supreme Court reports	$91,200.00
			salaries of court reporters	$873,400.00
			Administrative Office of the U.S. Courts	$500,800.00
			repair and improvements, D.C. District Court	$16,000.00
			repair and improvements, U.S. Court of Appeals for D.C.	$7,900.00
			salaries of referees	$879,000.00
			expenses of referees	$886,000.00
			Total	$22,499,200.00
October 10, 1949	Ch. 662, 81 Cong. (63 Stat. 738, 739)	Supreme Court of the United States	preparation of rules of civil procedure	$5,000.00
October 14, 1949	Ch. 694, 81 Cong. (63 Stat. 869, 870)	Miscellaneous Items of Expense	fees of jurors, FY 1949	$40,000.00
			transfer from salaries of criers, FY 1949 to fees for jurors	$(40,000.00)
			Total	$0
June 20, 1950	Ch. 405, 81 Cong. (64 Stat. 275, 279)	Other Courts and Services	salaries of judges	$175,000.00
			salaries of clerks	$100,000.00
			salaries of criers	$17,000.00
			miscellaneous salaries	$130,000.00
			travel expenses	$135,000.00
			salaries of court reporters	$45,000.00
			fees of jurors	$300,000.00
		Increased Pay Cost		
		Supreme Court of the United States	care of building and grounds	$3,600.00
		Customs Court	salaries and expenses	$5,000.00
		Other Courts and Services	probation system	$20,000.00
			Administrative Office of the U.S. Courts	$5,000.00
			Total	$935,600.00
			TOTAL APPROPRIATION	**$23,439,800.00**

1951

Statute (Citation)	Date Passed	Headings	Appropriation	Line-item Details
Ch. 896, 81 Cong. (64 Stat. 595, 629)	September 6, 1950	Supreme Court of the United States	$915,000.00	salaries of justices and all other officers and employees
			$91,200.00	printing and binding Supreme Court reports
			$52,100.00	miscellaneous expenses
			$159,200.00	care of building and grounds
		Court of Customs and Patent Appeals	$192,200.00	salaries and expenses
		Customs Court	$417,465.00	salaries and expenses
		Court of Claims	$575,000.00	salaries and expenses
			$10,700.00	building repair and improvements
		Other Courts and Services	$106,500.00	Hawaii, salaries of justices and circuit judges
			$5,095,000.00	salaries of judges
			$4,470,000.00	salaries and expenses of clerks
			$2,145,000.00	probation system
			$520,000.00	salaries of criers
			$475,000.00	fees of commissioners
			$2,700,000.00	fees of jurors
			$2,600,000.00	miscellaneous salaries
			$675,000.00	miscellaneous expenses
			$725,000.00	traveling expenses
			$972,000.00	salaries of court reporters
			$520,000.00	Administrative Office of the U.S. Courts
			$7,100.00	district court, District of Columbia
			$6,200.00	repair and improvements, U.S. Court of Appeals for D.C.
			$879,000.00	salaries of referees
			$995,000.00	expenses of referees
		Total	$25,303,665.00	
PL 82-45 (65 Stat. 52, 56)	June 2, 1951	Other Courts and Services	$25,000.00	fees of commissioners, FY 1950
			$200,000.00	fees of jurors, FY 1951
		Total	$225,000.00	
		TOTAL APPROPRIATION	$25,528,665.00	

1952

Statute (Citation)	Date Passed	Headings	Appropriation	Line-item Details
PL 82-188 (65 Stat. 575, 594)	October 22, 1951	Supreme Court of the United States	$928,000.00	salaries of justices and all other officers and employees
			$91,200.00	printing and binding
			$58,350.00	miscellaneous expenses
			$160,700.00	care of building and grounds
		Court of Customs and Patent Appeals	$194,500.00	salaries and expenses
		Customs Court	$433,165.00	salaries and expenses
		Court of Claims	$579,800.00	salaries and expenses
			$91,000.00	building repair and improvements
		Other Courts and Services	$120,000.00	Hawaii, salaries of justices and circuit judges
			$5,120,000.00	salaries of judges
			$4,520,000.00	salaries and expenses of clerks
			$2,180,000.00	probation system
			$542,300.00	salaries of criers
			$543,000.00	fees of commissioners
			$2,800,000.00	fees of jurors
			$2,670,000.00	miscellaneous salaries
			$750,000.00	miscellaneous expenses
			$715,000.00	traveling expenses
			$988,200.00	salaries of court reporters
			$535,000.00	Administrative Office of the U.S. Courts
			$7,100.00	repair and improvements, D.C. District Court
			$3,700.00	repair and improvements, U.S. Court of Appeals for D.C.
			$879,000.00	salaries of referees
			$1,090,000.00	expenses of referees
		Total	$26,000,015.00	
PL 82-253 (65 Stat. 736, 739)	November 1, 1951	Other Courts and Services	$70,000.00	fees of commissioners, FY 1951

Statute (Citation)	Date Passed	Headings	Line-item Details	Appropriation
PL 82-431 (66 Stat. 309, 310)	June 30, 1952	Other Courts and Services	fees of commissioners, FY 1952	$60,000.00
			fees of jurors, FY 1952	$260,000.00
		Total		$320,000.00
		TOTAL APPROPRIATION		**$26,390,015.00**

1953

Statute (Citation)	Date Passed	Headings	Line-item Details	Appropriation
PL 82-495 (66 Stat. 549, 567)	July 10, 1952	Supreme Court of the United States	salaries of justices and all other officers and employees	$1,017,900.00
			printing and binding	$91,200.00
			miscellaneous expenses	$46,450.00
			care of building and grounds	$174,100.00
		Court of Customs and Patent Appeals	salaries and expenses	$202,700.00
		Customs Court	salaries and expenses	$467,000.00
		Court of Claims	salaries and expenses	$613,800.00
			building repair and improvements	$3,700.00
		Other Courts and Services	Hawaii, salaries of justices and circuit judges	$120,000.00
			salaries of judges	$5,120,000.00
			salaries and expenses of clerks	$4,991,850.00
			probation system	$2,420,000.00
			salaries of criers	$600,000.00
			fees of commissioners	$543,000.00
			fees of jurors	$2,800,000.00
			miscellaneous salaries	$2,900,000.00
			miscellaneous expenses	$837,200.00
			traveling expenses	$715,000.00
			salaries of court reporters	$1,100,000.00
			Administrative Office of the U.S. Courts	$580,000.00
			repair and improvements, D.C. District Court	$7,100.00
			repair and improvements, U.S. Court of Appeals for D.C.	$3,700.00
			salaries of referees	$879,000.00
			expenses of referees	$1,165,000.00
		Total		$27,398,700.00

Statute (Citation)	Date Passed	Headings	Line-item Details	Appropriation
PL 83-11 (67 Stat. 8, 10)	March 28, 1953	Supreme Court of the United States	preparation of rules of civil procedure	$11,500.00
		Other Courts and Services	fees of commissioners	$107,000.00
			fees of jurors	$200,000.00
			miscellaneous salaries	$20,600.00
			salaries of court reporters	$15,700.00
			salaries of referees	$134,000.00
		Total		$488,800.00
PL 83-59 (67 Stat. 57, 59)	June 15, 1953	Other Courts and Services	fees of jurors	$350,000.00
		TOTAL APPROPRIATION		$28,237,500.00

1954

Statute (Citation)	Date Passed	Headings	Line-item Details	Appropriation
PL 83-178 (67 Stat. 318, 332)	August 1, 1953	Supreme Court of the United States	salaries of justices and all other officers and employees	$1,021,800.00
			printing and binding of Supreme Court reports	$91,200.00
			miscellaneous expenses	$48,950.00
			care of building and grounds	$174,100.00
		Court of Customs and Patent Appeals	salaries and expenses	$204,500.00
		Customs Court	salaries and expenses	$488,000.00
		Court of Claims	salaries and expenses	$618,000.00
			building repair and improvements	$15,600.00
		Courts of Appeals, District Courts, and Other Judicial Services	salaries of judges	$5,240,000.00
			salaries of supporting personnel	$12,369,970.00
			fees of jurors and commissioners	$3,675,000.00
			travel and miscellaneous expenses	$1,644,400.00
			Administrative Office of the U.S. Courts	$588,000.00
			salaries of referees	$1,058,750.00
			expenses of referees	$1,236,150.00
		Total		$28,474,420.00

Statute (Citation)	Date Passed	Headings	Appropriation	Line-item Details
PL 83-357 (68 Stat. 81, 84)	May 11, 1954	Courts of Appeals, District Courts, and Other Judicial Services	$115,000.00	fees of jurors and commissioners
			$36,000.00	travel and miscellaneous expenses
			$7,000.00	salaries of referees
			$71,600.00	expenses of referees
		Total	$229,600.00	
		TOTAL APPROPRIATION	$28,704,020.00	

1955

Statute (Citation)	Date Passed	Headings	Appropriation	Line-item Details
PL 83-470 (68 Stat. 396, 409)	July 2, 1954	Supreme Court of the United States	$1,016,000.00	salaries of justices and all other officers and employees
			$91,200.00	printing and binding Supreme Court reports
			$4,300.00	rules of civil procedure
			$52,650.00	miscellaneous expenses
			$338,300.00	care of building and grounds
		Court of Customs and Patent Appeals	$210,160.00	salaries and expenses
		Customs Court	$495,630.00	salaries and expenses
		Court of Claims	$618,000.00	salaries and expenses
			$8,000.00	building repair and improvements
			$5,472,500.00	salaries of judges
		Courts of Appeals, District Courts, and Other Judicial Services	$12,850,000.00	salaries of supporting personnel
			$3,950,000.00	fees of jurors and commissioners
			$1,800,000.00	travel and miscellaneous expenses
			$595,000.00	Administrative Office of the U.S. Courts
			$1,083,700.00	salaries of referees
			$1,443,550.00	expenses of referees
		Total	$30,028,990.00	

Statute (Citation)	Date Passed	Headings	Appropriation	Line-item Details
PL 83-663 (68 Stat. 800, 803)	August 26, 1954	Supreme Court of the United States	$5,835.00	automobile for Chief Justice
		Courts of Appeals, District Courts, and Other Judicial Services	$220,000.00	fees of jurors and commissioners, FY 1954
			$18,500.00	salaries of referees
		Total	$244,335.00	
PL 84-24 (69 Stat. 28, 36)	April 22, 1955	Supreme Court of the United States	$12,500.00	care of building and grounds
		Court of Customs and Patent Appeals	$13,300.00	salaries and expenses
		Courts of Appeals, District Courts, and Other Judicial Services	$900,000.00	salaries of judges
			$86,000.00	salaries of supporting personnel
			$380,000.00	fees of jurors and commissioners
			$45,000.00	travel and miscellaneous expenses
			$20,800.00	salaries of referees
			$34,575.00	expenses of referees
		Total	$1,492,175.00	
		TOTAL APPROPRIATION	$31,765,500.00	

1956

Statute (Citation)	Date Passed	Headings	Appropriation	Line-item Details
PL 84-133 (69 Stat. 264, 274)	July 7, 1955	Supreme Court of the United States	$1,022,400.00	salaries of justices and all other officers and employees
			$91,200.00	printing and binding Supreme Court reports
			$49,950.00	miscellaneous expenses
			$367,400.00	care of building and grounds
			$5,835.00	automobile for the chief justice
		Court of Customs and Patent Appeals	$235,755.00	salaries and expenses
		Customs Court	$598,270.00	salaries and expenses
		Court of Claims	$622,700.00	salaries and expenses
			$12,000.00	building repair and improvements

Public Law	Date	Court / Office	Amount	Purpose
		Courts of Appeals, District Courts, and Other Judicial Services	$5,728,000.00	salaries of judges
			$14,000,000.00	salaries of supporting personnel
			$4,500,000.00	fees of jurors and commissioners
			$2,276,750.00	travel and miscellaneous expenses
		Administrative Office of the U.S. Courts	$606,250.00	
			$1,151,400.00	salaries of referees
			$1,650,500.00	expenses of referees
		Total	$32,918,410.00	
PL 84-219 (69 Stat. 450, 464)	August 4, 1955	Supreme Court of the United States	$90,000.00	salaries
		Court of Customs and Patent Appeals	$40,000.00	salaries and expenses
		Customs Court	$67,500.00	salaries and expenses
		Court of Claims	$40,000.00	salaries and expenses
		Courts of Appeals, District Courts, and Other Judicial Services	$2,678,000.00	salaries of judges
			$70,000.00	salaries of referees
		Total	$2,985,500.00	
PL 84-533 (70 Stat. 161, 172)	May 19, 1956	Supreme Court of the United States	$900.00	miscellaneous expenses
		Courts of Appeals, District Courts, and Other Judicial Services	$225,000.00	travel and miscellaneous expenses
			$(225,000.00)	transfer from fees of jurors and commissioners to travel and miscellaneous expenses
			$8,375.00	salaries of referees
			$111,500.00	expenses of referees
		Increased Pay Costs		
		Supreme Court of the United States	$9,000.00	salaries
		Customs Court	$12,500.00	salaries and expenses

Headings	Appropriation	Line-item Details
Courts of Appeals, District Courts, and Other Judicial Services	$825,000.00	salaries of supporting personnel
	$36,500.00	Administrative Office of the U.S. Courts
Total	$1,003,775.00	
TOTAL APPROPRIATION	**$36,907,685.00**	

1957

Statute (Citation)	Date Passed	Headings	Appropriation	Line-item Details
PL 84-603 (70 Stat. 299, 308)	June 20, 1956	Supreme Court of the United States	$1,181,600.00	salaries of justices and all other officers and employees
			$91,200.00	printing and binding Supreme Court Reports
			$55,150.00	miscellaneous expenses
			$194,000.00	care of building and grounds
			$5,835.00	automobile for Chief Justice
		Court of Customs and Patent Appeals	$284,850.00	salaries and expenses
		Customs Court	$625,000.00	salaries and expenses
		Court of Claims	$693,000.00	salaries and expenses
			$9,000.00	building repair and improvements
		Courts of Appeals, District Courts, and Other Judicial Services	$8,406,000.00	salaries of judges
			$16,475,500.00	salaries of supporting personnel
			$4,250,000.00	fees of jurors and commissioners
			$2,721,800.00	travel and miscellaneous expenses
			$753,500.00	Administrative Office of the U.S. Courts
			$575,000.00	air conditioning for courtrooms
			$1,233,500.00	salaries of referees
			$1,874,200.00	expenses of referees
		Total	$39,429,135.00	

Statute (Citation)	Date Passed	Headings	Appropriation	Line-item Details
PL 84-814 (70 Stat. 678, 689)	July 27, 1956	Courts of Appeals, District Courts, and Other Judicial Services	$100,000.00	fees of jurors and commissioners, FY 1956
			$(100,000.00)	transfer from salaries of supporting personnel to fees of jurors and commissioners
		Total	$0	
		TOTAL APPROPRIATION	**$39,429,135.00**	

1958

Statute (Citation)	Date Passed	Headings	Appropriation	Line-item Details
PL 85-49 (71 Stat. 55, 64)	June 11, 1957	Supreme Court of the United States	$1,238,000.00	salaries of justices and all other officers and employees
			$90,000.00	printing and binding Supreme Court Reports
			$62,500.00	miscellaneous expenses
			$218,200.00	care of building and grounds
			$5,835.00	automobile for Chief Justice
		Court of Customs and Patent Appeals	$307,000.00	salaries and expenses
		Customs Court	$677,010.00	salaries and expenses
		Court of Claims	$810,855.00	salaries and expenses
			$9,000.00	building repair and improvements
		Courts of Appeals, District Courts, and Other Judicial Services	$8,800,000.00	salaries of judges
			$18,473,200.00	salaries of supporting personnel
			$4,250,000.00	fees of jurors and commissioners
			$2,780,000.00	travel and miscellaneous expenses
			$840,450.00	Administrative Office of the U.S. Courts
			$1,699,000.00	salaries of referees
			$2,199,700.00	expenses of referees
		Total	$42,460,750.00	
PL 85-58 (71 Stat. 176, 185)	June 21, 1957	Supreme Court of the United States	$7,500.00	care of building and grounds
supplemental, FY 1957		Court of Claims	$34,400.00	salaries and expenses

Statute (Citation)	Date Passed	Headings	Appropriation	Line-item Details
		Courts of Appeals, District Courts, and Other Judicial Services	$300,000.00	salaries of judges
			$(300,000.00)	transfer from salaries of supporting personnel to salaries of judges
			$160,000.00	fees of jurors and commissioners
			$253,000.00	salaries of referees
			$57,000.00	expenses of referees
		Total	$511,900.00	
PL 85-170 (71 Stat. 426, 436)	August 28, 1957	Courts of Appeals, District Courts, and Other Judicial Services	$10,000.00	salaries of referees
			$75,000.00	expenses of referees
supplemental, FY 1958		Total	$85,000.00	
PL 85-352 (72 Stat. 50, 59)	March 28, 1958	Courts of Appeals, District Courts, and Other Judicial Services	$275,000.00	salaries of judges
			$675,000.00	fees of jurors and commissioners
			$59,000.00	travel and miscellaneous expenses
			$46,000.00	salaries of referees
			$71,000.00	expenses of referees
		Total	$1,126,000.00	
		TOTAL APPROPRIATION	**$44,183,650.00**	

1959

Statute (Citation)	Date Passed	Headings	Appropriation	Line-item Details
PL 85-474 (72 Stat. 244, 253)	June 30, 1958	Supreme Court of the United States	$1,249,000.00	salaries of justices and all other officers and employees
			$90,000.00	printing and binding Supreme Court Reports
			$74,500.00	miscellaneous expenses
			$284,000.00	care of building and grounds
			$5,835.00	automobile for chief justice
		Court of Customs and Patent Appeals	$308,450.00	salaries and expenses

	Customs Court	$699,620.00	salaries and expenses
	Court of Claims	$812,655.00	salaries and expenses
		$9,000.00	building repair and improvements
	Courts of Appeals, District Courts, and Other Judicial Services	$9,358,500.00	salaries of judges
		$19,011,700.00	salaries of supporting personnel
		$4,995,000.00	fees of jurors and commissioners
		$2,975,000.00	travel and miscellaneous expenses
		$950,000.00	Administrative Office of the U.S. Courts
		$2,006,500.00	salaries of referees
		$2,625,550.00	expenses of referees
	Total	$45,455,310.00	
PL 86-30 (73 Stat. 33, 45) May 20, 1959 supplemental, FY 1959	Courts of Appeals, District Courts, and Other Judicial Services	$180,000.00	fees of jurors and commissioners
		$100,000.00	travel and miscellaneous expenses
		$91,000.00	Administrative Office of the U.S. Courts
		$(82,100.00)	transfer from judge's salaries, FY 1959
		$247,600.00	expenses of referees
	Increased Pay Costs Supreme Court of the United States	$70,000.00	salaries
		$7,200.00	care of building and grounds
		$465.00	automobile for the Chief Justice
	Customs Court	$38,680.00	salaries and expenses
	Court of Claims	$28,900.00	salaries and expenses
	Courts of Appeals, District Courts, and Other Judicial Services	$1,939,300.00	salaries of supporting personnel
		$(67,900.00)	transfer from salaries of judges to salaries of supporting personnel
	Total	$2,553,145.00	
	TOTAL APPROPRIATION	**$48,008,455.00**	

1960

Statute (Citation)	Date Passed	Headings	Appropriation	Line-item Details
PL 86-84 (73 Stat. 182, 190)	July 13, 1959	Supreme Court of the United States	$1,335,600.00	salaries of justices and all other officers and employees
			$90,000.00	printing and binding Supreme Court Reports
			$74,000.00	miscellaneous expenses
			$310,000.00	care of building and grounds
			$6,300.00	automobile for chief justice
		Court of Customs and Patent Appeals	$332,000.00	salaries and expenses
		Customs Court	$770,000.00	salaries and expenses
		Court of Claims	$875,000.00	salaries and expenses
			$9,500.00	building repair and improvements
		Courts of Appeals, District Courts, and Other Judicial Services	$9,128,000.00	salaries of judges
			$21,426,000.00	salaries of supporting personnel
			$4,620,000.00	fees of jurors and commissioners
			$3,250,000.00	travel and miscellaneous expenses
			$1,200,000.00	Administrative Office of the U.S. Courts
			$2,006,500.00	salaries of referees
			$3,000,000.00	expenses of referees
		Total	$48,432,900.00	
PL 86-213 (73 Stat. 437, 442) supplemental, FY 1960	September 1, 1959	Customs Court	$18,000.00	salaries and expenses
PL 86-424 (74 Stat. 42, 48) supplemental, FY 1960	April 13, 1960	Supreme Court of the United States	$37,400.00	care of building and grounds
		Courts of Appeals, District Courts, and Other Judicial Services	$57,000.00	salaries of judges
			$75,000.00	salaries of supporting personnel
			$200,000.00	fees of jurors and commissioners
			$250,000.00	travel and miscellaneous expenses

Federal Judiciary Appropriations: 1792–2010

1961

Statute (Citation)	Date Passed	Headings	Appropriation	Line-item Details
			$50,000.00	expenses of referees
		Total	$669,400.00	
		TOTAL APPROPRIATION	**$49,120,300.00**	
PL 86-678 (74 Stat. 555, 565)	August 31, 1960	Supreme Court of the United States	$1,370,000.00	salaries of justices and all other officers and employees
			$90,000.00	printing and binding Supreme Court Reports
			$69,800.00	miscellaneous expenses
			$287,200.00	care of building and grounds
			$6,365.00	automobile for Chief Justice
		Court of Customs and Patent Appeals	$343,000.00	salaries and expenses
		Customs Court	$799,260.00	salaries and expenses
		Court of Claims	$886,000.00	salaries and expenses
			$9,500.00	building repair and improvements
		Courts of Appeals, District Courts, and Other Judicial Services	$9,200,000.00	salaries of judges
			$22,085,000.00	salaries of supporting personnel
			$4,500,000.00	fees of jurors and commissioners
			$3,785,000.00	travel and miscellaneous expenses
			$1,292,940.00	Administrative Office of the U.S. Courts
			$2,125,000.00	salaries of referees
			$3,300,000.00	expenses of referees
		TOTAL APPROPRIATION	**$50,149,065.00**	

1962

Statute (Citation)	Date Passed	Headings	Appropriation	Line-item Details
PL 87-264 (75 Stat. 545, 554)	September 21, 1961	Supreme Court of the United States	$1,479,000.00	salaries of justices and all other officers and employees
			$92,000.00	printing and binding Supreme Court Reports
			$82,800.00	miscellaneous expenses

		$284,400.00	care of building and grounds
		$6,700.00	automobile for Chief Justice
	Court of Customs and Patent Appeals	$359,000.00	salaries and expenses
	Customs Court	$895,000.00	salaries and expenses
	Court of Claims	$955,000.00	salaries and expenses
		$9,500.00	building repair and improvements
	Courts of Appeals, District Courts, and Other Judicial Services	$9,200,000.00	salaries of judges
		$24,500,000.00	salaries of supporting personnel
		$4,500,000.00	fees of jurors and commissioners
		$4,407,500.00	travel and miscellaneous expenses
		$1,426,750.00	Administrative Office of the U.S. Courts
		$2,370,000.00	salaries of referees
		$4,210,000.00	expenses of referees
	Total	$54,777,650.00	
PL 87-332 (75 Stat. 733, 746) supplemental, FY 1962	September 30, 1961		
	Courts of Appeals, District Courts, and Other Judicial Services	$900,000.00	salaries of judges
		$1,145,000.00	salaries of supporting personnel
		$920,000.00	travel and miscellaneous expenses
		$15,000.00	Administrative Office of the U.S. Courts
		$135,000.00	fees of jurors and commissioners, FY 1961
	Total	$3,115,000.00	
PL 87-545 (76 Stat. 209, 214) supplemental, FY 1962	July 25, 1962		
	Supreme Court of the United States	$13,000.00	printing and binding Supreme Court Reports
	Courts of Appeals, District Courts, and Other Judicial Services	$300,000.00	fees of jurors and commissioners
		$110,000.00	travel and miscellaneous expenses
		$100,000.00	expenses of referees
	Total	$523,000.00	
	TOTAL APPROPRIATION	**$55,315,650.00**	

1963

Statute (Citation)	Date Passed	Headings	Appropriation	Line-item Details
PL 87-843 (76 Stat. 1080, 1097)	October 18, 1962	Supreme Court of the United States	$1,494,000.00	salaries of justices and all other officers and employees
			$108,000.00	printing and binding Supreme Court Reports
			$79,000.00	miscellaneous expenses
			$323,400.00	care of building and grounds
			$6,800.00	automobile for Chief Justice
			$35,000.00	books
		Court of Customs and Patent Appeals	$361,000.00	salaries and expenses
		Customs Court	$919,000.00	salaries and expenses
		Court of Claims	$1,025,000.00	salaries and expenses
			$9,500.00	building repair and improvements
		Courts of Appeals, District Courts, and Other Judicial Services	$10,860,000.00	salaries of judges
			$27,000,000.00	salaries of supporting personnel
			$5,800,000.00	fees of jurors and commissioners
			$4,600,000.00	travel and miscellaneous expenses
			$1,500,000.00	Administrative Office of the U.S. Courts
			$2,600,000.00	salaries of referees
			$4,850,000.00	expenses of referees
		Total	$61,570,700.00	
PL 88-25 (77 Stat. 20, 29)	May 17, 1963	Supreme Court of the United States	$30,000.00	printing and binding Supreme Court Reports
		Courts of Appeals, District Courts, and Other Judicial Services	$188,341.00	salaries of judges
supplemental, FY 1963		Increased Pay Costs	$70,000.00	travel and miscellaneous expenses
		Supreme Court of the United States	$9,000.00	salaries

Headings	Appropriation	Line-item Details
Court of Customs and Patent Appeals	$8,550.00	salaries
Customs Court	$12,350.00	salaries
Court of Claims	$9,500.00	salaries
Courts of Appeals, District Courts, and Other Judicial Services	$988,000.00	salaries of supporting personnel
Administrative Office	$30,000.00	Administrative Office
	$47,500.00	expenses of referees
	$(47,500.00)	transfer from salaries of referees to expenses of referees
Total	$1,345,741.00	
TOTAL APPROPRIATION	**$62,916,441.00**	

1964

Statute (Citation)	Date Passed	Headings	Appropriation	Line-item Details
PL 88-245 (77 Stat. 776, 793)	December 30, 1963	Supreme Court of the United States	$1,588,000.00	salaries of justices and all other officers and employees
			$138,000.00	printing and binding Supreme Court Reports
			$85,000.00	miscellaneous expenses
			$348,000.00	care of building and grounds
			$7,400.00	automobile for Chief Justice
			$35,000.00	books
		Court of Customs and Patent Appeals	$388,000.00	salaries and expenses
		Customs Court	$989,000.00	salaries and expenses
		Court of Claims	$1,100,000.00	salaries and expenses
			$9,500.00	building repair and improvements
		Courts of Appeals, District Courts, and Other Judicial Services	$11,200,000.00	salaries of judges
			$30,650,000.00	salaries of supporting personnel
			$5,500,000.00	fees of jurors and commissioners
			$4,500,000.00	travel and miscellaneous expenses
			$1,590,000.00	Administrative Office of the U.S. Courts

Statute (Citation)	Date Passed	Headings	Appropriation	Line-item Details
			$2,550,000.00	salaries of referees
			$5,250,000.00	expenses of referees
		Total	$65,927,900.00	
PL 88-317 (78 Stat. 204, 212)	June 9, 1964	Supreme Court of the United States	$6,900.00	care of building and grounds
		TOTAL APPROPRIATION	$65,934,800.00	

1965

Statute (Citation)	Date Passed	Headings	Appropriation	Line-item Details
PL 88-527 (78 Stat. 711, 728)	August 31, 1964	Supreme Court of the United States	$1,815,000.00	salaries of justices and all other officers and employees
			$138,000.00	printing and binding Supreme Court Reports
			$120,000.00	miscellaneous expenses
			$304,600.00	care of building and grounds
			$8,100.00	automobile for Chief Justice
			$35,000.00	books
		Court of Customs and Patent Appeals	$397,600.00	salaries and expenses
		Customs Court	$1,028,000.00	salaries and expenses
		Court of Claims	$1,140,000.00	salaries and expenses
		Courts of Appeals, District Courts, and Other Judicial Services	$11,100,000.00	salaries of judges
			$32,445,000.00	salaries of supporting personnel
			$5,500,000.00	fees of jurors and commissioners
			$4,710,000.00	travel and miscellaneous expenses
			$1,619,500.00	Administrative Office of the U.S. Courts
			$2,670,000.00	salaries of referees
			$5,750,000.00	expenses of referees
		Total	$68,780,800.00	

Statute (Citation)	Date Passed	Headings	Appropriation	Line-item Details
PL 89-16 (79 Stat. 81, 91)	April 30, 1965	Courts of Appeals, District Courts, and Other Judicial Services	$250,000.00	fees of jurors and commissioners
supplemental, FY 1965		Increased Pay Costs		
		Supreme Court of the United States	$79,000.00	salaries
			$400.00	automobile for Chief Justice
		Court of Customs and Patent Appeals	$43,000.00	salaries
		Customs Court	$91,000.00	salaries
		Court of Claims	$132,000.00	salaries
		Courts of Appeals, District Courts, and Other Judicial Services	$3,400,000.00	salaries of judges
			$1,105,000.00	salaries of supporting personnel
			$81,500.00	Administrative Office of the U.S. Courts
			$1,230,000.00	salaries of referees
			$205,000.00	expense of referees
		Total	$6,616,900.00	
		TOTAL APPROPRIATION	$75,397,700.00	

1966

Statute (Citation)	Date Passed	Headings	Appropriation	Line-item Details
PL 89-164 (79 Stat. 620, 636)	September 2, 1965	Supreme Court of the United States	$1,925,000.00	salaries of justices and all other officers and employees
			$138,000.00	printing and binding Supreme Court Reports
			$120,000.00	miscellaneous expenses
			$314,000.00	care of building and grounds
			$8,500.00	automobile for Chief Justice
			$38,000.00	books
		Court of Customs and Patent Appeals	$450,000.00	salaries and expenses
		Customs Court	$1,159,400.00	salaries and expenses
		Court of Claims	$1,300,000.00	salaries and expenses

Reference	Date	Court/Service	Purpose	Amount
		Courts of Appeals, District Courts, and Other Judicial Services	salaries of judges	$14,500,000.00
			salaries of supporting personnel	$34,292,000.00
			fees and expenses of court-appointed counsel	$3,000,000.00
			fees of jurors and commissioners	$6,000,000.00
			travel and miscellaneous expenses	$4,910,000.00
			Administrative Office of the U.S. Courts	$1,800,000.00
			salaries of referees	$4,314,000.00
			expenses of referees	$6,425,000.00
		Total		$80,693,900.00
PL 89–426 (80 Stat. 141, 149)	May 13, 1966	Courts of Appeals, District Courts, and Other Judicial Services	salaries of judges	$200,000.00
		Increased Pay Costs	fees of jurors and commissioners	$1,165,000.00
		Supreme Court of the United States	salaries	$41,000.00
		Court of Customs and Patent Appeals	care of building and grounds	$5,000.00
			salaries and expenses	$5,000.00
		Customs Court	salaries and expenses	$19,000.00
		Court of Claims	salaries and expenses	$13,300.00
		Courts of Appeals, District Courts, and Other Judicial Services	salaries of supporting personnel	$818,000.00
			Administrative Office of the U.S. Courts	$31,000.00
			expenses of referees	$125,000.00
		Total		$2,422,300.00
		TOTAL APPROPRIATION		**$83,116,200.00**

1967

Statute (Citation)	Date Passed	Headings	Appropriation	Line-item Details
PL 89-797 (80 Stat. 1479, 1497)	November 8, 1966	Supreme Court of the United States	$2,000,000.00	salaries of justices and all other officers and employees
			$138,000.00	printing and binding Supreme Court Reports
			$120,000.00	miscellaneous expenses
			$318,700.00	care of building and grounds
			$8,900.00	automobile for Chief Justice
			$38,000.00	books
		Court of Customs and Patent Appeals	$465,000.00	salaries and expenses
		Customs Court	$1,265,000.00	salaries and expenses
		Court of Claims	$1,425,000.00	salaries and expenses
		Courts of Appeals, District Courts, and Other Judicial Services	$15,857,000.00	salaries of judges
			$37,350,000.00	salaries of supporting personnel
			$3,000,000.00	fees and expenses of court-appointed counsel
			$7,700,000.00	fees of jurors and commissioners
			$6,000,000.00	travel and miscellaneous expenses
			$1,910,000.00	Administrative Office of the U.S. Courts
			$4,314,000.00	salaries of referees
			$6,760,000.00	expenses of referees
		Total	$88,669,600.00	
PL 90-21 (81 Stat. 30, 44)	May 29, 1967	Increased Pay Costs		
		Supreme Court of the United States	$5,600.00	care of building and grounds
		Court of Customs and Patent Appeals	$6,000.00	salaries and expenses
		Court of Claims	$15,000.00	salaries and expenses
		Courts of Appeals, District Courts, and Other Judicial Services	$940,000.00	salaries of supporting personnel
			$40,000.00	Administrative Office

1968

Statute (Citation)	Date Passed	Headings	Appropriation	Line-item Details
			$4,500.00	salaries of referees
			$170,000.00	expenses of referees
		Total	$1,181,100.00	
		TOTAL APPROPRIATION	**$89,850,700.00**	
PL 90-133 (81 Stat. 410, 426)	November 8, 1967	Supreme Court of the United States	$2,031,500.00	salaries of justices and all other officers and employees
			$155,000.00	printing and binding Supreme Court Reports
			$120,000.00	miscellaneous expenses
			$327,500.00	care of building and grounds
			$9,100.00	automobile for Chief Justice
			$40,000.00	books
		Court of Customs and Patent Appeals	$483,000.00	salaries and expenses
		Customs Court	$1,480,000.00	salaries and expenses
		Court of Claims	$1,500,000.00	salaries and expenses
		Courts of Appeals, District Courts, and Other Judicial Services	$16,300,000.00	salaries of judges
			$40,490,000.00	salaries of supporting personnel
			$3,150,000.00	fees and expenses of court-appointed counsel
			$7,800,000.00	fees of jurors and commissioners
			$6,113,000.00	travel and miscellaneous expenses
			$2,074,000.00	Administrative Office of the U.S. Courts
			$4,514,000.00	salaries of referees
			$7,360,000.00	expenses of referees
		Total	$93,947,100.00	
PL 90-392 (82 Stat. 307, 319)	July 9, 1968	Courts of Appeals, District Courts, and Other Judicial Services	$180,000.00	salaries for judges
		Federal Judicial Center	$350,000.00	fees for jurors and commissioners
			$40,000.00	salaries and expenses

Increased Pay Costs

Heading	Line-item Details	Appropriation
Supreme Court of the United States	care of building and grounds	$6,900.00
Court of Claims	salaries and expenses	$20,000.00
Courts of Appeals, District Courts, and Other Judicial Services	salaries of supporting personnel	$660,000.00
	expenses of referees	$60,000.00
Total		$1,316,900.00
TOTAL APPROPRIATION		**$95,264,000.00**

1969

Statute (Citation)	Date Passed	Headings	Appropriation	Line-item Details
PL 90-470 (82 Stat. 667, 683)	August 9, 1968	Supreme Court of the United States	$2,110,000.00	salaries of justices and all other officers and employees
			$155,000.00	printing and binding Supreme Court Reports
			$140,000.00	miscellaneous expenses
			$345,500.00	care of building and grounds
			$9,500.00	automobile for Chief Justice
			$40,000.00	books
		Court of Customs and Patent Appeals	$505,000.00	salaries and expenses
		Customs Court	$1,600,000.00	salaries and expenses
		Court of Claims	$1,595,000.00	salaries and expenses
		Courts of Appeals, District Courts, and Other Judicial Services	$16,795,000.00	salaries of judges
			$43,500,000.00	salaries of supporting personnel
			$3,150,000.00	fees and expenses of court-appointed counsel
			$11,900,000.00	fees of jurors and commissioners
			$6,450,000.00	travel and miscellaneous expenses
			$1,846,500.00	Administrative Office of the U.S. Courts
			$4,588,000.00	salaries of referees
			$8,200,000.00	expenses of referees
		Federal Judicial Center	$300,000.00	salaries and expenses
		Total	$103,229,500.00	

Statute (Citation)	Date Passed	Headings	Appropriation	Line-item Details
PL 91-47 (83 Stat. 49, 61) supplemental, FY 1969	July 22, 1969	Supreme Court of the United States	$27,000.00	printing and binding Supreme Court Reports
			$10,000.00	printing and binding Supreme Court Reports, FY 1968
		Customs Court	$113,000.00	salaries and expenses
		Courts of Appeals, District Courts, and Other Judicial Services	$1,948,000.00	salaries of judges
			$2,412,000.00	salaries of support personnel
			$850,000.00	court-appointed counsel, FY 1968
			$850,000.00	court-appointed counsel, FY 1969
			$400,000.00	travel and miscellaneous expenses
			$97,500.00	Administrative Office of the U.S. Courts
			$10,000.00	Administrative Office of the U.S. Courts
			$(10,000.00)	transfer from expenses of referees to Administrative Office
		Increased Pay Costs		
		Supreme Court of the United States	$120,000.00	salaries
			$15,900.00	care of building and grounds
		Court of Customs and Patent Appeals	$16,000.00	salaries and expenses
		Court of Claims	$64,000.00	salaries and expenses
		Courts of Appeals, District Courts, and Other Judicial Services	$248,000.00	salaries of referees
			$404,000.00	expenses of referees
		Total	$7,575,400.00	
		TOTAL APPROPRIATION	$110,804,900.00	

1970

Statute (Citation)	Date Passed	Headings	Appropriation	Line-item Details
PL 91-153 (83 Stat. 403, 418)	December 24, 1969	Supreme Court of the United States	$2,535,000.00	salaries of justices and all other officers and employees
			$195,000.00	printing and binding Supreme Court Reports
			$164,000.00	miscellaneous expenses
			$388,300.00	care of building and grounds

			automobile for Chief Justice	$9,900.00
			books	$40,000.00
	Court of Customs and Patent Appeals		salaries and expenses	$577,000.00
	Customs Court		salaries and expenses	$1,870,000.00
	Court of Claims		salaries and expenses	$1,872,000.00
	Courts of Appeals, District Courts, and Other Judicial Services		salaries of judges	$22,765,000.00
			salaries of supporting personnel	$47,957,000.00
			fees and expenses of court-appointed counsel	$3,150,000.00
			fees of jurors and commissioners	$15,000,000.00
			travel and miscellaneous expenses	$7,000,000.00
			Administrative Office of the U.S. Courts	$2,050,000.00
			salaries of referees	$6,203,000.00
			expenses of referees	$8,650,000.00
	Federal Judicial Center		salaries and expenses	$600,000.00
	Total			$121,026,200.00
PL 91-305 (84 Stat. 376, 384)	July 6, 1970	Customs Court	salaries and expenses	$18,000.00
		Courts of Appeals, District Courts, and Other Judicial Services	salaries and expenses, U.S. magistrates	$550,000.00
			court-appointed counsel	$1,150,000.00
			court-appointed counsel, FY 1969	$300,000.00
			fees of jurors and commissioners	$500,000.00
			travel and miscellaneous expenses	$500,000.00
			Administrative Office of the U.S. Courts	$15,000.00
		Increased Pay Costs		
		Supreme Court of the United States	salaries	$194,000.00
			care of building and grounds	$21,700.00
		Court of Customs and Patent Appeals	salaries	$22,000.00
		Customs Court	salaries	$128,500.00

Statute (Citation)	Date Passed	Headings	Appropriation	Line-item Details
		Courts of Appeals, District Courts, and Other Judicial Services	$4,370,000.00	salaries of supporting personnel
			$190,000.00	Administrative Office of the U.S. Courts
			$(20,000.00)	transfer from expenses of referees to Administrative Office
			$608,000.00	expenses of referees
		Total	$8,547,200.00	
		TOTAL APPROPRIATION	**$129,573,400.00**	

1971

Statute (Citation)	Date Passed	Headings	Appropriation	Line-item Details
PL 91-472 (84 Stat. 1040, 1055)	October 21, 1970	Supreme Court of the United States	$2,943,500.00	salaries of justices and all other officers and employees
			$215,000.00	printing and binding Supreme Court Reports
			$224,000.00	miscellaneous expenses
			$462,000.00	care of building and grounds
			$11,000.00	automobile for Chief Justice
			$46,000.00	books
		Court of Customs and Patent Appeals	$615,000.00	salaries and expenses
		Customs Court	$2,128,800.00	salaries and expenses
		Court of Claims	$1,941,000.00	salaries and expenses
		Courts of Appeals, District Courts, and Other Judicial Services	$22,975,000.00	salaries of judges
			$53,862,000.00	salaries of supporting personnel
			$4,300,000.00	fees and expenses of court-appointed counsel
			$14,930,000.00	fees of jurors
			$7,950,000.00	travel and miscellaneous expenses
			$2,375,000.00	Administrative Office of the U.S. Courts
			$4,560,000.00	salaries and expenses, U.S. magistrates
			$6,232,000.00	salaries of referees
			$9,400,000.00	expenses of referees
		Federal Judicial Center	$700,000.00	salaries and expenses
		Total	$135,870,300.00	

PL 91-665 (84 Stat. 1981, 1994) supplemental, FY 1971	January 8, 1971	Supreme Court of the United States	salaries	$54,000.00
			printing and binding Supreme Court Reports, FY 1970	$20,000.00
			printing and binding Supreme Court Reports	$63,000.00
			care of building and grounds	$25,000.00
			salaries of judges	$1,400,000.00
		Courts of Appeals, District Courts, and Other Judicial Services	salaries of supporting personnel	$1,900,000.00
			fees and expenses of court-appointed counsel	$5,700,000.00
			fees of jurors	$1,000,000.00
			travel and miscellaneous expenses	$1,360,000.00
			Administrative Office of the U.S. Courts	$70,000.00
		Commission on Bankruptcy Laws	salaries and expenses, derived from Referee's Salary and Expense Fund	$400,000.00
		Total		$11,992,000.00
PL 92-18 (85 Stat. 40, 57) supplemental, FY 1971	May 25, 1971	Increased Pay Costs		
		Supreme Court of the United States	salaries	$189,000.00
			care of building and grounds	$15,000.00
			automobile for the Chief Justice	$800.00
		Court of Customs and Patent Appeals	salaries and expenses	$32,000.00
		Customs Court	salaries and expenses	$146,000.00
		Court of Claims	salaries and expenses	$78,000.00
		Courts of Appeals, District Courts, and Other Judicial Services	salaries of judges	$25,000.00
			salaries of supporting personnel	$4,437,000.00
			Administrative Office of the U.S. Courts	$190,000.00
			salaries of referees	$10,000.00
			expenses of referees	$700,000.00
		Total		$5,822,800.00
		TOTAL APPROPRIATION		**$153,685,100.00**

1972

Statute (Citation)	Date Passed	Headings	Appropriation	Line-item Details
PL 92-77 (85 Stat. 245, 261)	August 10, 1971	Supreme Court of the United States	$3,482,000.00	salaries of justices and all other officers and employees
			$317,000.00	printing and binding Supreme Court Reports
			$318,000.00	miscellaneous expenses
			$13,400.00	automobile for Chief Justice
			$49,000.00	books
			$547,600.00	care of building and grounds
		Court of Customs and Patent Appeals	$664,000.00	salaries and expenses
		Customs Court	$2,355,000.00	salaries and expenses
		Court of Claims	$2,087,000.00	salaries and expenses
		Courts of Appeals, District Courts, and Other Judicial Services	$25,643,000.00	salaries of judges
			$68,654,000.00	salaries of supporting personnel
			$12,000,000.00	court-appointed counsel and operation of defender organizations
			$15,930,000.00	fees of jurors
			$9,600,000.00	travel and miscellaneous expenses
			$3,125,000.00	Administrative Office of the U.S. Courts
			$5,700,000.00	salaries and expenses, U.S. magistrates
			$6,416,000.00	salaries of referees
			$11,375,000.00	expenses of referees
		Federal Judicial Center	$1,255,000.00	salaries and expenses
		Total	$169,531,000.00	
PL 92-306 (86 Stat. 163, 172)	May 27, 1972	Supreme Court of the United States	$750.00	miscellaneous expenses
		Courts of Appeals, District Courts, and Other Judicial Services	$500,000.00	additional funds for retired judges
			$2,500,000.00	court-appointed counsel and operation of defender organizations
			$2,200,000.00	fees of jurors

Headings	Appropriation	Line-item Details
Increased Pay Costs		
Supreme Court of the United States	$13,000.00	care of building and grounds
Courts of Appeals, District Courts, and Other Judicial Services	$1,200,000.00	salaries of supporting personnel
	$40,000.00	Administrative Office of the U.S. Courts
	$120,000.00	expenses of referees
Total	$6,573,750.00	
TOTAL APPROPRIATION	**$176,104,750.00**	

1973

Statute (Citation)	Date Passed	Headings	Appropriation	Line-item Details
PL 92-544 (86 Stat. 1109, 1124)	October 25, 1972	Supreme Court of the United States	$3,784,000.00	salaries of justices and all other officers and employees
			$355,000.00	printing and binding Supreme Court Reports
			$423,000.00	miscellaneous expenses
			$14,600.00	automobile for Chief Justice
			$55,000.00	books
			$1,000,000.00	care of building and grounds
		Court of Customs and Patent Appeals	$684,000.00	salaries and expenses
		Customs Court	$2,341,000.00	salaries and expenses
		Court of Claims	$2,139,000.00	salaries and expenses
		Courts of Appeals, District Courts, and Other Judicial Services	$26,500,000.00	salaries of judges
			$76,008,000.00	salaries of supporting personnel
			$14,500,000.00	court-appointed counsel and operation of defender organizations
			$18,500,000.00	fees of jurors
			$10,626,000.00	travel and miscellaneous expenses
			$3,600,000.00	Administrative Office of the U.S. Courts
			$6,258,000.00	salaries and expenses, U.S. magistrates
			$6,991,000.00	salaries of referees
			$12,660,000.00	expenses of referees
		Federal Judicial Center	$1,544,000.00	salaries and expenses

Statute (Citation)	Date Passed	Headings	Appropriation	Line-item Details
PL 92-607 (86 Stat. 1498, 1516)	October 31, 1972	Commission on Bankruptcy Laws	$426,000.00	salaries and expenses
		Total	$188,408,600.00	
PL 93-50 (87 Stat. 113)	July 1, 1973	Courts of Appeals, District Courts, and Other Judicial Services	$432,000.00	salaries and expenses, U.S. magistrates
		Supreme Court of the United States	$61,000.00	printing and binding Supreme Court Reports
		Courts of Appeals, District Courts, and Other Judicial Services	$26,000.00	printing and binding, FY 1972
			$500,000.00	salaries of judges
			$2,972,000.00	court-appointed counsel and operation of defender organizations
		Comm. on Revision of Appellate System	$255,000.00	
		Increased Pay Costs		
		Supreme Court of the United States	$14,000.00	care of building and grounds
		Courts of Appeals, District Courts, and Other Judicial Services	$1,200,000.00	salaries of supporting personnel
			$(200,000.00)	transfer from fees of jurors to salaries of supporting personnel
			$82,000.00	Administrative Office of the U.S. Courts
			$(82,000.00)	transfer from fees of jurors to Administrative Office
			$236,000.00	expenses of referees
			$(236,000.00)	transfer from salaries of referees to expenses of referees
		Total	$4,828,000.00	
		TOTAL APPROPRIATION	$193,668,600.00	

1974

Statute (Citation)	Date Passed	Headings	Appropriation	Line-item Details
PL 93-162 (87 Stat. 636, 650)	November 27, 1973	Supreme Court of the United States	$3,964,000.00	salaries of justices and all other officers and employees
			$515,000.00	printing and binding Supreme Court Reports
			$560,000.00	miscellaneous expenses

Federal Judiciary Appropriations: 1792–2010

Public Law	Date	Court	Amount	Purpose
			$15,000.00	automobile for Chief Justice
			$63,000.00	books
			$1,100,000.00	care of building and grounds
		Court of Customs and Patent Appeals	$677,000.00	salaries and expenses
		Customs Court	$2,341,000.00	salaries and expenses
		Court of Claims	$2,154,000.00	salaries and expenses
		Courts of Appeals, District Courts, and Other Judicial Services	$27,300,000.00	salaries of judges
			$83,450,000.00	salaries of supporting personnel
			$16,500,000.00	court-appointed counsel and operation of defender organizations
			$18,500,000.00	fees of jurors
			$12,909,000.00	travel and miscellaneous expenses
			$3,906,000.00	Administrative Office of the U.S. Courts
			$7,837,000.00	salaries and expenses, U.S. magistrates
			$6,991,000.00	salaries of referees
			$12,660,000.00	expenses of referees
		Federal Judicial Center	$2,000,000.00	salaries and expenses
		Total	$203,442,000.00	
PL 93-245 (87 Stat. 1082)	January 3, 1974	Supreme Court of the United States	$45,000.00	miscellaneous expenses
			$377,000.00	care of building and grounds
		Total	$422,000.00	
PL 93-305 (88 Stat. 195, 209, 215)	June 8, 1974	Courts of Appeals, District Courts, and Other Judicial Services Increased Pay Costs	$2,000,000.00	court-appointed counsel and operation of defender organizations
		Supreme Court of the United States	$190,000.00	salaries
			$1,000.00	automobile for Chief Justice
			$16,300.00	care of building and grounds
		Customs Court	$83,000.00	salaries and expenses
		Court of Claims	$40,000.00	salaries and expenses
		Courts of Appeals, District Courts, and Other Judicial Services	$6,550,000.00	salaries of supporting personnel

Headings	Appropriation	Line-item Details
	$175,000.00	court-appointed counsel and operation of defender organizations
	$302,000.00	Administrative Office of the U.S. Courts
	$640,000.00	expenses of referees
Federal Judicial Center	$73,000.00	salaries and expenses
Total	$10,070,300.00	
TOTAL APPROPRIATION	**$213,934,300.00**	

1975

Statute (Citation)	Date Passed	Headings	Appropriation	Line-item Details
PL 93-433 (88 Stat. 1187, 1200)	October 5, 1974	Supreme Court of the United States	$4,450,000.00	salaries of justices and all other officers and employees
			$565,000.00	printing and binding Supreme Court Reports
			$642,000.00	miscellaneous expenses
			$687,300.00	care of building and grounds
			$16,300.00	automobile for Chief Justice
			$63,000.00	books
		Court of Customs and Patent Appeals	$782,000.00	salaries and expenses
		Customs Court	$2,479,000.00	salaries and expenses
		Court of Claims	$2,341,000.00	salaries and expenses
		Courts of Appeals, District Courts, and Other Judicial Services	$27,975,000.00	salaries of judges
			$101,822,000.00	salaries of supporting personnel
			$15,700,000.00	court-appointed counsel and operation of defender organizations
			$18,500,000.00	fees of jurors
			$15,100,000.00	travel and miscellaneous expenses
			$5,090,000.00	Administrative Office of the U.S. Courts
			$8,764,000.00	salaries and expenses, U.S. magistrates
			$6,990,000.00	salaries of referees
			$14,000,000.00	expenses of referees
		Federal Judicial Center	$2,400,000.00	salaries and expenses
		Space and Facilities, the Judiciary	$66,100,000.00	rent of space, tenant alterations, etc.
		Expenses, U.S. Court Facilities	$2,675,000.00	furniture and furnishings
		Total	$297,141,600.00	

PL 93-544 (88 Stat. 1771, 1779)	December 27, 1974	Supreme Court of the United States	$258,500.00	care of building and grounds
		Commission on Revision of Appellate System	$351,000.00	expenses
		Total	$609,500.00	
PL 94-32 (89 Stat. 173, 189)	June 12, 1975	Court of Appeals, District Courts	$112,000.00	Administrative Office of the U.S. Courts
			$(112,000.00)	transfer from space and facilities to Administrative Office
			$52,000.00	expenses of referees
			$2,500,000.00	speedy trial planning
			$10,000,000.00	pretrial services agencies
		Federal Judicial Center	$1,020,000.00	salaries and expenses
			$(1,020,000.00)	transfer from fees of jurors to salaries and expenses
		Expenses, U.S. Court Facilities	$1,200,000.00	furniture and furnishings
			$(1,200,000.00)	transfer from space and facilities to furniture and furnishings
		Increased Pay Costs Supreme Court of the United States	$155,000.00	salaries
			$500.00	automobile for Chief Justice
			$58,300.00	care of building and grounds
		Courts of Appeals, District Courts, and Other Judicial Services	$1,982,000.00	supporting personnel
			$(1,982,000.00)	transfer from space and facilities to supporting personnel
			$126,000.00	court-appointed counsel
			$(126,000.00)	transfer from space and facilities to court-appointed counsel
			$180,000.00	Administrative Office of the U.S. Courts
			$(180,000.00)	transfer from space and facilities to Administrative Office
			$538,000.00	expenses of referees
		Federal Judicial Center	$30,000.00	salaries and expenses
			$(30,000.00)	transfer from fees for jurors to Federal Judicial Center
		Total	$13,303,800.00	
		TOTAL APPROPRIATION	**$311,054,900.00**	

1976

Statute (Citation)	Date Passed	Headings	Appropriation	Line-item Details
PL 94-121 (89 Stat. 611, 629)	October 21, 1975	Supreme Court of the United States	$5,056,000.00	salaries of justices and all other officers and employees
			$1,314,000.00	salaries, July 1 to September 30, 1976
			$706,000.00	printing and binding Supreme Court Reports
			$737,000.00	miscellaneous expenses
			$178,000.00	miscellaneous expenses, July 1 to September 30, 1976
			$19,000.00	automobile for Chief Justice
			$4,700.00	automobile, July 1 to September 30, 1976
			$63,000.00	books
			$15,800.00	books, July 1 to September 30, 1976
			$1,429,000.00	care of building and grounds
			$195,500.00	care of building, July 1 to September 30, 1976
		Court of Customs and Patent Appeals	$853,000.00	salaries and expenses
			$213,000.00	salaries and expenses, July 1 to September 30, 1976
		Customs Court	$2,587,000.00	salaries and expenses
			$645,000.00	salaries and expenses, July 1 to September 30, 1976
		Court of Claims	$2,429,000.00	salaries and expenses
			$597,000.00	salaries and expenses, July 1 to September 30, 1976
		Courts of Appeals, District Courts, and Other Judicial Services	$28,750,000.00	salaries of judges
			$7,230,000.00	salaries of judges, July 1 to September 30, 1976
			$117,075,000.00	salaries of supporting personnel
			$29,700,000.00	salaries of supporting personnel, July 1 to September 30, 1976
			$16,590,000.00	court-appointed counsel and operation of defender organizations
			$4,148,000.00	court-appointed counsel, July 1 to September 30, 1976
			$18,000,000.00	fees of jurors
			$4,500,000.00	fees of jurors, July 1 to September 30, 1976
			$20,040,000.00	travel and miscellaneous expenses
			$4,883,000.00	travel and miscellaneous expenses, July 1 to September 30, 1976
			$10,510,000.00	salaries and expenses, U.S. magistrates

Public Law / Date	Category	Amount	Purpose
		$2,594,000.00	U.S. magistrates, July 1 to September 30, 1976
		$24,096,000.00	salaries and expenses of referees, with $600,000 transferred to Administrative Office for administration expenses of bankruptcy system
		$6,008,000.00	salaries and expenses of referees, July 1 to September 30, 1976, with $150,000 transferred to Administrative Office for administration expenses of bankruptcy system
	Administrative Office of the U.S. Courts	$7,233,000.00	salaries and expenses
	Federal Judicial Center	$1,823,000.00	salaries and expenses, July 1 to September 30, 1976
		$6,565,000.00	salaries and expenses
	Space and Facilities	$1,721,000.00	salaries and expenses, July 1 to September 30, 1976
		$64,000,000.00	rent of space, tenant alterations, etc.
		$16,000,000.00	rent of space, July 1 to September 30, 1976
	Expenses, U.S. Court Facilities	$4,570,000.00	furniture and furnishings
		$425,000.00	furniture and furnishings, July 1 to September 30, 1976
	Bicentennial Expenses	$2,000,000.00	
	Total	$415,503,000.00	
PL 94-157 (89 Stat. 826, 838) December 18, 1975	Courts of Appeals, District Courts, and Other Judicial Services	$4,100,000.00	court-appointed counsel and operation of defender organizations
		$575,000.00	court-appointed counsel, July 1 to September 30, 1976
		$404,000.00	salaries and expenses, U.S. magistrates
		$151,000.00	U.S. magistrates, July 1 to September 30, 1976
		$1,466,000.00	salaries and expenses of referees
		$661,000.00	salaries and expenses of referees, July 1 to September 30, 1976
	Total	$7,357,000.00	
PL 94-303 (90 Stat. 597, 622) June 1, 1976	Courts of Appeals, District Courts, and Other Judicial Services	$2,000,000.00	fees of jurors
		$500,000.00	fees of jurors, July 1 to September 30, 1976
		$313,000.00	salaries and expenses of referees
		$235,000.00	salaries and expenses of referees, July 1 to September 30, 1976
	Increased Pay Costs		
	Supreme Court of the United States	$500.00	automobile for chief justice
		$25,000.00	care of building and grounds

Headings	Appropriation	Line-item Details
Customs Court	$42,500.00	salaries and expenses
Court of Claims	$25,000.00	salaries and expenses
Courts of Appeals, District Courts, and Other Judicial Services	$2,400,000.00	salaries of supporting personnel
	$156,000.00	court-appointed counsel and operation of defender organizations
	$796,000.00	salaries and expenses of referees
Administrative Office of the U.S. Courts	$198,000.00	salaries and expenses
Increased Pay Costs		
Supreme Court of the United States	$63,000.00	salaries, July 1 to September 30, 1976
	$200.00	automobile for Chief Justice, July 1 to September 30, 1976
Court of Customs and Patent Appeals	$11,000.00	salaries and expenses, July 1 to September 30, 1976
Customs Court	$32,500.00	Customs Court, July 1 to September 30, 1976
Court of Claims	$26,000.00	Court of Claims, July 1 to September 30, 1976
Courts of Appeals, District Courts, and Other Judicial Services	$1,498,000.00	supporting personnel, July 1 to September 30, 1976
	$52,000.00	defender organizations, July 1 to September 30, 1976
	$112,000.00	salaries and expenses, U.S. magistrates, July 1 to September 30, 1976
	$275,000.00	referees, July 1 to September 30, 1976
Administrative Office of the U.S. Courts	$82,000.00	Administrative Office, July 1 to September 30, 1976
Federal Judicial Center	$18,000.00	FJC, July 1 to September 30, 1976
Total	$8,860,700.00	
TOTAL APPROPRIATION	**$431,720,700.00**	

1977

Statute (Citation)	Date Passed	Headings	Appropriation	Line-item Details
PL 94-362 (90 Stat. 937, 952)	July 14, 1976	Supreme Court of the United States	$7,482,000.00	salaries and expenses
			$800,000.00	care of building and grounds
		Court of Customs and Patent Appeals	$898,000.00	salaries and expenses

Customs Court	salaries and expenses	$2,705,000.00
Court of Claims	salaries and expenses	$2,536,000.00
Courts of Appeals, District Courts, and Other Judicial Services	salaries of judges	$29,782,000.00
	salaries of supporting personnel	$132,250,000.00
	defender organizations and court-appointed counsel	$20,686,000.00
	fees of jurors	$19,350,000.00
	travel and miscellaneous expenses	$24,380,000.00
	salaries and expenses, U.S. magistrates	$12,341,000.00
	salaries and expenses of referees	$30,201,000.00
Administrative Office of the U.S. Courts	salaries and expenses	$8,320,000.00
Federal Judicial Center	salaries and expenses	$7,650,000.00
Space and Facilities	space and facilities	$71,980,000.00
Expenses, U.S. Court Facilities	furniture and furnishings	$4,940,000.00
Total		$376,301,000.00

PL 95-26 (91 Stat. 61, 91)	May 4, 1977		
	Courts of Appeals, District Courts, and Other Judicial Services	fees of jurors	$2,150,000.00
	Increased Pay Costs	Judicial Survivors' Annuities Fund	$31,100,000.00
	Supreme Court of the United States	salaries and expenses	$250,000.00
		care of building and grounds	$30,600.00
	Court of Customs and Patent Appeals	salaries and expenses	$29,000.00
	Customs Court	salaries and expenses	$108,000.00
	Court of Claims	salaries and expenses	$59,000.00
	Courts of Appeals, District Courts, and Other Judicial Services	salaries of supporting personnel	$6,813,000.00
		defender organizations and court-appointed counsel	$314,000.00
		salaries and expenses, U.S. magistrates	$1,520,000.00
		salaries and expenses of referees	$815,000.00
	Administrative Office of the U.S. Courts	salaries and expenses	$354,000.00

Federal Judiciary Appropriations: 1792–2010

Statute (Citation)	Date Passed	Headings	Appropriation	Line-item Details
		Federal Judicial Center	$102,000.00	salaries and expenses
		Total	$43,644,600.00	
PL 95-86 (91 Stat. 419, 442)	August 2, 1977	Court of Customs and Patent Appeals	$41,000.00	salaries and expenses
		Customs Court	$73,000.00	salaries and expenses
		Court of Claims	$159,000.00	salaries and expenses
		Courts of Appeals, District Courts, and Other Judicial Services	$4,300,000.00	salaries of judges
			$249,000.00	salaries of supporting personnel
			$450,000.00	salaries and expenses, U.S. magistrates
			$1,435,000.00	salaries and expenses of referees
		Administrative Office of the U.S. Courts	$53,000.00	salaries and expenses
		Federal Judicial Center	$20,000.00	salaries and expenses
		Total	$6,780,000.00	
		TOTAL APPROPRIATION	$426,725,600.00	

1978

Statute (Citation)	Date Passed	Headings	Appropriation	Line-item Details
PL 95-86 (91 Stat. 419, 434)	August 2, 1977	Supreme Court of the United States	$8,391,000.00	salaries and expenses
			$800,000.00	care of building and grounds
		Court of Customs and Patent Appeals	$1,020,000.00	salaries and expenses
		Customs Court	$2,907,000.00	salaries and expenses
		Court of Claims	$3,000,000.00	salaries and expenses
		Courts of Appeals, District Courts, and Other Judicial Services	$39,700,000.00	salaries of judges
			$148,400,000.00	salaries of supporting personnel
			$24,000,000.00	defender services
			$23,250,000.00	fees of jurors
			$27,600,000.00	travel and miscellaneous expenses
			$17,500,000.00	salaries and expenses of magistrates

Date / Public Law	Office / Category	Amount	Description
		$33,500,000.00	salaries and expenses of referees
		$89,700,000.00	space and facilities
		$7,500,000.00	furniture and furnishings
	Administrative Office of the U.S. Courts	$10,500,000.00	salaries and expenses
	Federal Judicial Center	$6,550,000.00	salaries and expenses
	Total	$444,318,000.00	
PL 95-355 (92 Stat. 523, 540) September 8, 1978	Supreme Court of the United States	$750,000.00	care of building and grounds
	Courts of Appeals, District Courts, and Other Judicial Services	$2,000,000.00	special court under Rail Reorganization Act of 1973
	Federal Judicial Center	$55,000.00	salaries and expenses
	Increased Pay Costs		
	Supreme Court of the United States	$300,000.00	salaries and expenses
		$38,000.00	care of building and grounds
		$46,000.00	salaries and expenses
	Court of Customs and Patent Appeals	$78,000.00	salaries and expenses
	Customs Court	$4,000,000.00	salaries of supporting personnel
	Courts of Appeals, District Courts, and Other Judicial Services	$4,500,000.00	salaries of supporting personnel
		$(1,500,000.00)	transfer from salaries of judges
		$(2,500,000.00)	transfer from space and facilities
		$(500,000.00)	transfer from furniture and furnishings
		$500,000.00	salaries and expenses of referees
	Administrative Office of the U.S. Courts	$575,000.00	
	Federal Judicial Center	$144,000.00	
	Total	$8,486,000.00	
	TOTAL APPROPRIATION	**$452,804,000.00**	

1979

Statute (Citation)	Date Passed	Headings	Appropriation	Line-item Details
PL 95-431 (92 Stat. 1021, 1035)	October 10, 1978	Supreme Court of the United States	$9,690,000.00	salaries and expenses
			$1,450,000.00	care of building and grounds
		Court of Customs and Patent Appeals	$1,099,000.00	salaries and expenses
		Customs Court	$3,055,000.00	salaries and expenses
		Court of Claims	$3,520,000.00	salaries and expenses
		Courts of Appeals, District Courts, and Other Judicial Services	$40,258,000.00	salaries of judges
			$166,195,000.00	salaries of supporting personnel
			$24,800,000.00	defender services
			$20,750,000.00	fees of jurors and commissioners
			$31,914,000.00	travel and miscellaneous expenses
			$19,441,000.00	salaries and expenses of magistrates
			$35,300,000.00	salaries and expenses of referees
			$98,400,000.00	space and facilities
			$8,500,000.00	furniture and furnishings
			$5,000,000.00	pretrial services agencies
		Administrative Office of the U.S. Courts	$12,250,000.00	salaries and expenses
		Federal Judicial Center	$8,025,000.00	salaries and expenses
		Total	$489,647,000.00	
PL 96-38 (93 Stat. 97, 117)	July 25, 1979	Courts of Appeals, District Courts	$1,200,000.00	salaries of judges
			$1,800,000.00	salaries of supporting personnel
			$4,000,000.00	fees of jurors and commissioners
			$3,600,000.00	travel and miscellaneous expenses
			$4,200,000.00	furnishings and expenses for new judges under Omnibus Judgeship Act and Bankruptcy Reform Act
		Administrative Office of the Courts	$150,000.00	salaries and expenses

Headings	Appropriation	Line-item Details
Federal Judicial Center	$150,000.00	salaries and expenses
Increased Pay Costs	$25,000.00	care of building and grounds
Supreme Court of the United States	$22,000.00	salaries and expenses
Court of Customs and Patent Appeals	$40,000.00	salaries and expenses
Customs Court	$50,000.00	salaries and expenses
Court of Claims	$7,500,000.00	salaries of supporting personnel
Courts of Appeals, District Courts, and Other Judicial Services	$1,358,000.00	salaries of referees
Administrative Office of the U.S. Courts	$499,000.00	salaries and expenses
Federal Judicial Center	$104,000.00	salaries and expenses
Total	$24,698,000.00	
TOTAL APPROPRIATION	$514,345,000.00	

1980

Statute (Citation)	Date Passed	Headings	Appropriation	Line-item Details
PL 96-68 (93 Stat. 416, 427)	September 24, 1979	Supreme Court of the United States	$10,250,000.00	salaries and expenses
			$2,157,000.00	care of building and grounds
		Court of Customs and Patent Appeals	$1,719,000.00	salaries and expenses
		Customs Court	$4,850,000.00	salaries and expenses
		Court of Claims	$5,230,000.00	salaries and expenses
		Courts of Appeals, District Courts, and Other Judicial Services	$48,500,000.00	salaries of judges
			$195,700,000.00	salaries of supporting personnel
			$26,000,000.00	defender services
			$34,000,000.00	fees of jurors and commissioners
			$37,800,000.00	travel and miscellaneous expenses
			$22,000,000.00	salaries and expenses, U.S. magistrates
			$58,500,000.00	bankruptcy courts, salaries and expenses

		services for drug dependent offenders	$3,500,000.00
	Administrative Office of the U.S. Courts	space and facilities	$117,500,000.00
		salaries and expenses	$15,100,000.00
	Federal Judicial Center	salaries and expenses	$8,500,000.00
	Total		$591,306,000.00
PL 96-304 (94 Stat. 857, 900, 912) July 8, 1980	Courts of Appeals, District Courts, and Other Judicial Services	pretrial services agencies	$900,000.00
	Supreme Court of the United States	transfer from space and facilities	$(900,000.00)
		salaries and expenses	$113,000.00
		transfer from space and facilities	$(113,000.00)
		care of building and grounds	$25,000.00
		transfer from space and facilities	$(25,000.00)
	Court of Customs and Patent Appeals	salaries and expenses	$91,000.00
		transfer from bankruptcy courts	$(91,000.00)
	Customs Court	salaries and expenses	$91,000.00
		transfer from bankruptcy courts	$(91,000.00)
	Court of Claims	salaries and expenses	$239,000.00
		transfer from bankruptcy courts	$(239,000.00)
	Courts of Appeals, District Courts, and Other Judicial Services	salaries of judges	$3,600,000.00
		transfer from space and facilities	$(3,600,000.00)
		salaries of supporting personnel	$8,000,000.00
		transfer from space and facilities	$(8,000,000.00)
		salaries and expenses of magistrates	$800,000.00
		transfer from bankruptcy courts	$(800,000.00)
	Administrative Office of the U.S. Courts	salaries and expenses	$650,000.00
		transfer from bankruptcy courts	$(650,000.00)
	Federal Judicial Center	salaries and expenses	$117,000.00
		transfer from bankruptcy courts	$(117,000.00)
	Total		$0
	TOTAL APPROPRIATION		**$591,306,000.00**

1981

Statute (Citation)	Date Passed	Headings	Appropriation	Line-item Details
PL 96-369 (94 Stat. 3151)	October 1, 1980	Supreme Court of the United States	$11,140,000.00	salaries and expenses
PL 96-536 (94 Stat. 3166)	December 16, 1980		$1,526,000.00	care of building and grounds
continuing resolution		Court of Customs and Patent Appeals	$1,839,000.00	salaries and expenses
rates based on HR 7584		Customs Court	$5,036,000.00	salaries and expenses
		Court of Claims	$5,526,000.00	salaries and expenses
		Courts of Appeals, District Courts, and Other Judicial Services	$54,500,000.00	salaries of judges
			$214,181,000.00	salaries of supporting personnel
			$24,000,000.00	defender services
			$36,000,000.00	fees of jurors and commissioners
			$41,827,000.00	travel and miscellaneous expenses
			$23,851,000.00	salaries and expenses, U.S. magistrates
			$63,994,000.00	bankruptcy courts, salaries and expenses
			$3,645,000.00	services for drug dependent offenders
			$120,000,000.00	space and facilities
		Administrative Office of the U.S. Courts	$16,275,000.00	salaries and expenses
		Federal Judicial Center	$9,000,000.00	salaries and expenses
		Total	$632,340,000.00	
PL 97-12 (95 Stat. 14, 22)	June 5, 1981	Supreme Court of the United States	$42,000.00	care of building and grounds
			$645,000.00	acquisition of addition to grounds
		Courts of Appeals, District Courts, and Other Judicial Services	$2,000,000.00	bankruptcy
			$(2,000,000.00)	transfer from space and facilities
			$616,000.00	contribution to Judicial Survivors' Annuity Fund

Increased Pay Costs

Headings	Appropriation	Line-item Details
Supreme Court of the United States	$700,000.00	salaries and expenses
Court of Customs and Patent Appeals	$72,000.00	salaries and expenses
Court of International Trade	$114,000.00	salaries and expenses
Court of Claims	$267,000.00	salaries and expenses
Courts of Appeals, District Courts, and Other Judicial Services	$1,500,000.00	salaries of judges
	$18,750,000.00	salaries of supporting personnel
	$(12,500,000.00)	transfer from space and facilities to salaries of supporting personnel
	$700,000.00	salaries of salaries and expenses, U.S. magistrates
	$3,500,000.00	bankruptcy courts
Administrative Office of the U.S. Courts	$875,000.00	salaries and expenses
Federal Judicial Center	$222,000.00	salaries and expenses
Total	$15,503,000.00	
TOTAL APPROPRIATION	**$647,843,000.00**	

1982

Statute (Citation)	Date Passed	Headings	Appropriation	Line-item Details
PL 97-161 (96 Stat. 22)	March 31, 1982	Supreme Court of the United States	$11,208,000.00	salaries and expenses
continuing resolution rates based on H.R. 4169			$1,654,000.00	care of building and grounds
		Court of Customs and Patent Appeals	$1,950,000.00	salaries and expenses
		Court of International Trade	$5,200,000.00	salaries and expenses
		Court of Claims	$5,900,000.00	salaries and expenses
		Courts of Appeals, District Courts, and Other Judicial Services	$59,400,000.00	salaries of judges
			$263,400,000.00	salaries of supporting personnel
			$26,500.00	defender services
			$43,500,000.00	fees of jurors and commissioners

		operation and maintenance of the courts	$55,600,000.00
		bankruptcy courts, salaries and expenses	$81,200,000.00
		services for drug dependent offenders	$3,750,000.00
		space and facilities	$123,000,000.00
	Administrative Office of the U.S. Courts	salaries and expenses	$20,000,000.00
	Federal Judicial Center	salaries and expenses	$7,600,000.00
	Total		$683,388,500.00
PL 97-257 (96 Stat. 818, 825, 859)	September 10, 1982		
	Courts of Appeals, District Courts, and Other Judicial Services	defender services	$1,500,000.00
	Increased Pay Costs		
	Supreme Court of the United States	salaries and expenses	$427,000.00
	Court of Custom and Patent Appeals	salaries and expenses	$58,000.00
	Court of International Trade	salaries and expenses	$86,000.00
	Court of Claims	salaries and expenses	$270,000.00
	Courts of Appeals, District Courts, and Other Judicial Services	salaries of judges	$2,850,000.00
		salaries of judges	$50,000.00
		transfer from space and facilities	$(50,000.00)
		salaries of supporting personnel	$2,400,000.00
		salaries of supporting personnel	$4,500,000.00
		transfer from fees of jurors and commissioners	$(4,500,000.00)
		salaries of supporting personnel	$6,000,000.00
		transfer from space and facilities	$(6,000,000.00)
		defender services	$670,000.00
		bankruptcy courts	$3,500,000.00
	Administrative Office	salaries and expenses	$750,000.00
	Federal Judicial Center	salaries and expenses	$170,000.00
	Total		$12,681,000.00
	TOTAL APPROPRIATION		**$696,069,500.00**

1983

Statute (Citation)	Date Passed	Headings	Appropriation	Line-item Details
PL 97-377 (96 Stat. 1830, 1866, 1878) continuing resolution rates based on S. 2956	December 21, 1982	Supreme Court of the United States	$12,675,000.00	salaries and expenses
			$2,000,000.00	care of building and grounds
		Courts of Appeals, District Courts, and Other Judicial Services	$4,309,000.00	U.S. Court of Appeals for the Federal Circuit
		Court of International Trade	$5,372,000.00	salaries and expenses
		Courts of Appeals, District Courts, and Other Judicial Services	$64,500,000.00	salaries of judges
			$294,000,000.00	salaries of supporting personnel
			$32,215,000.00	defender services
			$42,500,000.00	jurors and commissioners
			$65,000,000.00	operation and maintenance of courts
			$89,000,000.00	bankruptcy courts, salaries and expenses
			$4,000,000.00	services for drug dependent offenders
			$132,412,000.00	space and facilities
			$12,000,000.00	court security
		Administrative Office of the U.S. Courts	$23,406,000.00	salaries and expenses
		Federal Judicial Center	$7,618,000.00	salaries and expenses
		Total	$791,007,000.00	
PL 98-63 (97 Stat. 301, 307)	July 30, 1983	Courts of Appeals, District Courts, and Other Judicial Services	$1,400,000.00	salaries of judges
		Increased Pay Costs	$1,400,000.00	defender services
			$2,500,000.00	bankruptcy courts
		Court of Appeals for the Federal Circuit	$97,000.00	salaries and expenses
		Court of International Trade	$129,000.00	salaries and expenses

Headings	Appropriation	Line-item Details
Courts of Appeals, District Courts, and Other Judicial Services	$2,510,000.00	salaries of judges
	$6,250,000.00	salaries of supporting personnel
	$9,000,000.00	salaries of supporting personnel
	$(2,000,000.00)	transfer from fees of jurors
	$(2,000,000.00)	transfer from operation and maintenance of courts
	$(5,000,000.00)	transfer from space and facilities
	$600,000.00	defender services
	$4,100,000.00	bankruptcy courts
Administrative Office	$660,000.00	salaries and expenses
Federal Judicial Center	$66,000.00	salaries and expenses
Total	$19,712,000.00	
TOTAL APPROPRIATION	**$810,719,000.00**	

1984

Statute (Citation)	Date Passed	Headings	Appropriation	Line-item Details
PL 98-166 (97 Stat. 1071, 1098)	November 28, 1983	Supreme Court of the United States	$13,635,000.00	salaries and expenses
			$1,971,000.00	care of building and grounds
		Court of Appeals for the Federal Circuit	$4,680,000.00	salaries and expenses
		Court of International Trade	$5,675,000.00	salaries and expenses
		Courts of Appeals, District Courts, and Other Judicial Services	$69,500,000.00	salaries of judges
			$330,000,000.00	salaries of supporting personnel
			$37,000,000.00	defender services
			$43,500,000.00	jurors and commissioners
			$75,350,000.00	operation and maintenance of courts
			$100,895,000.00	bankruptcy courts, salaries and expenses
			$5,000,000.00	services for drug dependent offenders
			$142,624,000.00	space and facilities
			$18,690,000.00	court security
		Administrative Office of the U.S. Courts	$26,775,000.00	salaries and expenses

Law	Date	Appropriation	Purpose	Amount
			transfer from pretrial services to Administrative Office	$(700,000.00)
		Federal Judicial Center	salaries and expenses	$8,445,000,000.00
		Total		$883,040,000.00
PL 98-396 (98 Stat. 1369, 1376, 1409)	August 22, 1984	Supreme Court of the United States	care of building and grounds	$600,000.00
		Courts of Appeals, District Courts, and Other Judicial Services	defender services	$4,000,000.00
			operation and maintenance	$1,125,000.00
			bankruptcy courts	$2,500,000.00
			bankruptcy courts	$1,000,000.00
			transfer from space and facilities to bankruptcy courts	$(1,000,000.00)
		Increased Pay Costs		
		Court of Appeals for the Federal Circuit	salaries and expenses	$50,000.00
			transfer from fees of jurors and commissioners	$(50,000.00)
		Court of International Trade	salaries and expenses	$50,000.00
			transfer from fees of jurors and commissioners	$(50,000.00)
		Courts of Appeals, District Courts, and Other Judicial Services	salaries of judges	$3,775,000.00
			transfer from operation and maintenance of courts to salaries of judges	$(3,625,000.00)
			transfer from space and facilities to salaries of judges	$(150,000.00)
			salaries of supporting personnel	$2,500,000.00
			transfer from fees of jurors and commissioners to salaries of supporting personnel	$(1,000,000.00)
			transfer from space and facilities to salaries of supporting personnel	$(1,500,000.00)
			defender services	$465,000.00
			transfer from operation and maintenance of courts to defender services	$(375,000.00)
			transfer from space and facilities to defender services	$(90,000.00)
			bankruptcy courts	$3,400,000.00
			transfer from space and facilities to bankruptcy courts	$(3,400,000.00)

			Appropriation	Line-item Details
		Federal Judicial Center, salaries and expenses	$120,000.00	
		transfer from space and facilities to Federal Judicial Center	$(120,000.00)	
		Total	$8,225,000.00	
		TOTAL APPROPRIATION	**$891,265,000.00**	

1985

Statute (Citation)	Date Passed	Headings	Appropriation	Line-item Details
PL 98-411 (98 Stat. 1545, 1570)	August 30, 1984	Supreme Court of the United States	$14,143,000.00	salaries and expenses
			$2,242,000.00	care of building and grounds
		Court of Appeals for the Federal Circuit	$5,150,000.00	salaries and expenses
		Court of International Trade	$6,070,000.00	salaries and expenses
		Courts of Appeals, District Courts, and Other Judicial Services	$75,540,000.00	salaries of judges
			$370,228,000.00	salaries of supporting personnel
			$42,000,000.00	defender services
			$42,000,000.00	jurors and commissioners
			$101,500,000.00	operation and maintenance of courts
			$116,950,000.00	bankruptcy courts, salaries and expenses
			$140,000,000.00	space and facilities
			$25,500,000.00	court security
		Administrative Office of the U.S. Courts	$28,250,000.00	salaries and expenses
		Federal Judicial Center	$9,330,000.00	salaries and expenses
		Total	$978,903,000.00	
PL 99-88 (99 Stat. 293, 309)	August 15, 1985	Courts of Appeals, District Courts, and Other Judicial Services	$3,098,000.00	salaries of judges
			$5,548,000.00	salaries of supporting personnel
			$21,992,000.00	defender services
			$1,700,000.00	jurors and commissioners
			$13,526,000.00	operation and maintenance of courts

Statute (Citation)	Date Passed	Headings	Appropriation	Line-item Details
			$(4,417,000.00)	rescission of available funds from "operation and maintenance of courts"
			$2,384,000.00	space and facilities
			$1,492,000.00	court security
		Administrative Office of the U.S. Courts	$86,000.00	salaries and expenses
		Federal Judicial Center	$51,000.00	salaries and expenses
		Total	$45,460,000.00	
		TOTAL APPROPRIATION	$1,024,363,000.00	

1986

Statute (Citation)	Date Passed	Headings	Appropriation	Line-item Details
PL 99-180 (99 Stat. 1136, 1153)	December 13, 1985	Supreme Court of the United States	$15,000,000.00	salaries and expenses
			$2,275,000.00	care of building and grounds
		Court of Appeals for the Federal Circuit	$5,500,000.00	salaries and expenses
		Court of International Trade	$6,400,000.00	salaries and expenses
			$103,000,000.00	salaries of judges
		Courts of Appeals, District Courts, and Other Judicial Services	$474,900,000.00	salaries of supporting personnel
			$61,800,000.00	defender services
			$43,400,000.00	jurors and commissioners
			$135,000,000.00	operation and maintenance of courts
			$147,000,000.00	space and facilities
			$32,750,000.00	court security
		Administrative Office of the U.S. Courts	$29,200,000.00	salaries and expenses
		Federal Judicial Center	$9,600,000.00	salaries and expenses
		Total	$1,065,825,000.00	
PL 99-349 (100 Stat. 710, 717)	July 2, 1986	Supreme Court of the United States	$46,000.00	care of building and grounds

		Headings	Appropriation	Line-item Details
		Courts of Appeals, District Courts, and Other Judicial Services	$1,200,000.00	salaries of supporting personnel
			$3,800,000.00	fees of jurors and commissioners
			$1,300,000.00	study of construction of office building
		Total	$6,346,000.00	
		TOTAL APPROPRIATION	**$1,072,171,000.00**	

1987

Statute (Citation)	Date Passed	Headings	Appropriation	Line-item Details
PL 99-591 (100 Stat. 3341–61)	October 30, 1986	Supreme Court of the United States	$14,600,000.00	salaries and expenses
			$2,279,000.00	care of building and grounds
		Court of Appeals for the Federal Circuit	$6,800,000.00	salaries and expenses
		Court of International Trade	$7,000,000.00	salaries and expenses
		Courts of Appeals, District Courts, and Other Judicial Services	$929,500,000.00	salaries and expenses
			$68,378,000.00	defender services
			$44,635,000.00	jurors and commissioners
			$36,000,000.00	court security
		Administrative Office of the U.S. Courts	$29,500,000.00	salaries and expenses
		Federal Judicial Center	$9,600,000.00	salaries and expenses
		Bicentennial	$1,000,000.00	
		Sentencing Commission	$5,800,000.00	salaries and expenses
		Total	$1,155,092,000.00	
PL 100-71 (101 Stat. 391, 395)	July 11, 1987	Courts of Appeals, District Courts, and Other Judicial Services	$37,800,000.00	salaries and expenses
		Administrative Office of the U.S. Courts	$100,000.00	salaries and expenses
		Federal Judicial Center	$1,000,000.00	salaries and expenses
		Total	$38,900,000.00	
		TOTAL APPROPRIATION	**$1,193,992,000.00**	

1988

Statute (Citation)	Date Passed	Headings	Appropriation	Line-item Details
PL 100-202 (101 Stat. 1329, 1329-24)	December 22, 1987	Supreme Court of the United States	$15,247,000.00	salaries and expenses
			$2,110,000.00	care of building and grounds
		Court of Appeals for the Federal Circuit	$7,430,000.00	salaries and expenses
		Court of International Trade	$7,768,000.00	salaries and expenses
		Courts of Appeals, District Courts, and Other Judicial Services	$1,081,447,000.00	salaries and expenses
			$85,100,000.00	defender services
			$43,135,000.00	jurors and commissioners
			$40,853,000.00	court security
		Administrative Office of the U.S. Courts	$31,167,000.00	salaries and expenses
		Federal Judicial Center	$10,548,000.00	salaries and expenses
		Sentencing Commission	$5,129,000.00	salaries and expenses
		TOTAL APPROPRIATION	**$1,329,934,000.00**	

1989

Statute (Citation)	Date Passed	Headings	Appropriation	Line-item Details
PL 100-459 (102 Stat. 2186, 2209)	October 1, 1988	Supreme Court of the United States	$15,901,000.00	salaries and expenses
			$2,131,000.00	care of building and grounds
		Court of Appeals for the Federal Circuit	$8,300,000.00	salaries and expenses
		Court of International Trade	$8,000,000.00	salaries and expenses
		Courts of Appeals, District Courts, and Other Judicial Services	$1,135,000,000.00	salaries and expenses
			$95,100,000.00	defender services
			$43,135,000.00	jurors and commissioners
			$41,423,000.00	court security

Statute (Citation)	Date Passed	Headings	Appropriation	Line-item Details
		Administrative Office of the U.S. Courts	$33,600,000.00	salaries and expenses
		Federal Judicial Center	$11,200,000.00	salaries and expenses
		Sentencing Commission	$5,183,000.00	salaries and expenses
		Total	$1,398,973,000.00	
PL 100-690 (102 Stat. 4181, 4541)	November 18, 1988	Courts of Appeals, District Courts, and Other Judicial Services	$35,000,000.00	salaries and expenses
			$15,000,000.00	defender services
			$1,000,000.00	fees of jurors and commissioners
		Total	$51,000,000.00	
PL 101-45 (103 Stat. 97, 98)	June 30, 1989		$4,000,000.00	fees of jurors and commissioners, to strengthen drug enforcement
		TOTAL APPROPRIATION	**$1,453,973,000.00**	

1990

Statute (Citation)	Date Passed	Headings	Appropriation	Line-item Details
PL 101-162 (103 Stat. 988, 1010)	November 21, 1989	Supreme Court of the United States	$17,434,000.00	salaries and expenses
			$4,400,000.00	care of building and grounds
		Court of Appeals for the Federal Circuit	$8,830,000.00	salaries and expenses
		Court of International Trade	$8,272,000.00	salaries and expenses
		Courts of Appeals, District Courts, and Other Judicial Services	$1,287,424,000.00	salaries and expenses
			$86,687,000.00	defender services
			$54,700,000.00	jurors and commissioners
			$43,090,000.00	court security
		Administrative Office of the U.S. Courts	$33,670,000.00	salaries and expenses
		Federal Judicial Center	$12,648,000.00	salaries and expenses
		Retirement Funds	$6,500,000.00	Judicial Officers Retirement Fund
		Sentencing Commission	$6,520,000.00	salaries and expenses
		Total	$1,570,175,000.00	

Statute (Citation)	Date Passed	Headings	Appropriation	Line-item Details
PL 101-302 (104 Stat. 213, 217)	May 25, 1990	Supreme Court of the United States	$63,000.00	salaries and expenses
		Courts of Appeals, District Courts, and Other Judicial Services	$25,503,000.00	salaries and expenses
			$4,500,000.00	salaries and expenses
			$(4,500,000.00)	transfer from defender services
		Sentencing Commission	$7,000,000.00	salaries and expenses
		Total	$32,566,000.00	
		TOTAL APPROPRIATION	**$1,602,741,000.00**	

1991

Statute (Citation)	Date Passed	Headings	Appropriation	Line-item Details
PL 101-515 (104 Stat. 2101, 2129)	November 5, 1990	Supreme Court of the United States	$19,029,000.00	salaries and expenses
			$3,453,000.00	care of building and grounds
		Court of Appeals for the Federal Circuit	$9,711,000.00	salaries and expenses
		Court of International Trade	$8,721,000.00	salaries and expenses
		Courts of Appeals, District Courts, and Other Judicial Services	$1,589,124,000.00	salaries and expenses
			$132,761,000.00	defender services
			$57,997,000.00	jurors and commissioners
			$(81,000.00)	transfer from jurors and commissioners to Court of International Trade
			$81,000.00	Court of International Trade
			$(4,919,000.00)	transfer from jurors and commissioners to Courts of Appeals, etc., to salaries and expenses
			$4,919,000.00	salaries and expenses
			$71,261,000.00	court security
		Administrative Office of the U.S. Courts	$37,400,000.00	salaries and expenses
		Federal Judicial Center	$13,918,000.00	salaries and expenses
		Retirement Funds	$5,000,000.00	Judicial Officers Retirement Fund

Statute (Citation)	Date Passed	Headings	Appropriation	Line-item Details
		Sentencing Commission	$8,422,000.00	salaries and expenses
		Total	$1,956,797,000.00	
PL 102-27 (105 Stat. 130, 136)	April 10, 1991	Supreme Court of the United States	$54,000.00	salaries and expenses
		Court of Appeals for the Federal Circuit	$51,000.00	salaries and expenses
		Court of International Trade	$36,000.00	salaries and expenses
		Courts of Appeals, District Courts, and Other Judicial Services	$68,730,000.00	salaries and expenses, with $750,000 for National Commission on Judicial Discipline and Removal
			$5,600,000.00	fees of jurors and commissioners
			$530,000.00	court security
		Administrative Office of the U.S. Courts	$2,450,000.00	salaries and expenses
		Federal Judicial Center	$1,633,000.00	salaries and expenses
		Total	$79,084,000.00	
PL 102-55 (105 Stat. 290, 294)	June 13, 1991	Courts of Appeals, District Courts, and Other Judicial Services	$(8,262,000.00)	rescission of salaries and expenses from PL 101-515
			$8,000,000.00	defender services
		Total	$(262,000.00)	
		TOTAL APPROPRIATION	$2,035,619,000.00	

1992

Statute (Citation)	Date Passed	Headings	Appropriation	Line-item Details
PL 102-140 (105 Stat. 782, 807)	October 28, 1991	Supreme Court of the United States	$20,787,000.00	salaries and expenses
			$3,801,000.00	care of building and grounds
		Court of Appeals for the Federal Circuit	$10,775,000.00	salaries and expenses
		Court of International Trade	$9,432,000.00	salaries and expenses
		Courts of Appeals, District Courts, and Other Judicial Services	$1,875,000,000.00	salaries and expenses
			$190,621,000.00	defender services

Federal Judiciary Appropriations: 1792–2010

Headings	Appropriation	Line-item Details
	$70,000,000.00	jurors and commissioners
	$81,048,000.00	court security
Administrative Office of the U.S. Courts	$44,681,000.00	salaries and expenses
Federal Judicial Center	$17,795,000.00	salaries and expenses
Retirement Funds	$6,000,000.00	Judicial Officers' Retirement Fund and Judicial Survivors' Annuity Fund
	$500,000.00	Federal Claims Judges' Retirement Fund
Sentencing Commission	$9,000,000.00	
Total	$2,339,440,000.00	

Statute (Citation)	Date Passed	Headings	Appropriation	Line-item Details
PL 102-368 (106 Stat. 1117, 1118)	September 23, 1992	Courts of Appeals, District Courts, and Other Judicial Services	$31,250,000.00	defender services
		TOTAL APPROPRIATION	$2,370,690,000.00	

1993

Statute (Citation)	Date Passed	Headings	Appropriation	Line-item Details
PL 102-395 (106 Stat. 1828, 1856)	October 6, 1992	Supreme Court of the United States	$22,286,000.00	salaries and expenses
			$3,320,000.00	care of building and grounds
		Court of Appeals for the Federal Circuit	$11,554,000.00	salaries and expenses
		Court of International Trade	$10,345,000.00	salaries and expenses
		Courts of Appeals, District Courts, and Other Judicial Services	$1,979,000,000.00	salaries and expenses
			$2,075,000.00	expenses of Claims Court, processing claims under National Childhood Vaccine Injury Act of 1986
			$215,121,000.00	defender services
			$68,820,000.00	jurors and commissioners
			$81,253,000.00	court security
		Administrative Office of the U.S. Courts	$45,100,000.00	salaries and expenses
		Federal Judicial Center	$17,500,000.00	salaries and expenses
		Retirement Funds	$8,000,000.00	Judicial Officers' Retirement Fund and Judicial Survivors' Annuity Fund

Statute (Citation)	Date Passed	Headings	Appropriation	Line-item Details
		Federal Claims Judges' Retirement Fund	$520,000.00	salaries and expenses
		National Comm. on Judicial Discipline	$443,000.00	
		Sentencing Commission	$9,000,000.00	salaries and expenses
		Total	$2,474,337,000.00	
PL 103-50 (107 Stat. 241, 246)	July 2, 1993	Courts of Appeals, District Courts, and Other Judicial Services	$55,000,000.00	defender services
			$5,500,000.00	fees of jurors and commissioners
		Total	$60,500,000.00	
		TOTAL APPROPRIATION	$2,534,837,000.00	

1994

Statute (Citation)	Date Passed	Headings	Appropriation	Line-item Details
PL 103-121 (107 Stat. 1153, 1177)	October 27, 1993	Supreme Court of the United States	$23,000,000.00	salaries and expenses
			$2,850,000.00	care of building and grounds
		Court of Appeals for the Federal Circuit	$12,900,000.00	salaries and expenses
		Court of International Trade	$11,000,000.00	salaries and expenses
		Courts of Appeals, District Courts, and Other Judicial Services	$2,156,000,000.00	salaries and expenses
			$2,160,000.00	expenses of Claims Court, processing claims under National Childhood Vaccine Injury Act of 1986
			$280,000,000.00	defender services
			$77,095,000.00	jurors and commissioners
			$86,000,000.00	court security
		Administrative Office of the U.S. Courts	$44,900,000.00	salaries and expenses
		Federal Judicial Center	$18,450,000.00	salaries and expenses
		Retirement Funds	$20,000,000.00	Judicial Officers' Retirement Fund and Judicial Survivors' Annuity Fund
			$545,000.00	Federal Claims Judges' Retirement Fund
		Sentencing Commission	$8,468,000.00	salaries and expenses
		Total	$2,743,368,000.00	

Statute (Citation)	Date Passed	Headings	Appropriation	Line-item Details
PL 103-211 (108 Stat. 3, 27)	February 12, 1994	Courts of Appeals, District Courts, and Other Judicial Services	($1,000,000.00)	defender services, rescission
		TOTAL APPROPRIATION	**$2,742,368,000.00**	

1995

Statute (Citation)	Date Passed	Headings	Appropriation	Line-item Details
PL 103-317 (108 Stat. 1724, 1749)	August 26, 1994	Supreme Court of the United States	$24,240,000.00	salaries and expenses
			$3,000,000.00	care of building and grounds
		Court of Appeals for the Federal Circuit	$13,438,000.00	salaries and expenses
		Court of International Trade	$11,685,000.00	salaries and expenses
		Courts of Appeals, District Courts, and Other Judicial Services	$2,340,127,000.00	salaries and expenses
			$2,250,000.00	expenses of Claims Court, processing claims under National Childhood Vaccine Injury Act of 1986
			$250,000,000.00	defender services
			$59,346,000.00	jurors and commissioners
			$97,000,000.00	court security
		Administrative Office of the U.S. Courts	$47,500,000.00	salaries and expenses
		Federal Judicial Center	$18,828,000.00	salaries and expenses
		Retirement Funds	$21,000,000.00	Judicial Officers' Retirement Fund
			$6,900,000.00	Judicial Survivors' Annuity Fund
			$575,000.00	Federal Claims Judges' Retirement Fund
		Sentencing Commission	$8,800,000.00	salaries and expenses
		Total	$2,904,689,000.00	
PL 104-19 (109 Stat. 194, 201)	July 27, 1995	Court of International Trade	($1,000,000.00)	salaries and expenses, rescission
		Courts of Appeals, District Courts, and Other Judicial Services	($9,500,000.00)	defender services, rescission
			($5,000,000.00)	fees of jurors and commissioners, rescission

Headings	Appropriation	Line-item Details
	$16,640,000.00	court security
Total	$1,140,000,000.00	
TOTAL APPROPRIATION	$2,905,829,000.00	

1996

Statute (Citation)	Date Passed	Headings	Appropriation	Line-item Details
PL 104-134 (110 Stat. 1321, 1321–32)	April 26, 1996	Supreme Court of the United States	$25,834,000.00	salaries and expenses
			$3,313,000.00	care of building and grounds
		Court of Appeals for the Federal Circuit	$14,288,000.00	salaries and expenses
		Court of International Trade	$10,859,000.00	salaries and expenses
		Courts of Appeals, District Courts, and Other Judicial Services	$2,433,141,000.00	salaries and expenses
			$2,318,000.00	expenses of Claims Court, processing claims under National Childhood Vaccine Injury Act of 1986
			$30,000,000.00	violent crime reduction programs
			$267,217,000.00	defender services
			$59,028,000.00	jurors and commissioners
			$102,000,000.00	court security
		Administrative Office of the U.S. Courts	$47,500,000.00	salaries and expenses
		Federal Judicial Center	$17,914,000.00	salaries and expenses
		Retirement Funds	$24,000,000.00	Judicial Officers' Retirement Fund
			$7,000,000.00	Judicial Survivors' Annuity Fund
			$1,900,000.00	Federal Claims Judges' Retirement Fund
		Sentencing Commission	$8,500,000.00	salaries and expenses
		TOTAL APPROPRIATION	$3,054,812,000.00	

1997

Statute (Citation)	Date Passed	Headings	Appropriation	Line-item Details
PL 104-208 (110 Stat. 3009, 3009–42)	September 30, 1996	Supreme Court of the United States	$27,157,000.00	salaries and expenses

Federal Judiciary Appropriations: 1792–2010

Statute (Citation)	Date Passed	Headings	Appropriation	Line-item Details
		Court of Appeals for the Federal Circuit	$2,800,000.00	care of building and grounds
			$15,013,000.00	salaries and expenses
		Court of International Trade	$11,114,000.00	salaries and expenses
		Courts of Appeals, District Courts, and Other Judicial Services	$2,556,000,000.00	salaries and expenses
			$(500,000.00)	transfer from salaries and expenses to Commission on Structural Alternatives for the Federal Courts of Appeals
			$500,000.00	Commission on Structural Alternatives for the Federal Courts of Appeals
			$325,111,000.00	defender services . . . [statute cuts off; amount reported in Administrative Office director's report]
			$2,390,000.00	expenses of Claims Court, processing claims under National Childhood Vaccine Injury Act of 1986
			$10,000,000.00	Antiterrorism and Effective Death Penalty Act of 1996
			$30,000,000.00	violent crime reduction programs
			$67,000,000.00	jurors and commissioners
			$127,000,000.00	court security
		Administrative Office of the U.S. Courts	$49,450,000.00	salaries and expenses
		Federal Judicial Center	$17,495,000.00	salaries and expenses
		Retirement Funds	$21,000,000.00	Judicial Officers' Retirement Fund
			$7,300,000.00	Judicial Survivors' Annuity Fund
			$1,900,000.00	Federal Claims Judges' Retirement Fund
		Sentencing Commission	$8,490,000.00	salaries and expenses
		TOTAL APPROPRIATION	**$3,279,220,000.00**	

1998

Statute (Citation)	Date Passed	Headings	Appropriation	Line-item Details
PL 105-119 (111 Stat. 2440, 2488)	November 26, 1997	Supreme Court of the United States	$29,245,000.00	salaries and expenses
			$3,400,000.00	care of building and grounds
		Court of Appeals for the Federal Circuit	$15,575,000.00	salaries and expenses
		Court of International Trade	$11,449,000.00	salaries and expenses

Statute (Citation)	Date Passed	Headings	Appropriation	Line-item Details
		Courts of Appeals, District Courts, and Other Judicial Services	$2,682,400,000.00	salaries and expenses
			$(900,000.00)	transfer from salaries and expenses to Commission on Structural Alternatives for the Federal Courts of Appeals
			$900,000.00	Commission on Structural Alternatives for the Federal Courts of Appeals
			$2,450,000.00	expenses of Claims Court, processing claims under National Childhood Vaccine Injury Act of 1986
			$40,000,000.00	violent crime reduction programs
			$329,529,000.00	defender services
			$64,438,000.00	jurors and commissioners
			$167,214,000.00	court security
		Administrative Office of the U.S. Courts	$52,000,000.00	salaries and expenses
		Federal Judicial Center	$17,495,000.00	salaries and expenses
		Retirement Funds	$25,000,000.00	Judicial Officers' Retirement Fund
			$7,400,000.00	Judicial Survivors' Annuity Fund
			$1,800,000.00	Federal Claims Judges' Retirement Fund
		Sentencing Commission	$9,240,000.00	salaries and expenses
		Total	$3,458,635,000.00	
PL 105-119 (111 Stat. 2493)	November 26, 1997		$5,000,000.00	salary adjustments for judges and justices
		TOTAL APPROPRIATION	**$3,463,635,000.00**	

1999

Statute (Citation)	Date Passed	Headings	Appropriation	Line-item Details
PL 105-277 (112 Stat. 2681, 2681–89)	October 21, 1998	Supreme Court of the United States	$31,059,000.00	salaries and expenses
			$2,364,000.00	care of building and grounds
		Court of Appeals for the Federal Circuit	$16,101,000.00	salaries and expenses
		Court of International Trade	$11,804,000.00	salaries and expenses
		Courts of Appeals, District Courts, and Other Judicial Services	$2,821,821,000.00	salaries and expenses

	Appropriation	Line-item Details
	$2,515,000.00	expenses of Claims Court, processing claims under National Childhood Vaccine Injury Act of 1986
	$41,043,000.00	violent crime reduction programs
	$360,952,000.00	defender services
	$66,861,000.00	jurors and commissioners
	$174,569,000.00	court security
Administrative Office of the U.S. Courts	$54,500,000.00	salaries and expenses
Federal Judicial Center	$17,716,000.00	salaries and expenses
Retirement Funds	$27,500,000.00	Judicial Officers' Retirement Fund
	$7,800,000.00	Judicial Survivors' Annuity Fund
	$2,000,000.00	Federal Claims Judges' Retirement Fund
Sentencing Commission	$9,487,000.00	salaries and expenses
TOTAL APPROPRIATION	**$3,648,092,000.00**	

2000

Statute (Citation)	Date Passed	Headings	Appropriation	Line-item Details
PL 106-113 (113 Stat. 1501, 1501A–33)	November 29, 1999	Supreme Court of the United States	$35,492,000.00	salaries and expenses
			$8,002,000.00	care of building and grounds
		Court of Appeals for the Federal Circuit	$16,797,000.00	salaries and expenses
		Court of International Trade	$11,957,000.00	salaries and expenses
		Courts of Appeals, District Courts, and Other Judicial Services	$2,958,138,000.00	salaries and expenses
			$2,515,000.00	expenses of Claims Court, processing claims under National Childhood Vaccine Injury Act of 1986
			$156,539,000.00	violent crime reduction programs
			$358,848,000.00	defender services
			$26,247,000.00	additional funds for defender services, derived from Violent Crime Reduction Trust Fund
			$60,918,000.00	jurors and commissioners
			$193,028,000.00	court security
		Administrative Office of the U.S. Courts	$55,000,000.00	salaries and expenses

Headings	Appropriation	Line-item Details
Federal Judicial Center		salaries and expenses
Retirement Funds	$18,000,000.00	Judicial Officers' Retirement Fund
	$29,500,000.00	Judicial Survivors' Annuity Fund
	$8,000,000.00	Federal Claims Judges' Retirement Fund
	$2,200,000.00	
Sentencing Commission	$8,500,000.00	salaries and expenses
TOTAL APPROPRIATION	$3,949,681,000.00	*less a .38 percent government-wide rescission of discretionary budget (PL 106-113, 113 Stat. 1501A-303)

2001

Statute (Citation)	Date Passed	Headings	Appropriation	Line-item Details
PL 106-553 (114 Stat. 2762, 2762A-80)	December 21, 2000	Supreme Court of the United States	$37,591,000.00	salaries and expenses
			$7,530,000.00	care of building and grounds
		Court of Appeals for the Federal Circuit	$17,930,000.00	salaries and expenses
		Court of International Trade	$12,456,000.00	salaries and expenses
		Courts of Appeals, District Courts, and Other Judicial Services	$3,359,725,000.00	salaries and expenses
			$2,602,000.00	expenses of Claims Court, processing claims under National Childhood Vaccine Injury Act of 1986
			$435,000,000.00	defender services
			$59,567,000.00	jurors and commissioners
			$199,575,000.00	court security
		Administrative Office of the U.S. Courts	$58,340,000.00	salaries and expenses
		Federal Judicial Center	$18,777,000.00	salaries and expenses
		Retirement Funds	$25,700,000.00	Judicial Officers' Retirement Fund
			$8,100,000.00	Judicial Survivors' Annuity Fund
			$1,900,000.00	Federal Claims Judges' Retirement Fund
		Sentencing Commission	$9,931,000.00	salaries and expenses
		Total	$4,254,724,000.00	
PL 107-38 (115 Stat. 220)	September 18, 2001		$95,000,000.00	allotted to the Judiciary for court security under the Emergency Supplemental Appropriations Act for Recovery from and Response to Terrorist Attacks Against the United States
		TOTAL APPROPRIATION	$4,349,724,000.00	*less .22 percent government-wide rescission of discretionary budget (PL 106-554, 114 Stat. 2763, 2763A-214)

2002

Statute (Citation)	Date Passed	Headings	Appropriation	Line-item Details
PL 107-77 (115 Stat. 748, 780)	November 28, 2001	Supreme Court of the United States	$39,988,000.00	salaries and expenses
			$37,530,000.00	care of building and grounds
		Court of Appeals for the Federal Circuit	$19,287,000.00	salaries and expenses
		Court of International Trade	$13,064,000.00	salaries and expenses
		Courts of Appeals, District Courts, and Other Judicial Services	$3,591,116,000.00	salaries and expenses
			$2,692,000.00	expenses of Claims Court, processing claims under National Childhood Vaccine Injury Act of 1986
			$500,671,000.00	defender services
			$48,131,000.00	jurors and commissioners
			$220,677,000.00	court security
		Administrative Office of the U.S. Courts	$61,664,000.00	salaries and expenses
		Federal Judicial Center	$19,735,000.00	salaries and expenses
		Retirement Funds	$26,700,000.00	Judicial Officers' Retirement Fund
			$8,400,000.00	Judicial Survivors' Annuity Fund
			$1,900,000.00	Federal Claims Judges' Retirement Fund
		Sentencing Commission	$11,575,000.00	salaries and expenses
		Total	$4,603,130,000.00	
PL 107-206 (116 Stat. 820, 829)	August 2, 2002	Supreme Court of the United States	$10,000,000.00	care of building and grounds: emergency expenses for security upgrades
		Courts of Appeals, District Courts, and Other Judicial Services	$7,115,000.00	salaries and expenses: emergency expenses to enhance security
		Total	$17,115,000.00	
		TOTAL APPROPRIATION	**$4,620,245,000.00**	

2003

Statute (Citation)	Date Passed	Headings	Appropriation	Line-item Details
PL 108-7 (117 Stat. 11, 82)	February 20, 2003	Supreme Court of the United States	$45,743,000.00	salaries and expenses
			$41,626,000.00	care of building and grounds
		Court of Appeals for the Federal Circuit	$20,313,000.00	salaries and expenses
		Court of International Trade	$13,687,000.00	salaries and expenses
		Courts of Appeals, District Courts, and Other Judicial Services	$3,800,000,000.00	salaries and expenses
			$2,784,000.00	expenses of Claims Court, processing claims under National Childhood Vaccine Injury Act of 1986
			$538,641,000.00	defender services
			$54,636,000.00	jurors and commissioners
			$268,400,000.00	court security
		Administrative Office of the U.S. Courts	$63,500,000.00	salaries and expenses
		Federal Judicial Center	$20,856,000.00	salaries and expenses
		Retirement Funds	$27,700,000.00	Judicial Officers' Retirement Fund
			$5,200,000.00	Judicial Survivors' Annuity Fund
			$2,400,000.00	Federal Claims Judges' Retirement Fund
		Sentencing Commission	$12,090,000.00	
		Total	$4,917,576,000.00	
PL 108-11 (117 Stat. 559, 561)	April 16, 2003	Supreme Court of the United States	$1,535,000.00	salaries and expenses; police enhancements
		United States Court of Appeals for the Federal Circuit	$973,000.00	salaries and expenses: court security
		United States Court of International Trade	$50,000.00	salaries and expenses: court security
		Total	$2,558,000.00	

Statute (Citation)	Date Passed	Headings	Appropriation	Line-item Details
PL 108-83 (117 Stat. 1007, 1036)	September 30, 2003	Courts of Appeals, District Courts, and Other Judicial Services	$12,187,000.00	salaries and expenses
			$17,228,000.00	defender services
			$2,778,000.00	fees of jurors and commissioners
		Total	$32,193,000.00	
		TOTAL APPROPRIATION	$4,952,327,000.00	

2004

Statute (Citation)	Date Passed	Headings	Appropriation	Line-item Details
PL 108-199 (118 Stat. 3, 76)	January 23, 2004	Supreme Court of the United States	$55,360,000.00	salaries and expenses
			$10,591,000.00	care of building and grounds
		Court of Appeals for the Federal Circuit	$20,662,000.00	salaries and expenses
		Court of International Trade	$14,068,000.00	salaries and expenses
		Courts of Appeals, District Courts, and Other Judicial Services	$3,994,176,000.00	salaries and expenses
			$3,193,000.00	expenses of Claims Court, processing claims under National Childhood Vaccine Injury Act of 1986
			$604,477,000.00	defender services
			$57,822,000.00	jurors and commissioners
			$277,500,000.00	court security
		Administrative Office of the U.S. Courts	$66,000,000.00	salaries and expenses
		Federal Judicial Center	$21,440,000.00	salaries and expenses
		Retirement Funds	$25,700,000.00	Judicial Officers' Retirement Fund
			$700,000.00	Judicial Survivors' Annuity Fund
			$2,600,000.00	Federal Claims Judges' Retirement Fund
		Sentencing Commission	$12,354,000.00	salaries and expenses
		TOTAL APPROPRIATION	$5,166,643,000.00	*less a government-wide rescission of .59 percent on discretionary accounts (118 Stat. 457)

2005

Statute (Citation)	Date Passed	Headings	Appropriation	Line-item Details
PL 108-447 (118 Stat. 2809, 2891)	December 8, 2004	Supreme Court of the United States	$58,122,000.00	salaries and expenses
			$9,979,000.00	care of building and grounds
		Court of Appeals for the Federal Circuit	$21,780,000.00	salaries and expenses
		Court of International Trade	$14,888,000.00	salaries and expenses
		Courts of Appeals, District Courts, and Other Judicial Services	$4,177,244,000.00	salaries and expenses
			$3,298,000.00	expenses of Claims Court, processing claims under National Childhood Vaccine Injury Act of 1986
			$676,385,000.00	defender services
			$61,535,000.00	jurors and commissioners
			$332,000,000.00	court security
		Administrative Office of the U.S. Courts	$68,200,000.00	salaries and expenses
		Federal Judicial Center	$21,737,000.00	salaries and expenses
		Retirement Funds	$32,000,000.00	Judicial Officers' Retirement Fund
			$2,000,000.00	Judicial Survivors' Annuity Fund
			$2,700,000.00	Federal Claims Judges' Retirement Fund
		Sentencing Commission	$13,304,000.00	salaries and expenses
		Total	$5,495,172,000.00	
PL 108-287 (118 Stat. 951, 1010)	August 5, 2004	Courts of Appeals, District Courts, and Other Judicial Services	$26,000,000.00	defender services: limited to panel attorney representations under the Criminal Justice Act
		TOTAL APPROPRIATION	**$5,521,172,000.00**	

2006

Statute (Citation)	Date Passed	Headings	Appropriation	Line-item Details
PL 109-115 (119 Stat. 2396, 2467)	November 30, 2005	Supreme Court of the United States	$60,730,000.00	salaries and expenses
			$5,624,000.00	care of building and grounds
		Court of Appeals for the Federal Circuit	$24,000,000.00	salaries and expenses
		Court of International Trade	$15,480,000.00	salaries and expenses
		Courts of Appeals, District Courts, and Other Judicial Services	$4,348,780,000.00	salaries and expenses
			$3,833,000.00	expenses of Claims Court, processing claims under National Childhood Vaccine Injury Act of 1986
			$717,000,000.00	defender services
			$61,318,000.00	jurors and commissioners
			$372,000,000.00	court security
		Administrative Office of the U.S. Courts	$70,262,000.00	salaries and expenses
		Federal Judicial Center	$22,350,000.00	salaries and expenses
		Retirement Funds	$36,800,000.00	Judicial Officers' Retirement Fund
			$600,000.00	Judicial Survivors' Annuity Fund
			$3,200,000.00	Federal Claims Judges' Retirement Fund
		Sentencing Commission	$14,400,000.00	salaries and expenses
		Total	$5,756,377,000.00	
PL 109-148 (119 Stat. 2680, 2781)	December 30, 2005	Courts of Appeals, District Courts, and Other Judicial Services	$18,000,000.00	emergency funds in response to Hurricane Katrina
		Rescission		*less 1 percent government-wide rescission of all discretionary accounts (PL 109-148, Sec. 3801)
		TOTAL APPROPRIATION	**$5,774,377,000.00**	

2007

Statute (Citation)	Date Passed	Headings	Appropriation	Line-item Details
PL 110-5 (121 Stat. 8, 9, 10, 55) Continuing Resolution Based on 2006 funding levels	February 15, 2007	Supreme Court of the United States	$60,730,000.00	salaries and expenses
			$5,624,000.00	care of building and grounds
		Court of Appeals, Federal Circuit	$24,000,000.00	salaries and expenses
		Court of International Trade	$15,480,000.00	salaries and expenses
		Courts of Appeals, District Courts, and Other Judicial Services	$4,498,130,000.00	salaries and expenses, of which $80,954,000 is available for transfer between all judicial accounts to maintain 2006 funding levels prior to that year's 1 percent government-wide rescission
			$3,833,000.00	expenses of Claims Court, processing claims under National Childhood Vaccine Injury Act of 1986
			$717,000,000.00	defender services
			$61,318,000.00	jurors and commissioners
			$372,000,000.00	court security
			indefinite	additional amounts to cover 50 percent of employee pay increases (government-wide)
		Administrative Office of the U.S. Courts	$70,262,000.00	salaries and expenses
		Federal Judicial Center	$22,350,000.00	salaries and expenses
		Retirement Funds	$36,800,000.00	Judicial Officers Retirement Fund
			$600,000.00	Survivor's Annuity
			$3,200,000.00	Federal Claims Judges Retirement
		Sentencing Commission	$14,400,000.00	salaries and expenses
		TOTAL APPROPRIATION	**$5,905,727,000.00**	

2008

Statute (Citation)	Date Passed	Headings	Appropriation	Line-item Details
PL 110-161 (121 Stat. 1844, 1986)	December 26, 2007	Supreme Court of the United States	$66,526,000.00	salaries and expenses
			$12,201,000.00	care of building and grounds
		Court of Appeals for the Federal Circuit	$27,072,000.00	salaries and expenses
		Court of International Trade	$16,632,000.00	salaries and expenses

Headings	Appropriation	Line-item Details
Courts of Appeals, District Courts, and Other Judicial Services	$4,604,762,000.00	salaries and expenses
	$4,099,000.00	expenses of Claims Court, processing claims under National Childhood Vaccine Injury Act of 1986
	$14,500,000.00	immigration enforcement
	$835,601,000.00	defender services
	$10,500,000.00	expenses of attorneys in immigration enforcement cases
	$63,081,000.00	jurors and commissioners
	$410,000,000.00	court security
Administrative Office of the U.S. Courts	$76,036,000.00	salaries and expenses
Federal Judicial Center	$24,187,000.00	salaries and expenses
Retirement Funds	$59,400,000.00	Judicial Officers' Retirement Fund
	$2,300,000.00	Judicial Survivors' Annuity Fund
	$3,700,000.00	Federal Claims Judges' Retirement Fund
Sentencing Commission	$15,477,000.00	salaries and expenses
TOTAL APPROPRIATION	$6,246,074,000.00	

2009

Statute (Citation)	Date Passed	Headings	Appropriation	Line-item Details
PL 111-8 (123 Stat. 524, 644)	March 11, 2009	Supreme Court of the United States	$66,777,000.00	salaries and expenses
			$18,447,000.00	care of building and grounds
		Court of Appeals for the Federal Circuit	$30,384,000.00	salaries and expenses
		Court of International Trade	$19,605,000.00	salaries and expenses
		Courts of Appeals, District Courts, and Other Judicial Services	$4,801,369,000.00	salaries and expenses
			$4,253,000.00	expenses of Claims Court, processing claims under National Childhood Vaccine Injury Act of 1986
			$849,400,000.00	defender services
			$62,206,000.00	jurors and commissioners
			$428,858,000.00	court security

Statute (Citation)	Date Passed	Headings	Appropriation	Line-item Details
		Administrative Office of the U.S. Courts	$79,049,000.00	salaries and expenses
		Federal Judicial Center	$25,725,000.00	salaries and expenses
		Retirement Funds	$65,340,000.00	Judicial Officers' Retirement Fund
			$6,600,000.00	Judicial Survivors' Annuity Fund
			$4,200,000.00	Federal Claims Judges' Retirement Fund
		Sentencing Commission	$16,225,000.00	salaries and expenses
		Total	$6,478,438,000.00	
PL 111-320 (123 Stat. 1859, 1879)	June 24, 2009	Courts of Appeals, District Courts, and Other Judicial Services	$10,000,000.00	salaries and expenses: immigration enforcement
		TOTAL APPROPRIATION	$6,488,438,000.00	

2010

Statute (Citation)	Date Passed	Headings	Appropriation	Line-item Details
PL 111-117 (123 Stat. 3034, 3173)	December 16, 2009	Supreme Court of the United States	$74,034,000.00	salaries and expenses
			$14,525,000.00	care of building and grounds
		Court of Appeals for the Federal Circuit	$32,560,000.00	salaries and expenses
		Court of International Trade	$21,350,000.00	salaries and expenses
		Courts of Appeals, District Courts, and Other Judicial Services	$5,011,018,000.00	salaries and expenses
			$5,428,000.00	expenses of Claims Court, processing claims under National Childhood Vaccine Injury Act of 1986
			$977,748,000.00	defender services
			$61,861,000.00	jurors and commissioners
			$452,607,000.00	court security
		Administrative Office of the U.S. Courts	$83,075,000.00	salaries and expenses
		Federal Judicial Center	$27,328,000.00	salaries and expenses
		Retirement Funds	$71,874,000.00	Judicial Officers' Retirement Fund
			$6,500,000.00	Judicial Survivors' Annuity Fund
			$4,000,000.00	Federal Claims Judges' Retirement Fund

	Sentencing Commission	$16,837,000.00	salaries and expenses
	Total	$6,860,745,000.00	
PL 111-230 (124 Stat. 2485, 2487) August 13, 2010	Courts of Appeals, District Courts, and Other Judicial Services	$10,000,000.00	salaries and expenses: immigration enforcement
	TOTAL APPROPRIATION	$6,870,745,000.00	